ARCHITECTURE IN HIGH RESOLUTION

MARK FOSTER GAGE

ARCHITECTURE IN HIGH RESOLUTION

ORO EDITIONS

TABLE OF CONTENTS

ACKNOWLEDGMENTS

It takes an immense amount of effort to invent an entirely new, yet historically and culturally derived architectural language from scratch using artificial intelligence and high-end mathematics software. It takes downright Brobdingnagian effort to then form it all into a working building design that is meant solely for accessing a hidden ancient civilization in a vast and remote desert, halfway around the world, in a country that historically has forbidden western visitors. Why put so much effort into it? Why make it so complicated that it requires a five hundred page book to document? Why not just throw some minimalist boxes down, take the money and run? The short answer is that...well I don't have an answer. I just cannot do the thing that everyone else is doing that allows them to get so many things built. Being programmed to do architecture that's seemingly slightly out of reach of the imagination of the world is a blessing and a curse and I thank everyone who's been along for this particular ride. We got close—very close this time. Endeavors such as this project would not be possible without extensive collaboration and effort, culminating in this case not as built architectural form but rather as a book. The ambition for this project—to produce an architecture that is uncannily familiar by being both historic and contemporary via the subtle estranged qualities of its formal language, came from discussions over the years with my peers. All architectural projects emerge from somewhere, and this one likely emerged from the part of my brain most in contact with Peter Eisenman, Michael Young, Kutan Ayata, Karel Klein, David Ruy, Ferda Kolatan, Tom Wiscombe, and Graham Harman, to name only a few. To Michael, Kutan, and Ferda, thanks for all the steak, and to Graham, thanks for being willing to wander around Tibet for a week talking architecture and philosophy in our quest for both nirvana and non-yak-based, vegetarian entrees. To all of the people who worked on this project or helped develop the fractal and artificial intelligence techniques used on it at Mark Foster Gage Architects, I offer profound, gratitude-filled thanks, and as always, I enjoyed the effort—this one especially. That very long MFGA dramatis personae includes: Evan Mason and Ryan Wilson (senior designers), Jean-Emanuel Tremblay (JET for short, the editorial assistant of this book), Alex Tihanos, Bashayer Bahmosen, Chad Miller, Christopher Pin, Dylan Pero, Kate Gesing, Keira Li, Kevin Li, Keyur Mistry, Langdon Drewett, Lauren Hunter, Lorents-Kristian Blomseth, Łukasz Leja, Megan Ann York, Rotana Hok, Shelley Luo, Yunling Xie, Zach Beale, Zach Hoffman, and Zehua Zhang. A belated thanks to Andrew Hommick who I forgot to thank in our last monograph (sorry Andrew). I also extend my gratitude the thanks to all of the collaborating companies that we worked with who provided their incredible expertise and talent to this unusual endeavor, including at Stantec (architect of record, engineering, construction): Frederick Kramer, Jay Jacoby, Wessam Daoud, and especially Rula Sadik who was there co-piloting the project at every step of the way. At Balmori Associates (landscape design): Noemie Lafaurie-Debany and to Javier González-Campaña—thanks for flying halfway around the world with me at a moment's notice, (but at least we got first class and a killer water menu...), at Transsolar (sustainability engineering): Eric Olsen, Krista Palen, and Adrian Turcato; at Front (facade engineering): Marc Simmons and Reina Kawakami; at Organica (water recycling): Alejandro Roman, and Antonio Agnelli; at Focus Lighting (exterior lighting) Brett Anderson; at Via Domani (digital fabrication): Mathieu Victor; at Mobility Chain (transportation and vehicle infrastructure): Francesco Maria Cerroni; at Picksell rendering (renderings): Michał Puchalski; and at Arqui9 (rendering): Timon Van Wynsberghe, Matteo Ferrari, Lukasz Mildner, Kelly Torres. Last but not least, family is pretty great for free help and allowing me to occasionally pilfer ideas—thanks Mom, Dad, Jarron, Eric, Katherine, Soren, Truman, and Gizmo. Soren, you can't read this yet, but since it has a lot more pictures than text, this one's dedicated to you.

FOREWORD

Graham Harman

While reading Mark Foster Gage's extraordinary book *Architecture in High Resolution*, I found myself torn between two differing analogies. Throughout the early portions of the work, it felt strangely reminiscent of the Warren Report on the assassination of President John F. Kennedy. With Gage, as with the Warren Commission, the reader finds a meticulous effort at exhaustive documentation of facts surrounding a specific incident. Although many conspiracy theorists have questioned whether the Commission was sincerely committed to the truth, I doubt anyone will have a similar worry about Gage: if anything, his candor is so pronounced as to be disarming. After countless hours of research and design work, Gage openly admits the failure of his entry in the competition to build the showcase desert resort. Though his thoroughness resembles that of a homicide detective surveying a crime scene, the only "crime" at issue was that victory in this competition went to another firm. Yet this is the usual fate of architects, including the most celebrated ones. A competition often draws thousands of entries; by necessity, the experience of winning is rare. Although one would expect considerable frustration in a professional life of this kind, Gage will have his share of victories in the decades to come: his prodigious imagination and meticulous eye for detail will see to that. In the meantime, he and others in his position will take comfort from the fact that failed competition entries do not drop dead on the spot or pass into some black hole of non-being. As Gage already notes in the book, many of the ideas rejected by the firm nonetheless seem like promising solutions to be held in reserve for efforts still unknown. As for the resort project as a whole, some of the most influential works in architecture are ones that were never built. As Jeffrey Kipnis once put it about an especially well-known architect: "[a] curious feature of [Rem] Koolhaas' career is the unusual number of [failed] competition entries it has produced that have come to assume the status of paradigmatic projects, even contemporary masterworks."[1] One might imagine that Koolhaas is far from alone in this respect.

The second analogy that came to mind while reading Gage's book was that of musical "outtakes." With the advent of compact disc boxed sets in the 1990s, and later with the Babel-like catalog of YouTube, it has become increasingly common to hear multiple variants and rejected or abortive studio takes of well-known hit songs. I love the music of John Coltrane, but never much cared for his overly polished and forcedly upbeat "Like Sonny" until I heard the rejected versions, many of them featuring soulful grooves as platforms for explosive improvisation by Trane. The same for the Beatles and "Strawberry Fields Forever," long dismissed in my mind as the irrelevant nostalgia of Liverpool autobiography: until I heard the outtakes, ruled by organ riffs imported from some evil calliope out of Ray Bradbury. Though I deeply regret the decisions made by producers to release the tamer versions of these songs, there is something enjoyable about savoring the alternates in private. So too for Gage's numerous discarded forms, although many are mocked in the book by the architect himself. Whenever Gage writes something like "this one was rejected as inappropriate due to the Nabatean historical context of the project," we immediately want to imagine some alternate context in which his twisted smokestack forms or overly ornate wall patterns *would* be appropriate. While the weight of his historical research is palpable in the book, Gage adds a somewhat otherworldly twist to the patterns favored by the ancient desert peoples, one that quickly leaves us disoriented. As H. P. Lovecraft's narrator tells us when examining a strange piece of headwear in a local museum:

> *All other art objects I had ever seen either belonged to some known racial or national stream, or else were consciously modernistic defiances of every recognized stream. This*

tiara was neither. It clearly belonged to some settled technique of infinite maturity and perfection, yet that technique was utterly remote from any...which I had ever heard of or seen exemplified. [2]

Anyone who has seen Gage's unbuilt proposals for the Helsinki Guggenheim or a wild winged skyscraper in Manhattan will feel the relevance of this Lovecraftian passage.

So much for analogies, which always fall short of their target. Let's now speak briefly about Object-Oriented Ontology (OOO), whose traces appear more than once in the book. At one point Gage proposes "moving beyond the Deleuzian tendency toward single surface modeling techniques." Here he cites Patrik Schumacher, who would no doubt identify Niklas Luhmann rather than Deleuze as his intellectual model. Even so, this would simply mean that Luhmann has been imported to do the same sort of architectural work that Deleuze did for a bygone generation: the elimination of corners, the blurring of distinction between continuous surface and aperture, the replacement of sudden cuts and ruptures with smooth gradients that tend further to efface the boundary between edifice and environment. Gage belongs to a generation of rising architects who suddenly tired of the Deleuzean atmosphere of their youth and turned to OOO largely because of its renewed embrace of discreteness, determinate articulation, and an unashamed focus on the aesthetic.

Earlier in the book, Gage invokes another pillar of the OOO lexicon: "My sketching, illustrating the design to use the site to hide our structures from view—making them more mysterious and withdrawn, as opposed to making them overly visible as louder 'iconic' structures that didn't respect the venerable desert context." The term "withdrawal" was taken by OOO from the writings of Martin Heidegger, and is often depicted by exaggerating critics as the only idea in OOO's toolbox. It is certainly an important one, and Gage makes impressive use of it in this book, as when he decides to cut down on poolside vegetation to turn the guest's attention toward the surrounding desert context itself. Of course, withdrawal does not just mean hiding within a given context, but also refers to hidden interior spaces concealed from an initial view, but explorable at length once we run across them. Gage delivers on this front as well, establishing numerous intricate hollows both inside and near the resort.

The problem with deeming OOO a theory of withdrawal is that this is merely a view from one side of the central problem. That problem, rooted as deeply as Aristotle's theory of substance, is the strangely loose relation that objects have with their own qualities. Socrates can be happy at one moment and sad at another while still being Socrates, which makes one wonder whether Socrates has any stable qualities at all. An apple remains one and the same thing even when rotated endlessly in one's hand, seen in midday sun and later at dusk, or in varying moods of euphoria or despair. Saul, the persecutor of Christians, becomes Paul the Apostle who revives and expands the Church, with some mysterious core of personal energy the only evident constant in these opposed phases. This tension between objects and their qualities is generally effaced in architectural Modernism, with its tendency—shared by Modernisms in every field—to mistake the idea for the thing, and the idea in turn with its instantaneous presence in a flash of insight. One of the benefits of the return to historical forms (as seen for instance in Gage's resort) is its rediscovery of architecture as a genre destined to unfold across time, in the serial wanderings of the one who explores it. Other aesthetic disciplines are inherently temporal as well, yet cinema jettisons objects in favor of serial viewpoints, and literary works achieve unity primarily in the reader's mind. Sculpture may take five or ten minutes to consider from all vantage points, but is still not quite a temporal art. It is architecture, above all, that allows for the temporally enacted tension of objects and qualities on a vast scale, coupling a massive overall physical object with a drawn-out sequence of sometimes very heterogeneous experiences. If we shift our temporal framework from that of an individual strolling the grounds, hallways, and secret rooms of a building to that of a collective shaped by the force of monuments (Aldo Rossi) then we are reminded that architecture is also intensely historical in a way quite different from that of the other arts. Though the typical intellectual also spends a great deal of time amidst the monuments of philosophy and literature and the history of science, these landmarks exist quite apart from the kinetic activities of daily life, and this is why architectural monuments are unique. The Nabatean carved buildings at Petra are already fairly accessible—like Gage, I have visited them in person—but those in Saudi Arabia have basically remained Martian monuments due to the absence of any feasible nearby human nest. To launch their renewed history as "urban" monuments may be seen as the mission of the resort whose design was in question here.

Whether or not this project reflects a new stage in Gage's career, I am not in a position to say. However, what struck me about such earlier efforts as the Guggenheim and the Manhattan skyscraper is that they had relatively little to do with "withdrawal." Most of the energy went into the façades, which let loose the needed unruly tension between objects and qualities. But the objects at issue in these cases were not of the dark, hidden, or inscrutable sort. Instead, they were the kinds of objects that Husserl calls "intentional" and that OOO calls "sensual." They were elements of the façade, and therefore objects in the sense that the apple in my hand is an object too. Stated differently, there was nothing remotely Heideggerian about Gage's earlier work. His sense of humor has nothing in common with mournful Black Forest hikes, and neither does his early aesthetics. With the Saudi resort project, his jesterly moments still appear here and there, but now they are accompanied by a quieter deference to genius loci. Both the specific decorum of Islam and the force of the blazing sun lead Gage to place things in concealment that might once have been plastered in public view on the Guggenheim surface. As a long-time admirer of his work, I look forward to seeing what comes next along this trajectory.

I have already mentioned Gage's sense of humor: not only his personal wit, but even his designs have the uncommon ability to make me laugh out loud. Sometimes his mere ideas for projects are enough to summon mirth: draining the East River and turning it into a valley? At other times, it might be his mock medieval gall in encrusting Teletubbies onto the face of building or playing some other perverse trick in the midst of a project that could hardly be more serious. But there is also his omnivorous intellect, visible enough in the pages of this book, but even more so for those who are able to spend some time with the man. There was no better colleague with whom to travel in Tibet, and no better teacher to observe in the studio. In the years to come, a wider public will become familiar with Gage's magic bag of gifts.

[1] Kipnis, "Recent Koolhaas," p. 137. In Jeffrey Kipnis, *A Question of Qualities: Essays in Architecture*. Cambridge, MA: MIT Press, 2013.)

[2] H. P. Lovecraft, "The Shadow Over Innsmouth," p. 595. In *H. P. Lovecraft, Tales*. (New York: Library of America, 1995.)

INTRODUCTION

Mark Foster Gage

"I say, play your own way. Don't play what the public wants. You play what you want and let the public pick up on what you're doing—even if it does take them fifteen, twenty years" - *Thelonious Monk*

From 1932–2019, the Kingdom of Saudi Arabia was largely closed to international tourists. On September 17, 2019, Crown Prince Mohammed bin Salman, as part of his Vision 2030 program that aims to reduce the country's reliance on oil and diversify its economy by way of tourism, decreed that the country would immediately begin to issue tourist visas to visitors from 49 countries for the first time in its national history. One of the Kingdom's most valuable cultural attractions is the UNESCO world heritage site of Mada'in Salih, a collection of extraordinary ancient Nabatean structures carved into solid stone and perfectly preserved in the remote and uninhabited desert. For nearly two millennia, these structures have remained unseen, unvisited by the world. The combination of these two factors—a stunning cultural destination and the fact that the country has little experience with tourism as an industry, nor any of the associated tourist infrastructure required (hotels, restaurants, and sometimes even roads) presented a problem—how to open this globally significant area to a new generation of global visitors and still retain its remote, isolated, mysterious, and undisturbed status? The answer was to hold an architectural competition.

An international invitation-only architectural competition was launched to find an architecture firm to design what would be the first resort open to non-Muslim tourists not only in Mada'in Salih, but within the Kingdom of Saudi Arabia. From this competition there were five architectural firms selected, each hailing from a different country, with Mark Foster Gage Architects as the sole firm selected from the United States. Mark Foster Gage Architects' involvement with this vast endeavor would ultimately extend past the initial competition and into an effort to imagine some designs for not only the resort, but also the associated cultural and tourist infrastructure of the region. After nearly 18 months, including multiple trips to Saudi Arabia, client visits to New York City, the assembly of a vast team of twelve consulting companies and fifty people, the production of books, pamphlets, videos, presentation boards, a physical model with parts 3D-printed in solid bronze, the creation of thousands of images documenting design ideas—and no fewer than twenty people working on the project at different points in the process from Mark Foster Gage Architects *alone*...we lost and built absolutely nothing.

Yet in failure there is often hope. From this defeat arose opportunity—this book, gorgeously published by ORO Press. With overflowing hard drives of visual records that documented the design process in incredible detail, coupled with the fact that the design process itself involved the extensive use of innovative technologies such as 3D fractal software and artificial intelligence, the office decided to produce the architectural version of a post-mortem anatomical autopsy.

HIGH RESOLUTION ANATOMY

From the Greek root anatomē, the term refers to a dissection, or a way of studying a body that involves intensive scrutiny of its individual parts in order to better understand the whole. Anatomical texts have little to no hierarchy—giving the same attention of study to the skeletal framework of one's finger bones as they do to the human heart. In anatomy books, as with Pre-Raphaelite art, the whole is not championed over the part—rather each part is equal and important and treated with the same careful observational status in the interest of curiosity and discovery. This is also another way of saying that such books show the human body in *high resolution*, not only focusing on the "important" parts, but illustrating the entirety of the body in exquisite detail. To produce an architecture book using this anatomical format, so we believed, would allow for the display of every aspect of the design process with equal vigor and dignity. Rather than merely splashing the final seductive images on Instagram, this book is an extensive documentation of all of the project's parts—beautiful, ugly, discarded, exiting, not-quite-right, and everything in between.

A high-resolution-anatomy book on architecture is certainly an unusual conceit and offers the literal opposite of architecture's standard repertoire of design publications—the monograph. In 2018, Rizzoli Press published our office's own monograph, titled: *Mark Foster Gage: Projects and Provocations*, but as with all monographs it is only a careful selection of the very best images from a wide range of projects. It shows the sizzle of the steak—but no butchery. This gives readers the impression that our architecture is, perhaps, easy—as the difficulty of the process of design is erased in favor of emphasizing the glamour of the final images and photographs. This earlier monograph, cradled in a beautiful custom slipcase with a gold stamped fabric cover, lushly presents thirty projects on over 250 pages of color images. The book you now hold in your hand documents not thirty projects, but one, and uses not 250 pages, but rather, 500. That is to say it is twice as long and focuses on 97 percent fewer projects. In this sense we have produced an "anti-monograph," a book that goes deep into a single process of design rather than surveying numerous projects in only the most flattering of lights. This is the opposite of what the world today requests—for it is Instagram-resistant and cumbersome, and shows not the ease of a glamorous architectural life of design, but the drudgery of consistent brute-force effort over long periods of time. However, the office holds that this is not a negative, as it celebrates that an architecture, even in superficial times such as our own, can still be imagined with complexity, difficulty, experimentation, and hard effort. At least we think so. But then again, we lost.

THE ARCHITECTURAL BODY

Architecture's first architectural theorist, although by trade actually a Roman military engineer *(praefectus fabrum)*, Marcus Vitruvius Pollio, was the first of many writers throughout time to metaphorically compare the architectural project to the human body. In producing an anatomy book on an architectural project, we've taken this concept rather literally. The use of a high-resolution anatomical format was, as with all such medical texts, developed to inform rather than persuade; to document rather than dazzle. As we do with nearly everything, we got obsessed with this idea and dove into the deep end of anatomical publishing—its history, cultural effects, and protagonists. To learn more about such anatomy books we went back into medical and publishing history, where nearly all roads lead to the Ur-anatomy book; *De Humani Corporis Fabrica* (*On the Fabric of the Human Body*), written in 1543 by Andreas Vesalius and published by Johannes Oporinus. This, among the world's first illustrated anatomical texts, dominated the field of medicine for centuries through its extensive use of visual illustrations to convey complex 3D content. This collection of books was based on Vesalius's Paduan lectures, during which he deviated from common practice by actually dissecting a corpse *live* to illustrate what he was lecturing on. Dissections had previously been performed by a barber surgeon under the direction of a Doctor of Medicine, who was not expected to perform manual labor. Vesalius' magnum opus presents a careful examination of the organs and the complete structure of the human body. This would not have been possible without the many advances that had been made during the Renaissance, including artistic developments in literal visual representation and technical developments in printing. Because of these developments and his careful involvement, Vesalius was able to produce illustrations superior to any produced previously. The *Fabrica* was 660 pages long and featured a simple layout, primarily with limited illustrations per page. These descriptions were straightforward and written simply, avoiding theoretical and medical jargon. For the book you hold in your hand we adopted this model, as we also privileged visual imagery over jargoned text, as well as the equal status given to all parts in their explanation—as opposed to only speculation about the cultural greatness of the whole. In fact, we became so obsessed with the *Fabrica* that we Nancy Drewed our way into discovering its original 1543 typeface, *Basel Antiqua*. For a recent reprint of the *Fabrica,* this historic typeface was updated for digital use by font designer Christian Mengelt and released as Mengelt Basel Antiqua. It is used nearly exclusively in the interior text of this book, including the part which you are now reading.

If we were only slightly more pretentious, we may have gone so far as to name this book: *De Architectura Corporis Fabrica* (*On the Fabric of the Architectural Body*), yet we were unconvinced about the current consumer yearning for Latin-titled books. Instead we more loosely present it as a distant descendant to the original 1543 *Fabrica*. As the project the book documents was itself a re-invention of history, we thought the relationship between this book and its historic precedent was warranted—especially as we neither had any Nabatean books to use, nor speak that particular language. Although for our inscriptions in the project we did find someone who did—Dr. Hani Hayajneh. We have all become amateur Nabatean archaeologists, or at least aficionados, and found this ancient civilization to be alien, mysterious, and wonderful source material for the curious and exploratory mind.

THE NABATEAN CIVILIZATION

Some history of the Nabatean Kingdom is warranted in order to better understand the nature of this book and project. The Nabatean Kingdom reached its peak roughly at the same time as the emerging Roman Empire, dominating the areas surrounding the Mediterranean farther east. Nabatean influence was focused on the far eastern edge of the Mediterranean, more specifically on the Arabian peninsula, spanning between their then capital, Petra—in modern-day Jordan, to the southern tip of the Arabian peninsula—modern-day Yemen. Although documents of a Greek invasion indicate that a wealthy community was thriving in the immediate vicinity of Petra as early as 312 BCE, most scholars date the Nabatean Kingdom from 168 BCE—the date of their first known king—to 106 CE when it was annexed by the Roman Empire under the emperor Trajan. This is to say it was a powerful, influential, wealthy and culturally advanced civilization—but a short one. This brevity helps to explain the limits of its architectural footprint, evidence of which can only significantly be found in two locations—Petra and Mada'in Salih.

Nabateans were a nomadic people who amassed their wealth primarily via the incense trade and its routes, which stretched from Yemen to present day Gaza. Their domination of these routes was not because of their military might—but rather their unique skills with finding, preserving and *hiding* water. The Nabatean city of Hegra, known today as Mada'in Salih, is now located in the larger oasis city of Al Ula. These names are somewhat interchangeable as Hegra was its Nabatean name and Mada'in Salih is Arabic and now refers to the specific site of the ruins. Al Ula is the larger modern town which encompasses it all. Hegra was the "second city" of the Nabateans, only less important than Petra, which is today world renowned for having numerous structures carved directly into the sandstone cliffs and not easily accessible—an important part of their longevity. Hegra was the key to Petra's wealth, as it was the largest city between the source of the valuable incense from Yemen and the capital city. There exists 1,500 miles of harsh and unforgiving desert terrain between the two. Hegra, therefore, for Nabatean traders and travelers was an oasis city, as it had natural water springs, but was also a source of all other resources in an otherwise barren environment. As such Hegra was a center for trade, learning, worship and business—the taxing of which was another income source for the Nabatean Kingdom. Hegra assured the continued existence of the incense trade which was the primary source of Nabatean wealth.

While Roman civilization was built on military might and roads, the Nabatean Kingdom was based on the unlikely mirepoix of water and fragrances.

While Petra was a city with monumental structures carved into a system of canyons and ravines, Hegra was the reverse—a city in a vast desert landscape, carved into rocky outcroppings of objects that often appear as if they were dropped from the sky. While one is immersed in canyons when one visits Petra and views the carved buildings only from up close, in Hegra, the similarly styled rock-carved buildings are instead visible from vast distances, eerily hovering over an otherwise empty desert horizon. Coming upon the ruins of Mada'in Salih, one feels as if they are perhaps on a different planet—confronted with the remains of a lost and powerful species that carved their structures into massive building-sized boulders. Among these structures there remains hardly any additional evidence of human life—which, in Nabatean times, would have consisted of vast fields of nomadic tents and wooden structures primarily made from palm trees. It is however, in stone, where the Nabateans made their presence known across time. Their skill in masonry, as can be seen in the existing structures of Petra and Mada'in Salih, was unmatched in the ancient world. It was a premise of our project that the city of Al Ula could, once again, become a center for international stone-carving with investment into robotic carving technologies—as the geological resources are vast and evidence of the regional expertise in the subject is overwhelmingly evident.

THE POLITICS OF KINGDOMS

Nabatean women in Hegra were considered equal to men, contrary to the much different political status of women in Saudi Arabia today. Nabatean inscriptions indicate that women were priestesses, co-rulers, monarchs, could inherit, dispose of property, own their own tombs, bring lawsuits and represent themselves in courts of law. Some women were depicted on coins. That women in Saudi Arabia only recently received the right to both drive a car and vote in the last decade illustrates some of the vast differences between these Kingdoms that have occupied the same land. We believe, however, that this project is an act of political progress, of opening the Kingdom up to the larger world and making available for global access these incredible cultural artifacts. We learned immensely from this exchange and experience and can only hope that future generations of curious visitors, as well as the Saudi Arabian communities that welcome them, can also benefit from such exchange of ideas.

In the nineteenth century CE, European explorers began to visit formerly Nabatean territories and cities like Petra were rediscovered. Interest in the Nabateans grew during the late twentieth century with scholars and archaeologists visiting the region and excavating the ancient sites—primarily located in Jordan. In 1985, Petra was declared a World Heritage Site and selected as one of the "New Seven Wonders of the World" in 2007. The rediscovery of the monuments of Mada'in Salih, given their far more remote location, took significantly longer, particularly since the Saudi government only made them available for archaeological study in 2000. The archaeological site was proclaimed as a UNESCO World Heritage Site in 2008 and made available for extremely limited tourism in 2019 with plans to significantly upgrade the infrastructure, including the resort of our competition, by 2030. The problem was how to enable this transition to happen, while maintaining the dignity and feeling of otherworldliness produced by this largely human-free, extraordinary, and monumental landscape.

A STARTING PREMISE

In addressing this problem, we began with the premise that a feeling of otherworldliness cannot be produced using the common tools of our own everyday world. In order to move beyond this limitation and into the realm of the fascinating, mysterious and awe-inspiring, our office proposed a question—what if the Nabateans were still with us today?

What might their architecture have evolved into given an additional 1,800 years to mature and incorporate all that has developed since? This is the resort we wanted to design, a New Nabatea of sorts, a complex that merged the design techniques from this ancient civilization with those that preceded and followed, including those of the twenty-first century. The result is, we believe, a fantastic fusion of not only landscape and architecture, as called for in the project brief, but also of history—all enabled through the innovative use of advanced technologies. One thing is clear of the Nabateans of Hegra—their society was not only one of wealth and power, but one that also exchanged ideas with neighboring cultures. This is seen in the architecture that remains at Mada'in Salih today, in even singular buildings such as the masterpiece tomb of Qasr al-Farid, there is not only the exquisite precision of Nabatean stonecutting and innovations such as the Nabatean column capital found nowhere else in the world—but there can also be found the clever reinterpretation of entablatures, triglyphs, and metopes from Greek antiquity, curved stone cornices from ancient Egypt, and the stepped merlon motifs of early Mesopotamia. Nabatean design culture was one of beautiful fusions. To imagine a New Nabatea in the twenty-first century, we must imagine that, above all, they would have continued to combine into their architecture aspects of design from more recent regional Islamic and Saudi design traditions. We have, therefore, imagined a counterfactual resort—fusing Nabatean patterns and proportions with other influences ranging from the details of Bedouin jewelry and the patterns of early Islamic architecture to the contemporary graphic design aesthetics of Saudi Arabia today. In order to accomplish this fusion of cultures, patterns, materials, technologies, and forms in our design, we turned to the emerging technologies of artificial intelligence. It was our hope in doing so that we could produce an architecture that was as rooted in the deep past as it was in the emerging technologies and cultural developments of the twenty-first century.

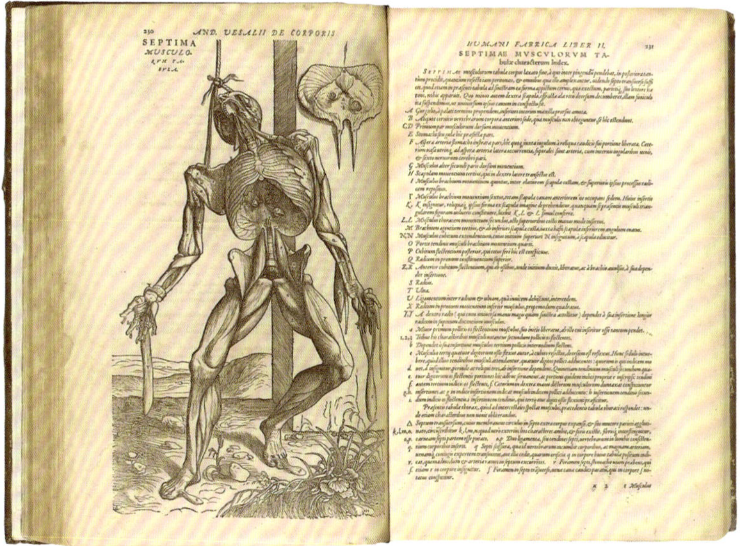

230 AND. VESALII DE CORPORIS

SEPTIMA MVSCVLORVM TABVLA.

HUMANI FABRICA LIBER II. 231

SEPTIMAE MVSCVLORVM TAbulæ characterum Index.

De Humani Corporis Fabrica Libri Eptem (On the Fabric of the Human Body) Andreas Vesalius, 1543.

I

SOJOURN TO SAUDI ARABIA
1–9

Meetings in Riyadh
Historic Ad Diriyah

Opposite page : A photo of the Kingdom Center in Riyadh built in 2002 by Ellerbe Becket Architects.

2

RIYADH, SAUDI ARABIA

Flying from New York City to Riyadh on Saudia Airlines. Saudia, being the national airline of Saudi Arabia, a devoutly Islamic country, does not serve alcohol. However in first class they did have a "water menu" that featured no less than fourteen different types of bottled water.

3

MEETINGS IN RIYADH

Above is an image of our first meeting regarding the project. When we were there this hotel where we also stayed was rather empty, which often meant that my assistant and I were the only guests dining in the various (albeit wonderful) restaurants. Luxury with a twist of loneliness. Other meeting participants masked for anonymity.

THE EDGE OF THE WORLD

On an earlier trip to Saudi Arabia, I hired a driver to take me to *Jebel Fihrayn*, aka "The Edge of the World," a rocky escarpment several hours northwest of Riyadh. This photograph shows our truck, the road, and the sublimely empty context of the drive. As the Kingdom only began to allow tourist visas in 2019—three years after these photos were taken—this photo is a representative of the need for an updated tourist infrastructure as these historic and cultural destinations open up to the larger global community. At the moment, no Starbucks.

6

AD DIRIYAH

On the outskirts of Riyadh lies Ad Diriyah, a small town and its historic ruins. Diriyah's Turaif district was the first capital of the Saudi family and was declared a UNESCO World Heritage Site in 2010. The ruins, unlike those in Egypt or other countries, have a haunting quality in that they are nearly empty of tourists. While most of the roof structures are gone, the existing walls, towers and materials gave us a sense of the qualities of space that we wanted to emulate—where one is compressed in narrow, shaded corridors and released into larger, grander spaces as part of a choreography of spatial surprises.

Some areas of Diriyah have been reconstructed, such as this wall that has very small arrays of triangular windows that shade users from direct sunlight. These same windows were also shaped for defensive purposes to prevent the entry of invaders and projectiles. The wall is entirely made of mud brick and its thickness both resists heat during the day and stores it to combat the cool desert nights.

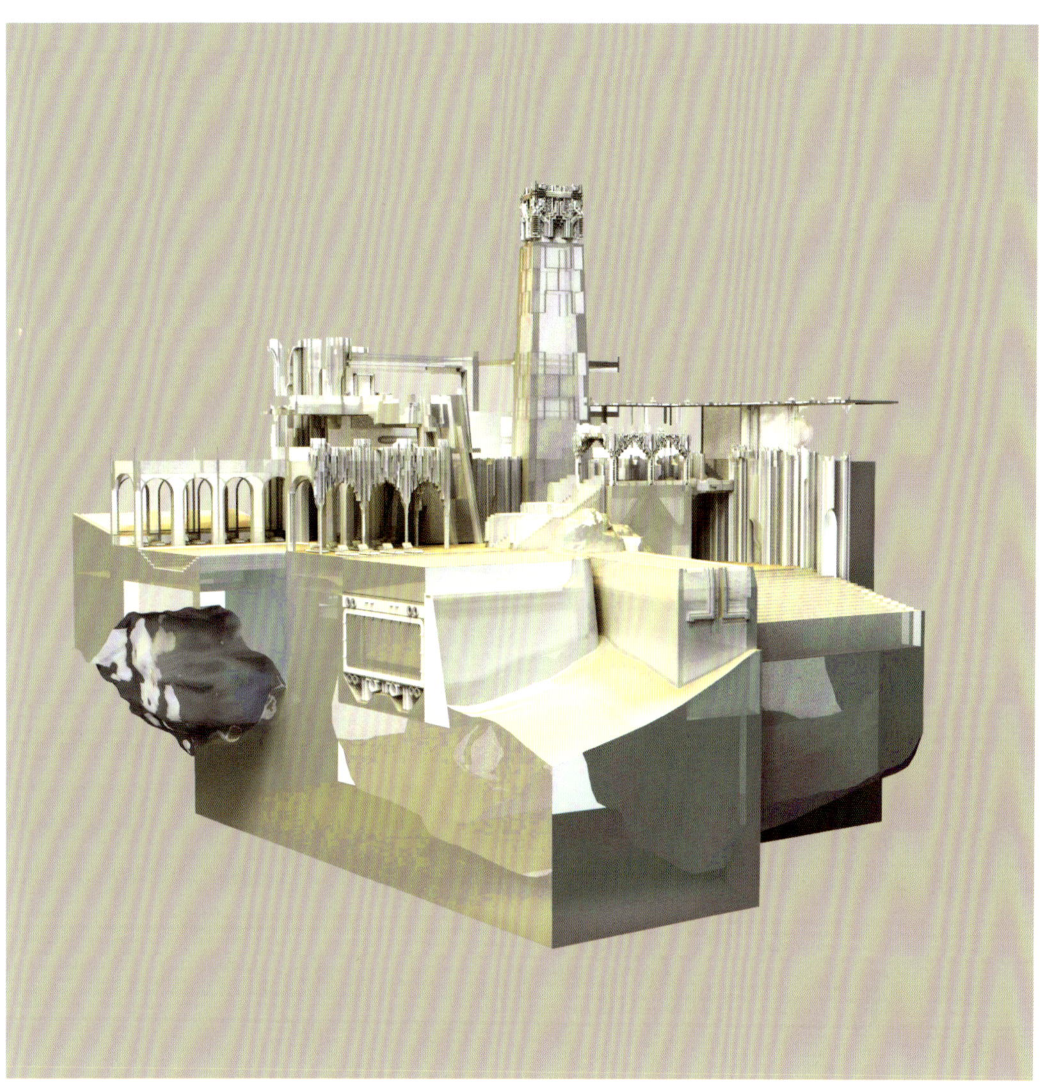

9

POST IPSO FACTO REPRESENTATION

This image was done after the project was complete as a way to better understand how continually evolving techniques of representation can reveal more information about our work. This particular image was done by using an iridescent material to capture the full complexity of the geometries present in the design, as would happen in an X-ray, including individual monolithically stacked stones.

THE CONTEXT OF ANTIQUITY
10–35

Opposite page : Residential façade in Al-Balad, a historic area within Jeddah that has been continuously occupied since the 7th century CE. This residential window type with painted wood screens that block the sun and wind by projecting forward from the façade came to our attention in our research about Saudi housing types.

LIHYAN / DADĀN / HEGRA / AL ULA

With four significant civilizations occupying this desert oasis, even proper naming of the region can be difficult. The first recorded occupants of this area were the Lihyanites, which many believe to be the same as the Dadanites. References to this area by both of these names were made in the Hebrew Bible, where it was identified as a major trading center on the Arabian peninsula. The Dadanite/Lihyanite kingdom ruled for two centuries prior to occupation by the Nabateans in the first century BCE, who named it Hegra. It later became known as Al Ula, with the Arabic name Mada'in Salih referring primarily to the site of the Nabatean architectural antiquities.

The above image is an aerial view of the historic Al Ula showing the interconnected homes. Occupied continuously since the twelfth century, the Old Town district of Al Ula housed residents up until the 1980s when it was finally abandoned. The over 900 mud-brick houses are all attached to one another for both shading and defensive reasons. Densely packed, the town has only fourteen access gates. Given that the houses share walls, there is less surface area per-house to collect heat from the sun, making the interiors rather temperate in the over one hundred degree heat. With narrow exterior circulation and woven palm shading devices, one could walk around most of the town without encountering direct sunlight, which is a strategy we would also later use in our design of the desert resort.

MADA'IN SALIH

The Qasr al-Farid, translated as "The Lonely Castle," is one of over at least 110 monumental tombs scattered around the landscape of Mada'in Salih. Unlike most of the other tomb façades that are carved out of similar sandstone, Qasr al-Farid is unique in that it is isolated, carved out of a single massive stone outcropping and is so large that it has four columns across its façade as opposed to the more typical two. Inscriptions indicate that the sculptor was named Hoor ibn Ahi for Hani ibn Tafsy, and it was nearly completed in the fortieth year of the reign of the Nabatean King Aretas I, thereby dating it to 31 BCE. As a western visitor it's a bewildering experience to have such a massive historic and cultural artifact nearly completely to oneself, as the entire area has no tourist infrastructure to speak of, leaving one to reach the tombs casually via drivers often across untamed desert.

16

QASR AL-FARID

This is a photo of the Qasr al-Farid from ground level looking upward, with our team wandering into the solid carved interior room in nearly stunned disbelief. Our resort proposal sought to renew Al Ula as a new global center for advanced stone carving through the use of robotic carving techniques. Our design proposed to take advantage of this expertise and use the resort as a showcase for such next-generation construction technologies that could aim to redefine the use of stone in architecture for a new millennium of regional construction. With the deep history regarding this craft, we thought there would be no better place in the world to lead this category of technology and innovation than Al Ula.

At the base of the Qasr al-Farid, myself in the white shirt, pondering who could have possibly created such a massive hybrid of architecture and geology—and why. The carvings on this particular tomb façade are stunning, evidence of which can be seen above the door in the form of wings from what would have originally been a harpy-like guardian figure. Nabatean stone carvers worked from top to bottom with their architectural carvings (i.e. whole buildings), leaving archaeologists to speculate that this tomb was never quite finished—as one can see a rougher layer of stone, yet unsmoothed, remaining toward the bottom.

18

QASR AL BINT NECROPOLIS

Like Russian dolls unpacked and placed side by side, the formation shown is the site of nearly twenty-five carved stone façades, decreasing in size as the solid sandstone outcroppings diminishes in height. The tomb façade farthest to the left reaches a height of sixteen meters and is known as Qasr al Bint, or "Palace of the Maiden." Above the doorway an inscription plaque indicates that the largest façade dates to circa 31 CE, coincidentally estimated to be the same year Roman architect and engineer Vitruvius is said to have written the *Ten Books on Architecture*—the first book on architectural theory and practice that survives from antiquity. Given that they were in power simultaneously, there would likely have been extensive trade between the Nabateans and Romans, seemingly affirmed by the classical pilasters, columns, and entablatures of nearly all of the tomb façades, which are more often abstracted versions of Roman, not Greek, classical elements.

19

AREA "C"

Above is a photograph of two of the smaller carved tombs within the Mada'in Salih site, dating from 16–61 CE. While some of the tombs were elevated, carved higher into the sandstone faces, some were built on the ground level, which has since further eroded, leaving the façades without a bottom edge. This causes some of the classical components to succumb to gravity and simply fall off, as is likely the case in this image.

CULTURES OF PRECISION

In the history of architectural antiquity, the names of only a few master stone carvers are known to us—for instance that of Rabez Malco—found carved into a façade at Mada'in Salih. This speaks volumes to the value the Nabateans placed on the art of stone carving. Unlike most civilizations, it was only theirs where a stone carver was allowed to sign his work. This should, perhaps, come as no surprise—as the stonework is unrivaled, as the rare paired and offset pilaster/column structures here indicate.

One can also see faint evidence of more detailed and delicate carving in the top image inscribed into the face of the curved pilaster capital. To my knowledge, this genre of classical capital is unique to the Nabateans, resembling neither the Tuscan, Doric, Ionic, Corinthian, nor Composite orders of western classicism. The opposite image shows a similar descendant precision found in early twentieth century Bedouin jewelry from the same region.

22

POST IPSO FACTO REPRESENTATION

This image was done after the project was complete as a way to better understand how evolving techniques of representation can reveal more information about our projects. This particular image was completed using the technique of cel shading. The image brings attention to the depth created by the inscriptions along the covered walkway found at the top of the projects ceremonial stair entrance.

23

POST IPSO FACTO REPRESENTATION

Shown here are the highly articulated arch structures found along the front elevation of the pool area. They are contrasted against the interior arched façades of the chilled pool which are more abstract in terms of design, and get their aesthetic identity from their natural material and color as seen in upcoming images.

24

JABAL ALFIL

While Al Ula is known for its cultural artifacts, the same general area is home to some equally unbelievable, naturally-occurring geological formations such as Jabal Al Fil, or "Elephant Rock," which has a massive three-story extension that, as one can see in this photograph, looks like an elephant's trunk. The "trunk" and "body" of this monolithic sandstone structure were shaped by millions of years of wind, sand, and water erosion.

25

JABAL ITHLIB / AL DIWAN

Religion and ritual at Mada'in Salih were concentrated in a hidden area within Jabal Ithlib, which can only be accessed via a narrow passageway through the gorge known as the Siq. To the right of the Siq is a massive carved cubic volume, pictured, known as the *Diwan*, a dining triclinium where elite or ritual banqueting would have occurred. The open front of the Diwan indicates that it may have had a public element, with observers of ritual feasts watching in from outside of the room. In lieu of an exhibitionist ritual or banquet, this image merely shows our drivers and team stealing some shade from the staggering heat. *Following pages:* Fast forward to one of our early designs showing everything carved in the reddish sandstone of the site and region at large.

DESERT NATURE RESERVE

Unlike most architectural competitions and projects that we've been involved in since opening our office in 2002, for this one we were allowed to *pick* our exact site—from anywhere within a very large area. The problem with the area we were allowed to select from was that it was too large to cover on foot, or even in an SUV, meaning that we needed to use a helicopter to get a sense of the possibilities. Each competitor was given access to the surroundings via the helicopter above, with which they could more specifically identify areas for further on-ground scrutiny over the following days.

29

WATERFALL ROCK

Once each finalist team had identified potential sites they were interested in exploring in more detail, they were assigned two SUVs—one to drive them and one in the event that the other broke down—so that nobody would be stranded in the waterless desert. Various groups would occasionally rendezvous for Saudi coffee, or Qahwa, a combination of green coffee beans and cardamom heated in small campfires on a *dallah*, a fusion of a teapot and pitcher with an oversized Toucan-like beak. The above images give a sense of the scale of some of the geological formations, including "waterfall rock," shown here, which was very close to the site our team selected and would have been the primary view seen from many of our guest residences.

30

QUWEIRA SANDSTONE

Above is an extended group portrait taken on a precariously anchored, million-year-old chunk of crumbling sandstone. After millions of years of wear, many of the sandstone outcroppings are suffering from a type of honeycomb weathering that crumbles the surfaces of the rocks. The hollowing may result from the variations in the rocks' properties as they interact with salt weathering, sandstorms, and repeated wetting and drying cycles over eons. Scientists are currently studying the mechanism of honeycomb formation at the Al-Hijr archaeological site to attempt to preserve it for centuries to come.

31

SIQ GEOLOGY

The documented human history of the Al Ula region is deep, spanning far beyond the Nabateans to a pre-history of ancient carvings indicating possible human occupation as far back as 200,000 BCE. This pales in comparison to the timescales of the region's geological history. The Al Ula desert region possesses a wealth of untouched Siq and Quweira geology—among the most pristine examples of Precambrian igneous and metamorphic basement rock structures in the world. Our proposal set as a principle that all guest suites would have unobstructed views to the horizon—beyond desert rocks, into the untouched deeper mysteries made newly visible to the naked eye.

32

THE GROUND TEXTURES OF MADA'IN SALIH

These are photographs of my feet on the different rock textures of the extended site. I often take photos of my feet on site visits, as they automatically provide a sense of scale for the sand, stone, rock and other textures of the ground. They illustrate everything from siq, quiwera, igneous and metamorphic geological substrates—to man-made flooring of the same materials made from the millennia of civilizations that have occupied the region.

SITE HUNTING BY HELICOPTER

The above image is the helicopter view of the actual site we selected for our resort location. The site became affectionately known as the "Hand" because of its spindly finger-like outcroppings and deep ravines that we later used to nestle our buildings into. This particular site also gave the resort a high vantage point that we felt would provide better views and a cooler environment than others in the areas. The site exists miles from the current Al Ula town area toward the west, and thousands of miles from the next significant town if heading east.

DRAWING TERROIR
36–59

Opposite page : View of the narrow passageway through the gorge known as the Siq that leads to the religious area of Jabal Ithlib. The previously described dining diwan or triclinium is visible to the right of the figures in the photograph.

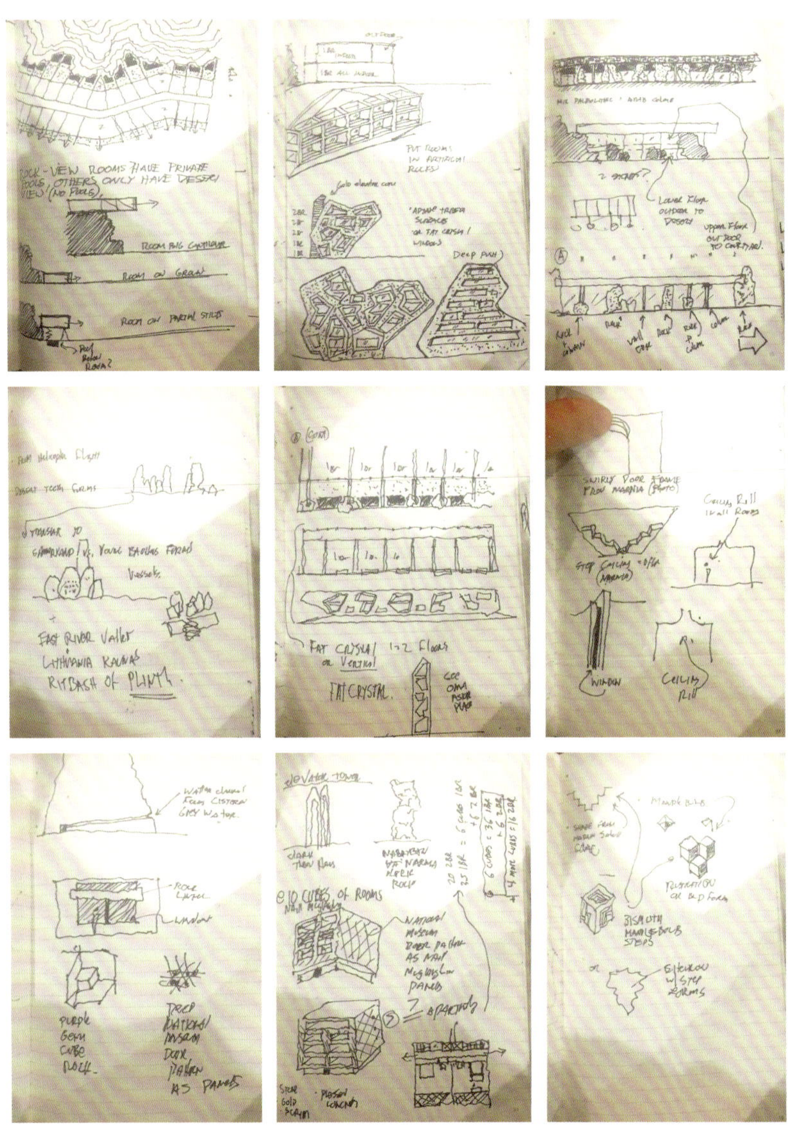

SITE IDEATION

Here are quick hand sketches of various ideas I had for the design while helicoptering and SUV-ing around the extended site over the course of several days. Some of them convey a sense of scale and possible views from the site. Others convey ideas of form, program and access—using an array of representational types; diagrams, plans, elevations, sections and axonometrics.

39

DEEP GEOLOGY

Sketching how we could take our SUV to a location protected by massive sandstone escarpments. Al Ula's geological structures, some well over 500 million years old, not only predate human civilization, but predate the very existence of life on earth itself. While such formations exist in many places on earth, they are particularly pristine and picturesque in the Al Ula desert. What this means is that to gaze across the vast landscapes of the site is to not only see the far vistas of the historic desert, but also to look unobstructed—back farther into the deep timescales of the very formation of the world. A lot of responsibility for a fine-point Sharpie.

DESIGN FAST FORWARD: THE HORIZON POOL

The above image illustrates an early design of the relationship between our reception building, the horizon pool, and its associated arcade. One of our earliest responses to the site was to provide relief from the desert heat, by making our resort into a more lush, garden oasis. Upon further reflection we realized that it was the harsh desert atmosphere that gave the region not only its visual identity but also its cultural identity. Accordingly, we abandoned the excessive planting of greenery and grouped the plantings into a single garden of native species that was discrete and contained, allowing the rest of the resort to be more deeply immersed in the experience of the remote desert.

DESIGN FAST FORWARD: TOWER CIRCULATION

As previous images illustrate, the site we selected was topographically dramatic, with very steep inclines. As such, we knew we would need to use well-placed structures for vertical circulation. Instead of embedding elevators in existing buildings—and thereby making them wider, we opted to place vertical circulation into dedicated tower structures that would both connect different program levels, and also form wayfinding features and elements to compose special views within the escarpments and outcroppings. The above etching, testing the height of a tower, is taken from an actual location with no modification to the site or foregrounded balanced boulder.

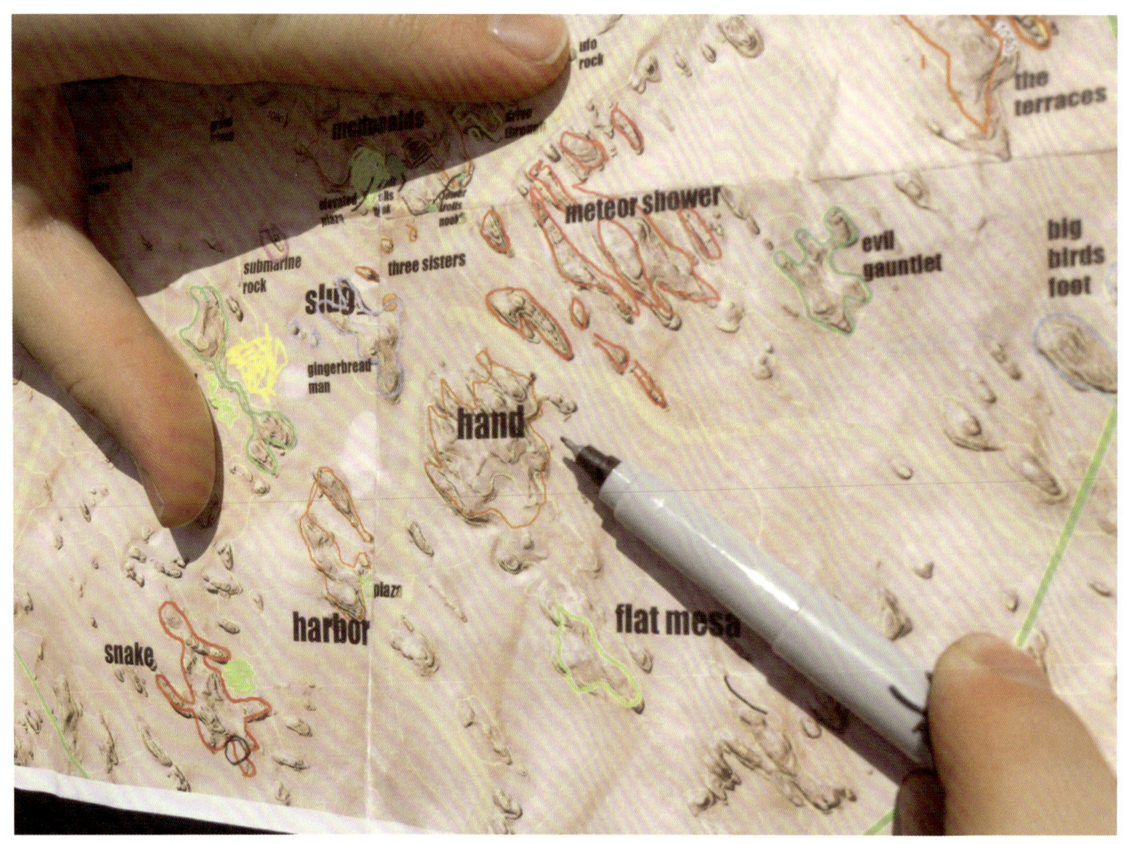

THE MAP

This image shows a photoshop "guide map" we made prior to the site visits, in anticipation of the helicopter flight. We knew we would need shorthand names to help us to speak about particular areas that otherwise had no names. You'll notice the obviousness of the names we gave to certain areas as they appeared from the air—serious and scholarly titles such as "Big Birds Foot," "Evil Gauntlet," "Meteor Shower," "McDonald's," "Gingerbread Man," "Submarine Rock," "Slug," "Three Sisters," "Snake," and ultimately "Hand," which my Sharpie is pointing toward—the site we ultimately selected for our resort design. "Big Birds Feet" was a close runner-up.

AND THE TERRITORY

Above is a view from the top of our site, aka the "Hand," showing the scale of the sandstone structures that would be viewed by the rooms located in the area from where the photo was taken. A white SUV can be seen in the middle-right that gives as sense of the vast scale of the rocky areas. The tracks of multiple days of crisscrossing between possible locations can be seen indexed in the sand. In the resort design, however, we limited desert vehicle traffic to specific corridors so that such man-made intrusions would never be seen from guest areas.

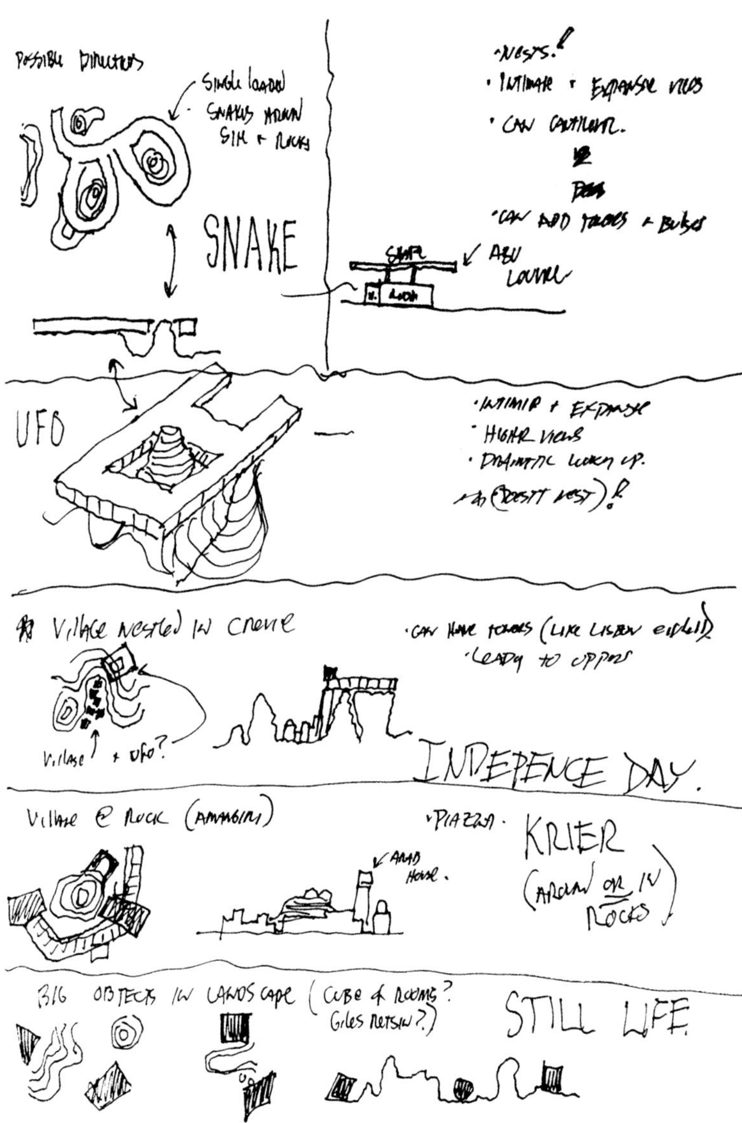

MORE INITIAL IDEAS

These sketches illustrate the desire to use the site to hide our structures from view—making them more mysterious and withdrawn as opposed to making them overtly visible as louder "iconic" structures that didn't respect the venerable desert context. Another sketch illustrates the related desire to have the site provide different levels of activities for users, rather than artificially making different levels by simply stacking floor plates.

CUBUS MUNDANA

Above are more of my sketches that show how elevating the residential suite buildings off the desert floor would provide access to view corridors that would allow guests to view farther into the sublime surroundings. These drawings also illustrate the desire to make reference to the original Nabatean structures by using similarly proportioned masses—namely squares, cubes and very simple massing structures that are not complex by themselves, but made complex through their details and relationships to the rocky surroundings.

VIEW ALONG CEREMONIAL ENTRANCE AXIS

The above rendering and collage, done in-house, was an early attempt to imagine how the resort's central core would look to a guest when driving by a specific rock formation and seeing a nearly head-on view of the resort's central core. This helped us to further determine our building arrangements, as we liked the aesthetic balance provided by the foreground rock on the left, the massive sandstone outcroppings on the far right, and the resorts central observation and water filtration tower, centered, which seemed to be the visual fulcrum on which both balanced.

It was likely common practice for Nabatean stone carvers to start their façades and work from top to bottom. Occasionally, given that they were working with monolithic geological structures, mistakes were made. Areas of stone were sometimes not sufficiently strong to accept the carvings—so the carvers would simply stop and begin a new tomb structure elsewhere. The surrounding desert is peppered with numerous "false starts," which are unique in architecture, as one rarely sees the tops of buildings completed with the bottoms never having been started.

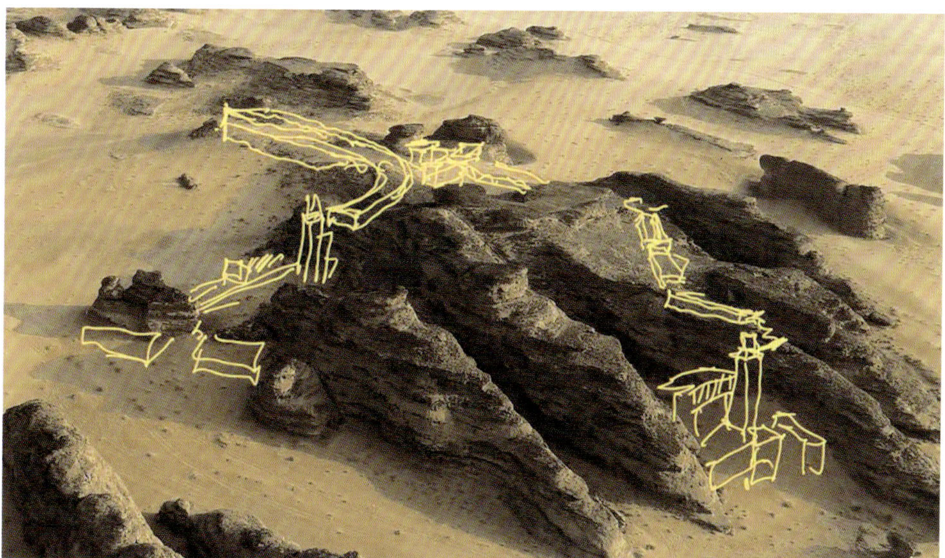

A CARVED AND NESTLED CITY

These digital sketches illustrate potential sites for building placement, and interconnectivity between ravines. With such sketches we sought to, at the broader scale, consider the buildings as carved into and out of the rocky outcroppings. Ultimately, we would take a much more restrained approach than shown here—making a greater effort to minimize our visual impact on the site. Building our design more directly *into* the site, as opposed to on top of it, had the additional advantage of allowing us to use the rocky walls of the outcroppings inside the residential buildings themselves—mixing architectural and geological structures to produce interiors.

RESORT ON TOP OF OUTCROPPINGS OR ON HOT DESERT FLOOR

NO

RESORT NESTLED INSIDE ROCK OUTCROPPINGS

YES!

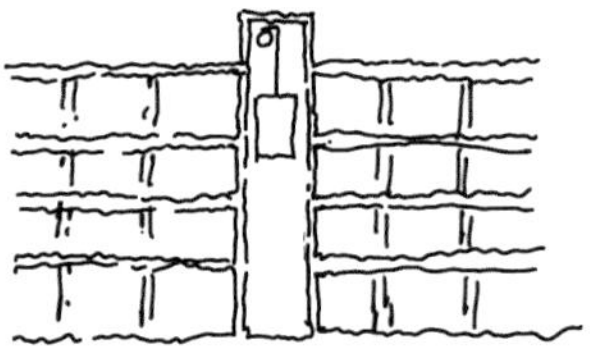

STRUCTURE PROVIDES DIFFERENT LEVELS

NO

SITE PROVIDES DIFFERENT LEVELS

YES!

SOME INITIAL IDEAS (TRIBUTE TO LEON KRIER)

Here are simplistic drawings from my on-site sketchbook that were used to communicate our thoughts to the larger non-architect team. These were not part of the presentation process and were only for internal use, as we tend to eschew over-simplifying or infantilizing our design ideas. That is to say that our ultimate design may have been driven by such sketches, but it is in no way represented by them in its final, complex, form. While we realize that simplistic sketches are all the rage to make architecture consumable in an Instagram world. We figured if such things need to be done, they should be done in the manner of the master himself, Leon Krier, whom I had the pleasure of teaching a design studio with at Yale.

ELEVATING PROJECT ABOVE DESERT FLOOR PROVIDES MUCH BETTER VIEWS AND IS BENEFICIAL FOR WATER RECYCLING AND COLLECTION

YES!

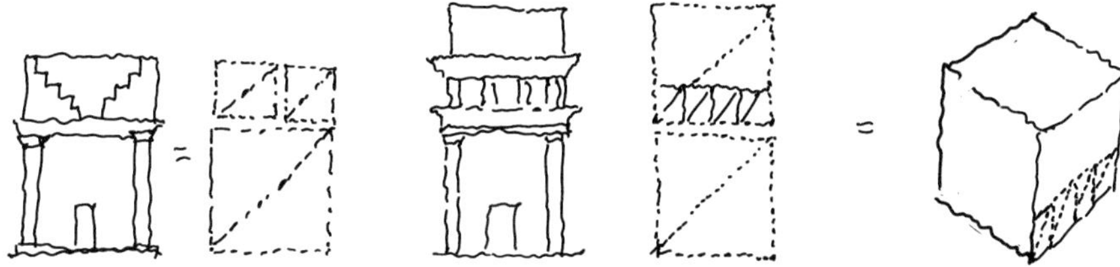

PROJECT USES REGIONAL HISTORIC GEOMETRIES AND PROPORTIONS FOR SHAPES OF ALL NEW BUILDINGS

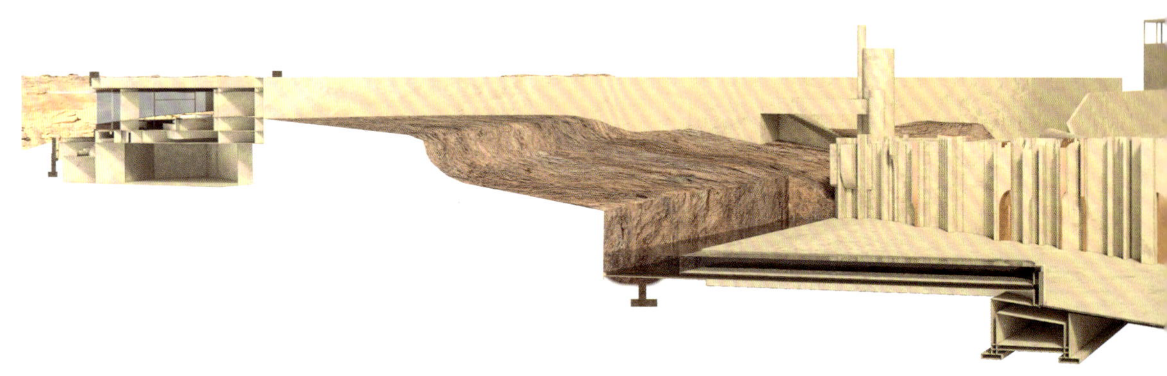

PRELIMINARY SITE SECTIONS

Shown above are two preliminary site section drawings that show the stepped terrain of our basin that would later house the water-recycling oasis garden. This slope would naturally allow cleaned water to flow directly into the horizon pool toward the right of the image. Sectional drawings on this particular project were far less useful than they are on more typical projects—thus the lack of them in the design process documentation. One of the reasons for this was that many buildings were single volumes and didn't warrant sections to understand their spatial relationships. Furthermore, the hundreds of different topographical and volumetric relationships present meant that there were no standard section drawings that could be applied to standard types. These site sections, however, rather clearly show the general stepping of the project geography.

NESTLING INTO THE SITE

These ground-level digital sketches illustrate how buildings might be embedded into the site with thin tower wayfinding markers peeking out above the outcroppings. This was the design direction we ultimately pursued—one landed on rather early in the site-visit process. The dashed lines indicated occupiable programmed volumes or circulation areas that are excavated from the solid sandstone escarpments.

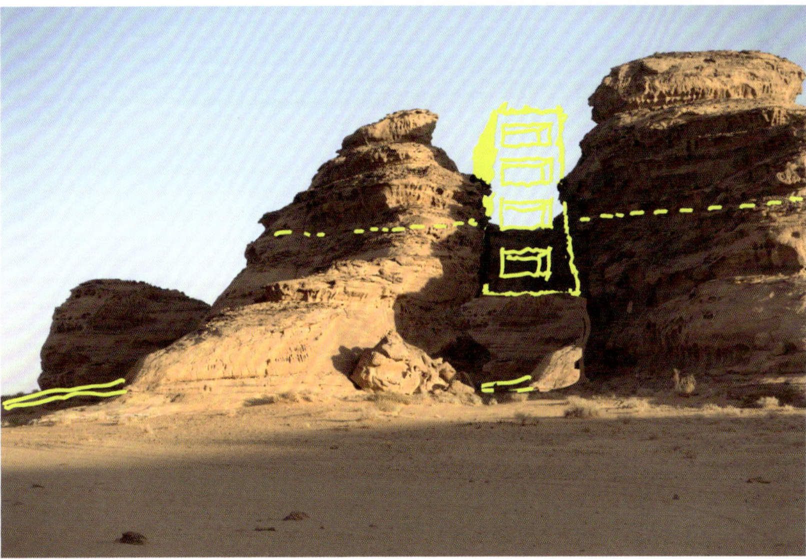

Above are additional digital sketches that show how views of the architecture might be composed with the geological formations in mind, such that one could not see architecture or geology independent of the other.

RESORT IS A SINGLE BUILDING

RESORT IS MULTIPLE BUILDINGS WITH MULTIPLE EXPERIENCES

YES!

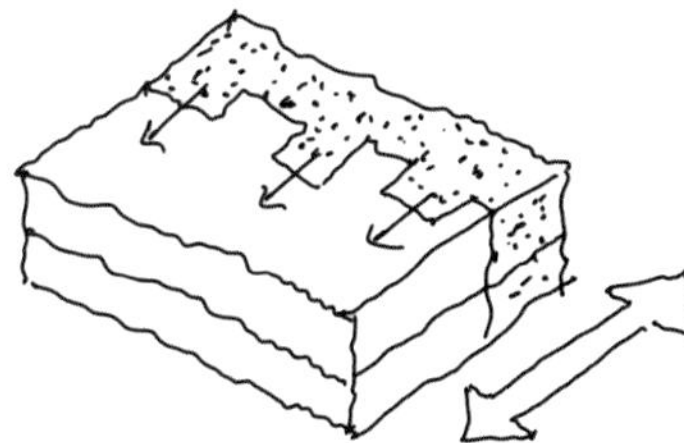

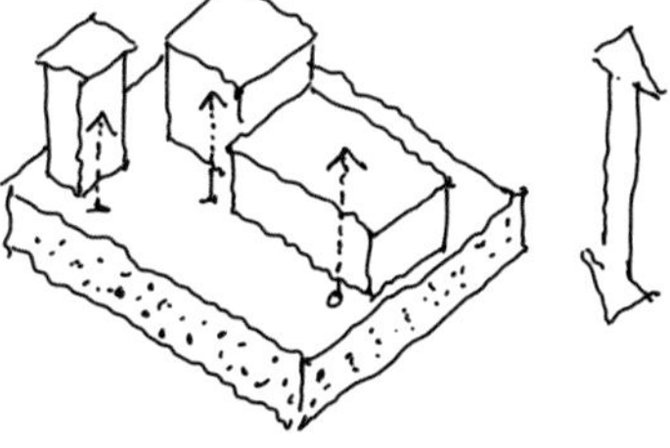

BACK OF HOUSE SERVICES PROGRAMS HORIZONTALLY

NO

BACK OF HOUSE SERVICES PROGRAMS VERTICALLY

YES!

GEOLOGY, MASSING, AND ROOM SERVICE

The top sketches show our desire to produce not a single, monumental building, but rather a composed, mini-Neo-Nabatean city nestled in the rocky surroundings. This strategy required the use of towers as vertical circulation elements that interconnect discrete buildings. This allowed us to also create different aesthetic experiences for the interior and exteriors of various resort program areas. For the larger parts of the project these discrete buildings would be placed on a "plinth," which would house all service functions and would access the buildings through dedicated vertical service circulation devices such as dumbwaiters and service elevators.

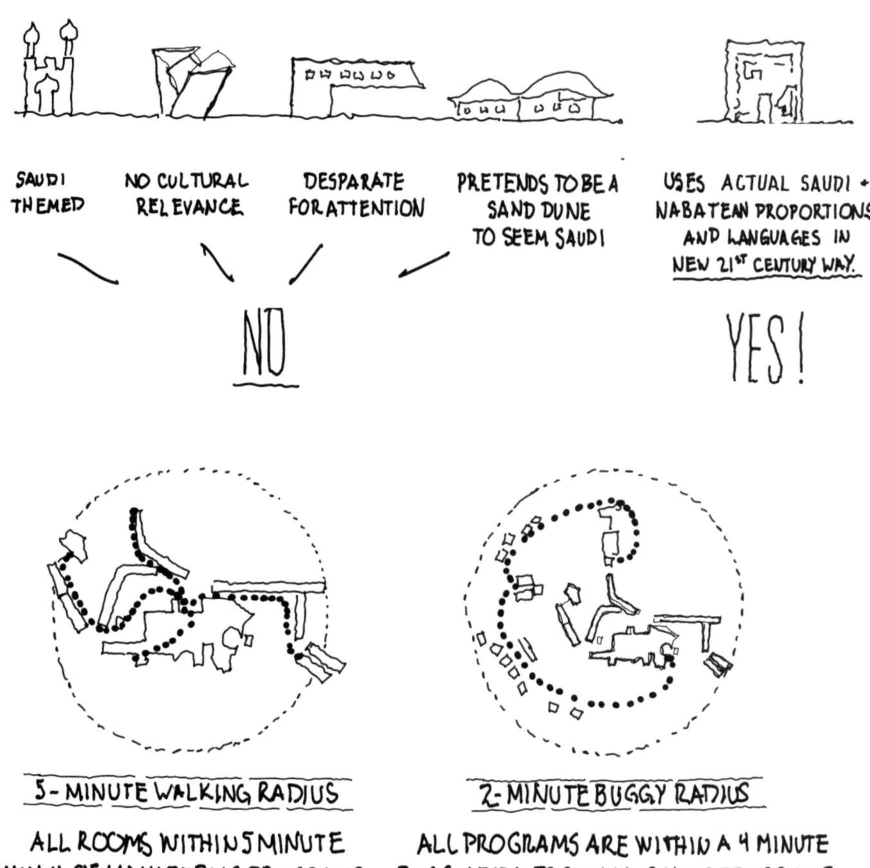

HISTORIC VS EGOTISTICAL IDENTITY

This was not a location for architectural hubris and wildly iconic monuments to the human ego. These sketches illustrate the ultimate direction we would take, which relied on Nabatean geometries—squares, cubes, stepped structures, and stacking—as a way to let the desert and sandstone escarpments shine against a language of more restrained building geometries. These simple geometries, however, would later be developed with high-resolution architectural detail that provide a man-made contrapposto to the textures of the rocky outcroppings. The lower drawings show initial strategies for internal circulation and external approach. *Following pages:* This concept sketch rendering shows how architecture blends into the geological formations rather than becoming the center of attention. The concept sketch image is of a horizon pool with unobstructed views of the surrounding desert.

A VENERABLE GEOLOGY

Opposite page : This photo shows the dramatic vertical canyons of the surrounding Al Ula desert. Our competition was centered on flatter areas and was occurring simultaneous to another competition for a canyon resort, ultimately won by Jean Nouvel.

GUEST CLUBHOUSE

Reception
(additionally annotated within color block)

Business Center
(additionally annotated within color block)

Resteraunts
(additionally annotated within color block)

Spa
(additionally annotated within color block)

Guest Prayer Rooms

Kids' Club

Annotated Guest Services

GUEST DESTINATIONS

Outdoor pursuits and games
(additionally annotated within color block)

Observatory

GUEST RESIDENCES

Guest Suites

Guest Tents

Resort Villas

SERVICE PROGRAMS

Back of House
and Staff Accomodations
(additionally annotated within color block)

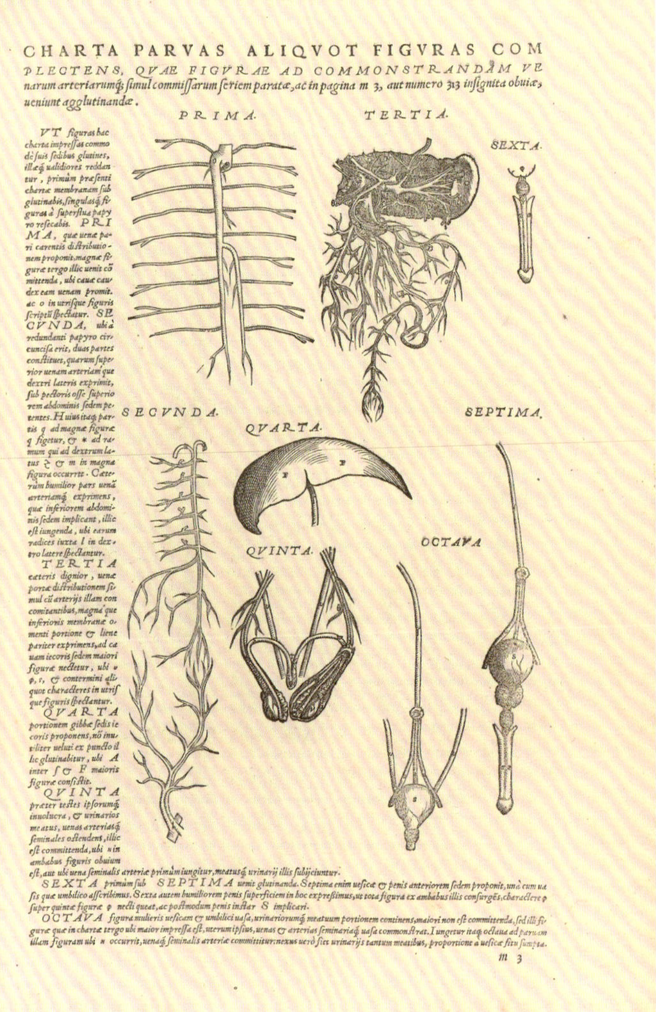

CHARTA PARVAS ALIQVOT FIGVRAS COMPLECTENS, QVAE FIGVRAE AD COMMONSTRANDAM VEnarum arteriarumq; ſimul commiſſarum ſeriem paratæ, ac in pagina m 3, aut numero 313 inſignita obuiæ, ueniunt agglutinandæ.

PRIMA. TERTIA. SEXTA. SECVNDA. QVARTA. SEPTIMA. QVINTA. OCTAVA.

VT figuras hac charta impreſſas commodè ſuis ſedibus glutines, illæq; ualidiores reddantur, primùm præſenti chartæ membranam ſubglutinabis, ſingulasq; figuras à ſuperſlua papyro reſecabis. PRIMA, quæ uenæ pari carentis diſtributionem proponit, magnæ figuræ tergo illic uenit cōmittenda, ubi cauæ caudex eam uenam promit. ac o in utriſque figuris ſcriptū ſpectatur. SECVNDA, ubi à redundanti papyro circuncifa erit, duas partes conſtituet, quarum ſuperior uenam arteriamq́ue dextri lateris exprimit, ſub pectoris oſſe ſuperiorem abdominis ſedem petentes. Huius itaq; partis q ad magnæ figuræ q figetur, & * ad ramum qui ad dextrum latus ≀ & m in magna figura occurrit. Cæterùm humilior pars uenā arteriamq; exprimens, quæ inferiorem abdominis ſedem implicant, illic eſt iungenda, ubi earum radices iuxta l in dextro latere ſpectantur.

TERTIA cæteris dignior, uenæ portæ diſtributionem ſimul cū arterijs illam concomitantibus, magnā que inferioris membranæ omenti portione & liene pariter exprimens, ad cauam iecoris ſedem maiori figuræ nectetur, ubi υ φ, τ, & contermini aliquot characteres in utriſque figuris ſpectantur.

QVARTA portionem gibbæ ſedis iecoris proponens, nō inutiliter ueluti ex puncto illic glutinabitur, ubi A inter ſ & F maioris figuræ conſiſtit.

QVINTA præter teſtes ipſorumq; inuolucra, & urinarios meatus, uenas arteriasq; ſeminales oſtendens, illic eſt committenda, ubi κ in ambabus figuris obuium eſt, aut ubi uena ſeminalis arteriæ primùm iungitur, meatusq; urinarij illis ſubijciuntur.

SEXTA primùm ſub SEPTIMA uenit glutinanda. Septima enim uesicæ & penis anteriorem ſedem proponit, unà cum uaſis quæ umbilico aſſcribimus. Sexta autem humiliorem penis ſuperficiem in hoc expreſsimus, ut tota figura ex ambabus illis conſurgēs, charactere φ ſuper quintæ figuræ φ necti queat, ac poſtmodum penis inſtar S implicari.

OCTAVA figura mulieris ueſicam & umbilici uaſa, urinariorumq; meatuum portionem continens, maiori non eſt committenda, ſed illi figuræ quæ in chartæ tergo ubi maior impreſſa eſt, uterum ipſius, uenas & arterias ſeminariaq; uaſa commonſtrat. Iungetur itaq; octaua ad paruam illam figuram ubi κ occurrit, uenaq; ſeminalis arteriæ committitur: nexus uerò fiet urinarijs tantum meatibus, proportione a ueſicæ ſitu ſumpta.

m 3

During the design process, as is also the case with the design of this book, we tend to treat the program anatomically. This means that program elements are divorced from one another which allows us to think of their ideal character as individual entities separate from the larger whole. Current trends tend to treat space as uniformly generic, and program as something that is later applied to such spaces.

In order to produce architectural difference, we think of the reverse-- that each program requires certain qualities, and only later are these assembled into a larger whole. The above page from the aforementioned *Fabrica* exists in an interesting side-by-side with the adjacent page, an anatomical array of program elements in their individual configurations.

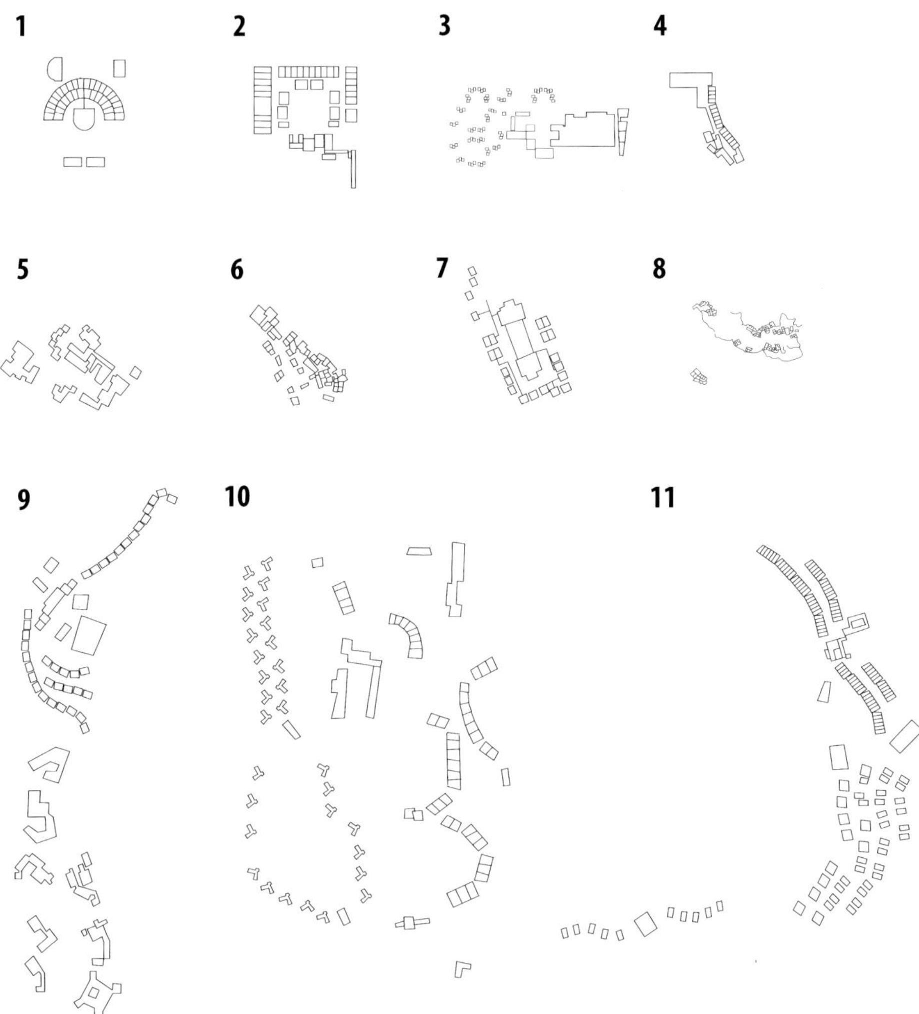

DATA AND DEVIATIONS

Often, after receiving a program and visually breaking it down into properly sized boxes, we'll go through a "clumping" phase, where certain sympathetic programs are placed into proximity with one another, but treated independently for the purposes of design. *Following pages:* This is an early concept rendering and collage of how we imagined the architecture would be composed within the site. This collage was done prior to visiting the site and was intended only to show the interest in the architecture "peeking" out from the rocky escarpments, rather than dominating the compositions through being "iconic" forms.

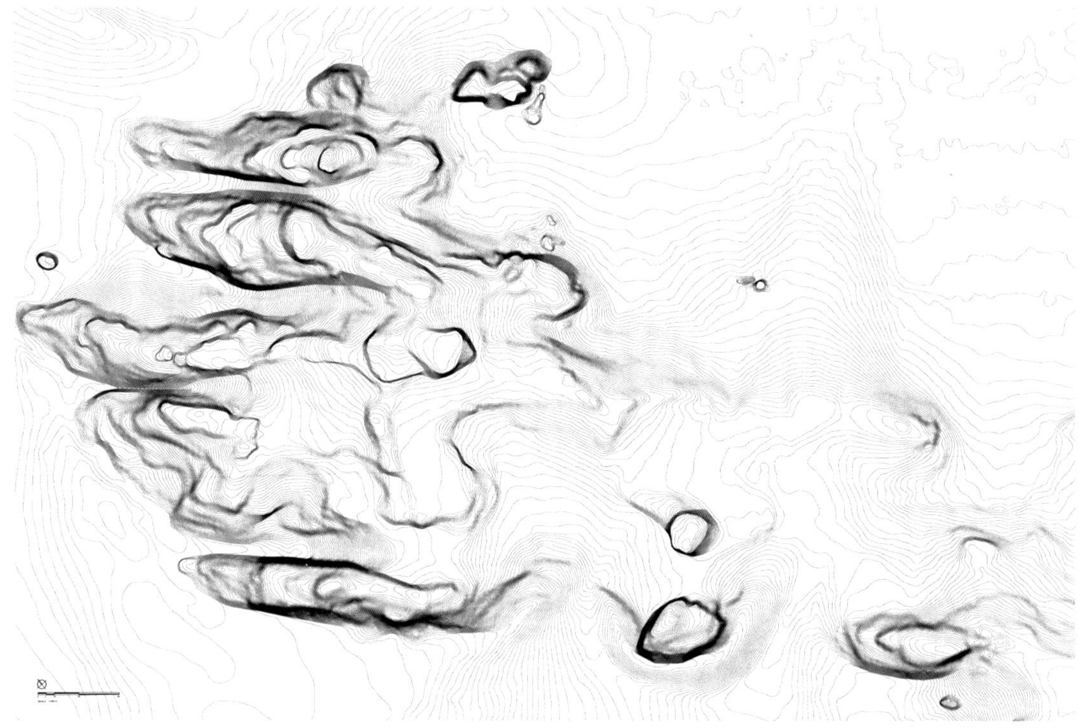

66

SITE TOPOGRAPHICAL ANALYSIS

This shows the first high resolution drawing of our site with topographical lines that indicate height. One can see the extensive ridges and ravines formed by the "fingers" of the hand-like site we had selected. The site also has an elevated, but visually protected "basin" in the lower center of the image which would become the functional core of our resort—housing communal programs such as the pools, spa, gardens, restaurants and reception areas. This site was selected because it was topographically rich—offering vast possibilities for creating spaces and generating rich relationships between the buildings and geological structures in which they were embedded.

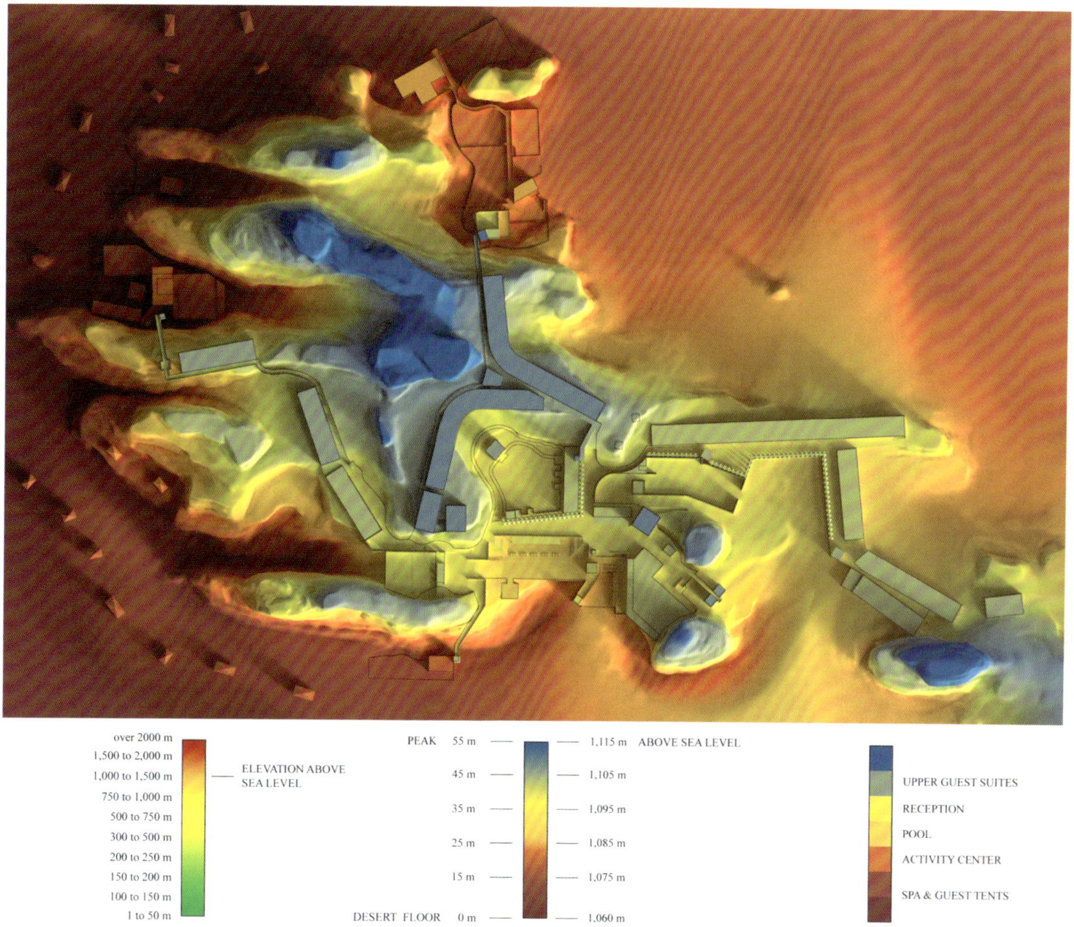

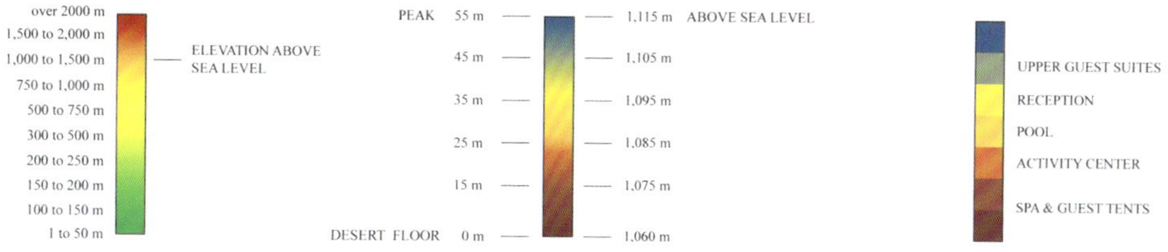

67

SITE HEAT ANALYSIS

One of our earliest concerns in this project was heat—and how to avoid it. This heat map study of the site illustrates how the strategy of elevating our buildings off the desert floor and into the sandstone structures would provide them with natural cooling. Redder areas are hotter and blue areas are cooler. Our goal was to have no residential units in red areas and to aim for light orange to yellow areas, which would require less mechanical assistance to become comfortably habitable. The remote villas, located on the desert floor in the lower left, were moved to a cooler location because of the results of this analysis.

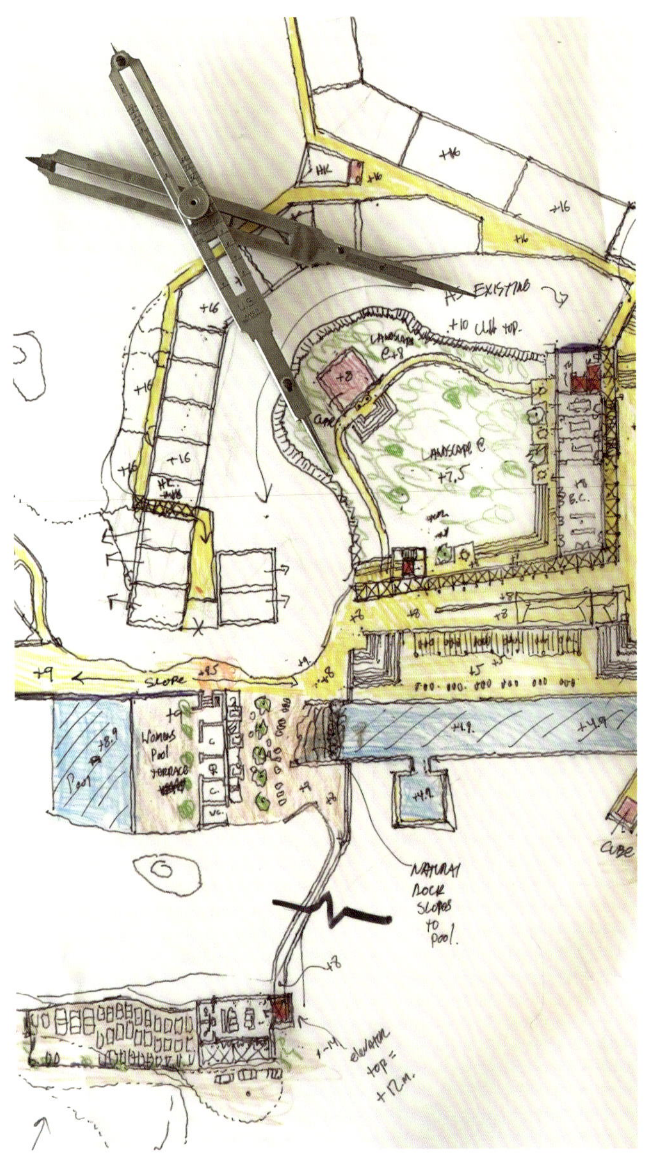

Preceding pages: Once we returned to our offices in New York, we broke out our highest-tech equipment—colored pencils and my proportional divider that I inherited from my Grandpa Delmar, who was an Air-Force navigator. It is a strange twist of fate that Air Force navigators and classically trained architects both rely on the same tools. Proportional dividers such as these are famously represented in art history in association with architects, notably in Albrecht Durer's masterwork engraving "Melancholia I," from 1513–1514. *This page:* Above is a hand sketch detail of the pool and oasis areas.

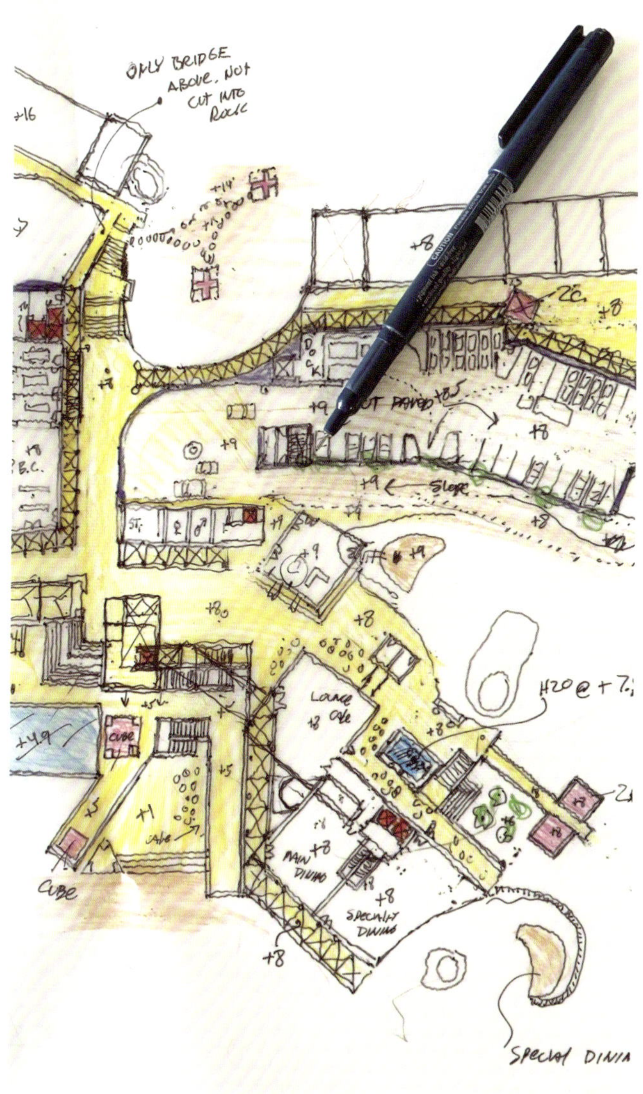

71

YES. COLORED PENCILS

Despite our office's significant reliance on advanced technologies and the astronomical amount of money we spend on computers and related equipment, I find that there is nothing quite as quick as a rudimentary colored-pencil sketch, although we never show them as presentation drawings. Designing with translucent vellum—or if I'm feeling particularly wealthy, mylar—remains the best way to quickly develop design iterations, especially in plan through multiple layers of drawings stacked on top of one another. Hardly the sexy imagery one sees on Instagram, but a necessary step in the process of actually designing something that works programatically.

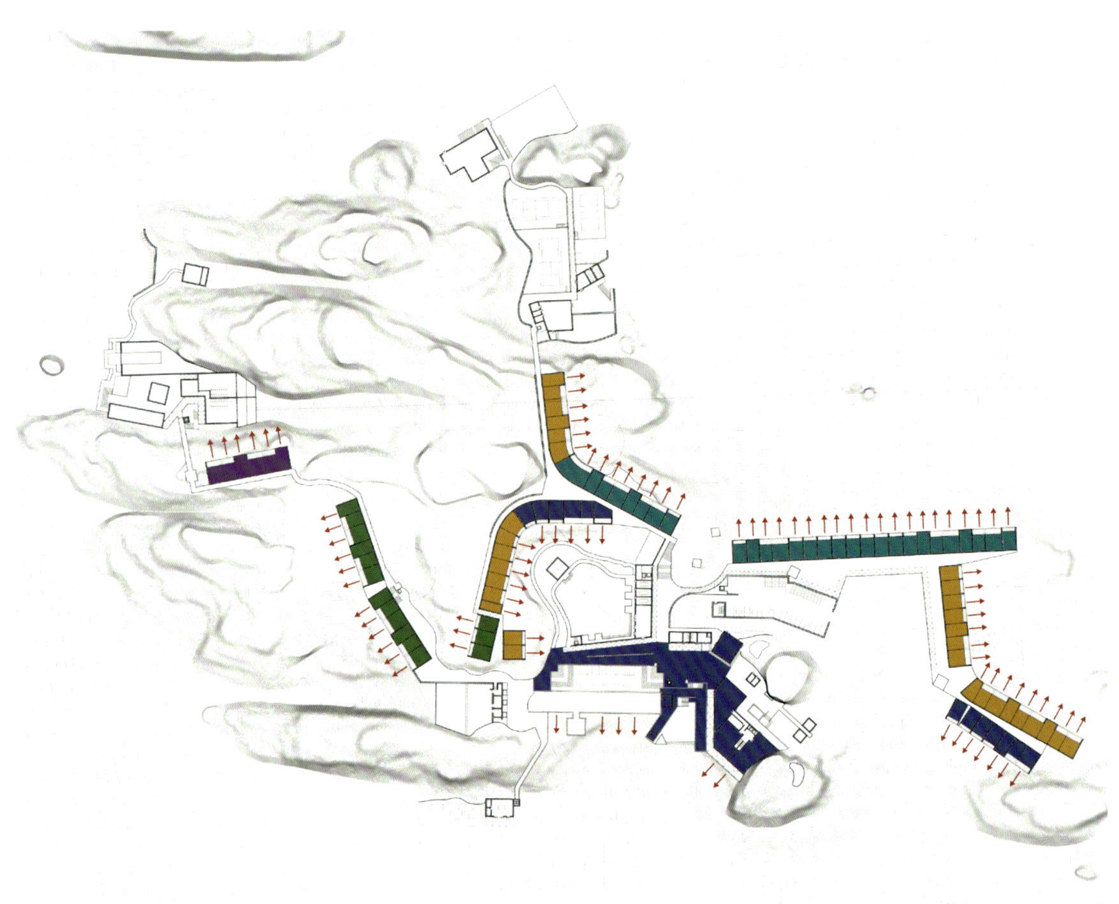

VIEW ORIENTATIONS

Our proposal placed significant emphasis on the fact that no residential suites would have a view of any other residential suites. Instead, all rooms would have unobstructed views over the desert horizon. This proved to be a rather tricky puzzle, requiring diagrams such as this one that illustrate, with colors and arrows, the exact panoramic view that each of the room groupings would see. *Opposite page:* These are the desert vistas that would be visible from the different rooms—managing these view corridors required a complex calculus of visibility, which we expected on our site visit and accordingly documented them in incredible detail.

THE SATELLITE CAMPUS

This master plan shows not only our primary resort site, but also our "satellite site" that was the location for a solar field for power generation and the staff residential quarters. Each staff unit has frontage on the resort's plant nursery, dedicated to re-introducing native plant species to the region. The staff buildings form a barrier to protect the plant life from consumption by wild camels. The stepped form of the solar field was a play on the stepped forms present in almost all of the carved façade structures in Mada'in Salih—playfully making the geometric forms favored by the Nabateans visible from satellites. I don't know if Nabatean deities live up there, but if they do I'm sure they'd be just tickled.

To truly experience the site we thought that it would be best if one was "in" it—meaning that our resort could not be a singular large building merely surrounded by a perimeter of sandy and rocky "nature." Instead, ours was an unraveled building, with smaller pieces embedded within the site—all high above the desert floor yet nestled and protected within rocky clefts, ridges and miniature valleys. Guests can experience nature in multiple ways, through close proximity to the stone of the site and through being elevated, and therefore visually connected to the vast and magnificent unobstructed horizon. We therefore describe our guest suites as being "within the rocks, above the sky"—a seeming impossibility made possible through the unique and otherworldly site.

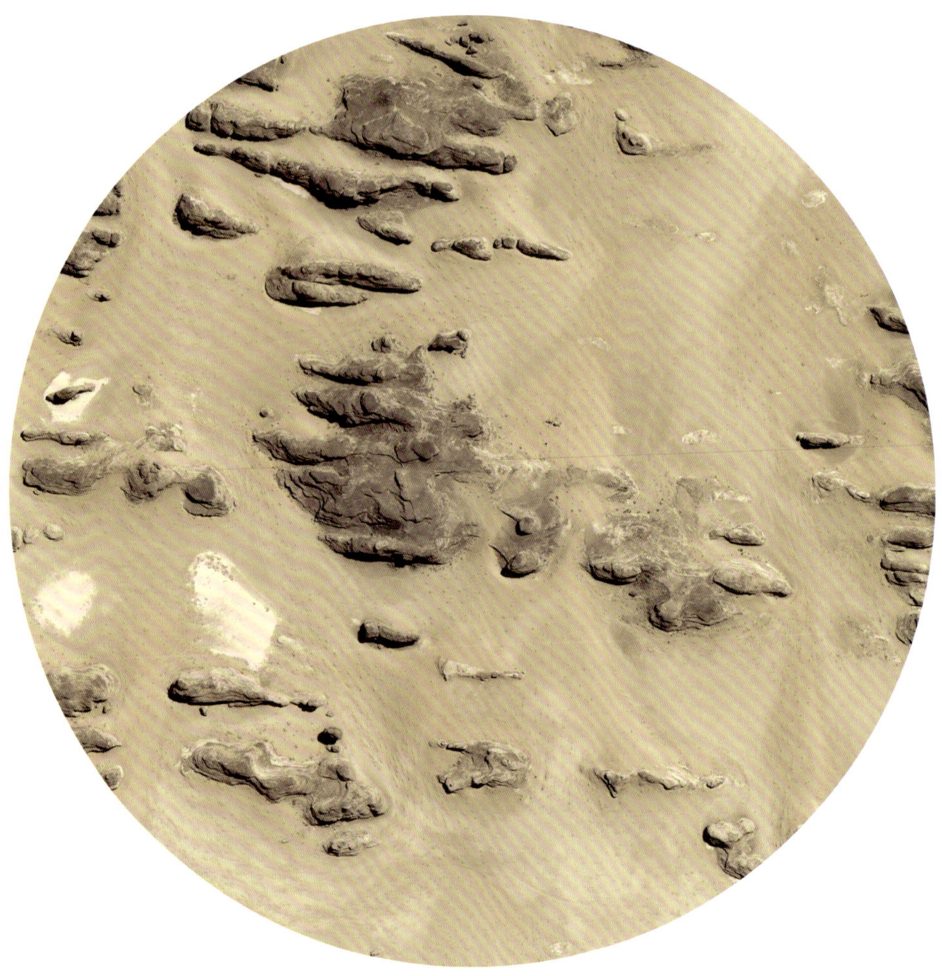

THE SITE FROM SATELLITE

Preceding pages: The image is an aerial view of our design showing embedded buildings and the centralized core of the communal programs. The central tower was an observation tower with the double function of acting as a giant gravity-fed water filter, intended to recycle gray water for additional uses. A domed lattice covers the "oasis"—a functional native species garden used to further recycle water for use in the swimming pools, which it would trickle into over the course of the day to counter evaporation. *This page:* Above is a satellite view of our site.

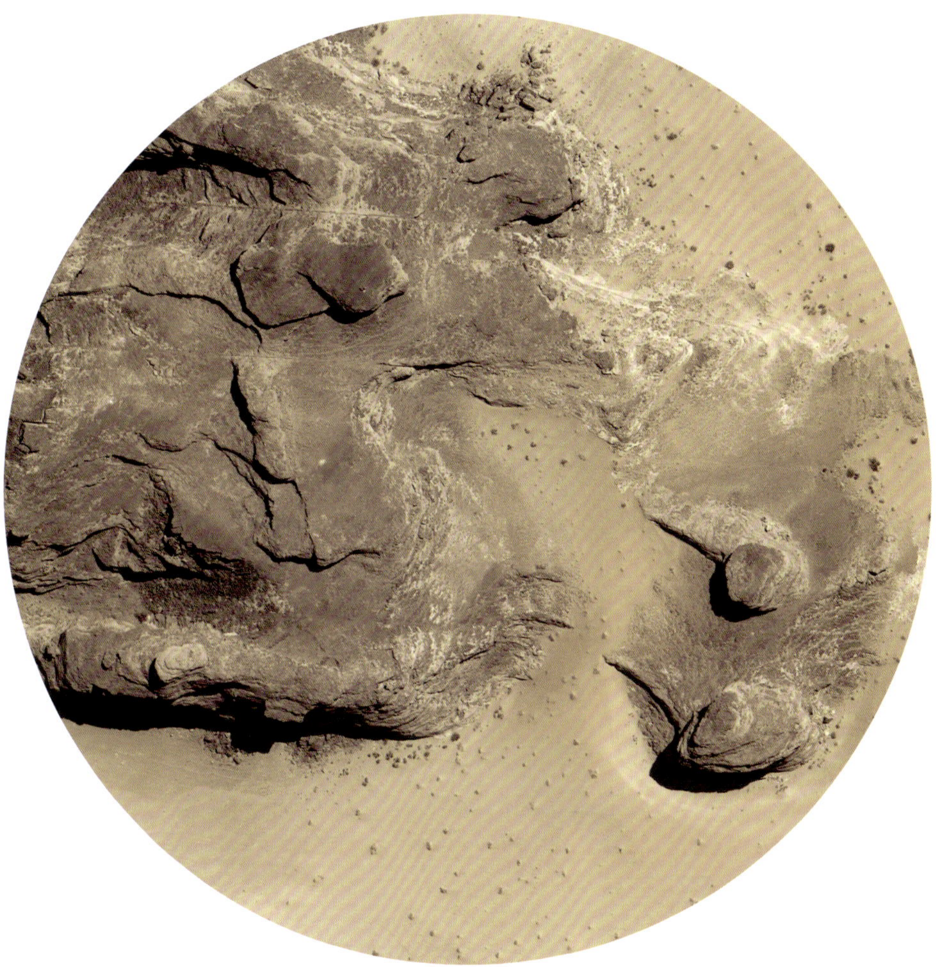

79

WORKING ON MARS

The above image shows the areas of our central core magnified in greater detail. Visible is the central "basin" that is defined by the sandy patch surrounded by the darker sandstone outcroppings and the two isolated stone masses visible in the lower right of the image. We had these images hanging up in our office and more than one person walking by in our building asked if we were working on something involving Mars. While the answer was no, the geological and aesthetic quality of the site probably wasn't far off from that of the Martian landscape.

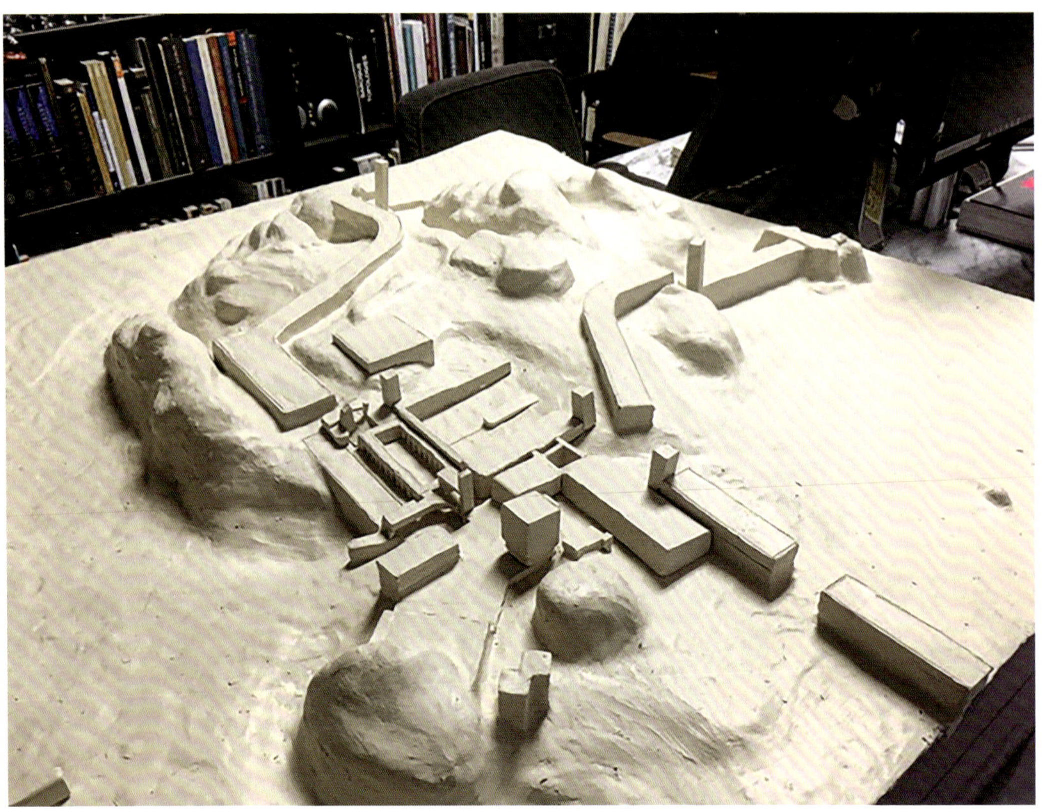

CLAY STUDY MODEL

Due to the incredible complexity of the site topography, we found it necessary to build a rather old-school clay model of the site that we could hack into as a way to visualize the interactions between buildings and site. This particular iteration showed us that our buildings were actually rather ugly on the site—too visible and too linear. Making models such as this one is helpful not because they reinstate that our intuitions about certain things are right, but because they show us where we are wrong. This particular model caused a rather substantial redesign of the residential building locations.

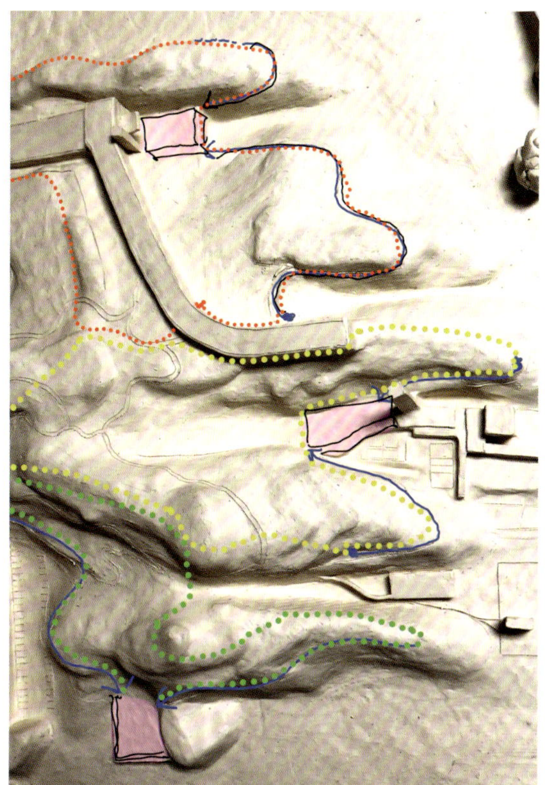

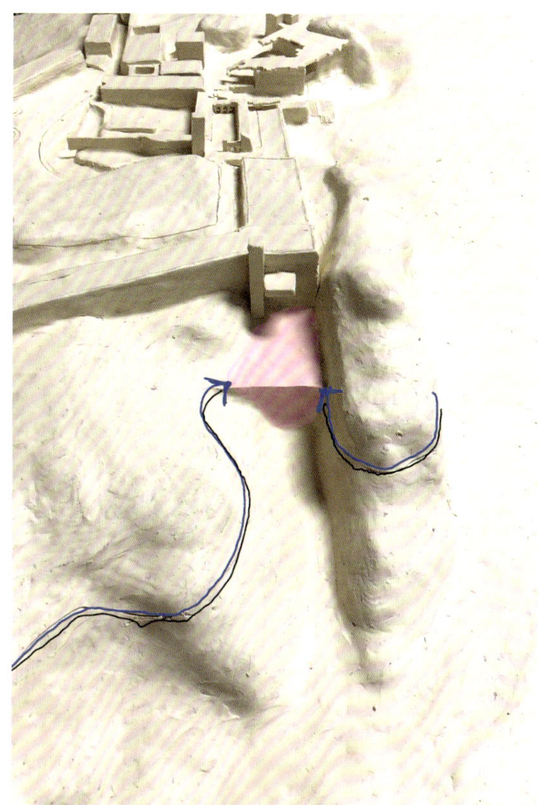

HYDRAULIC CHANNELING—ANCIENT EDITION

After using our sloppy clay model as a means to study the siting of our buildings, we later used it to predict the flows of rainwater. Al Ula is prone to massive deluges of short-term rain, which can be incredibly useful and ecologically sensible if the water can be captured before it hits the desert floor and is absorbed by the sand. As such we designed a series of etched mini-canals into the sandstone outcroppings in a manner similar to that of the Nabateans. This channeled rain water goes into a series of storage reservoirs located underneath some of our building structures. The stored water would later be filtered and re-used for resort functions.

Opposite page: This image is an early sketch of an isolated shade and refreshment pavilion located within a naturally occurring sandstone nook. The language of intersecting domes would continue to be used in our final design for the restaurant pavilion. *This page:* The interior of these freestanding pavilions would not only be programmed with the necessities for tourism, but would also be stunning volumes covered with fractal/AI-generated tile patterns based on Nabatean geometries—such as the image above, which combines step-forms and diagonals with a vibrant explosion of greens and teals.

MAIN VAGETATION TYPES OF THE ARABIAN PENINSULA

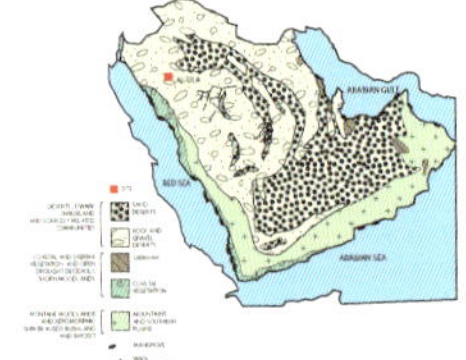

PRINCIPAL TOPOGRAPHICAL FEATURES OF THE ARABIAN PENINSULA

TOPOGRAPHICAL TRANSECT ACROSS ARABIAN PENINSULA

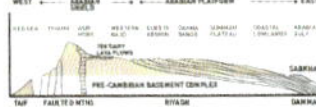

Al Ula's Rich ecosystem

The Royal Commission for AlUla (RCU) has set outstanding objectives in terms of natural integrity and diversity with the designation of the Sharaan Nature Reserve. The project focuses on restoration AlUla's natural ecosystem and indigenous vegetation. The landscape spaces associated with the Sharaan Retreat will showcase the RCU's effort. Integrated into the overall plan, a nursery will grow the most emblematic species of the plants community for distribution in the landscape.

The commonest physiographic features over vast areas of the Arabian Peninsula are rock and gravel deserts. These are of two main types: 1.- Rock and stone deserts (hamadas) where all fine weathering products have been removed by the wind; and 2.- Gravel deserts (regs) where the parent material consists of heterogeneous deposits, such as alluvium, and where all the fine material has been removed by the wind.

The vegetation of these deserts forms a mosaic which is very difficult to classify. Large areas are very thinly vegetated with plants restricted to rock crevices and to drainage channels and wadis where sand and soil accumulate. An annual 'meadow' often develops in areas where soil and water collect after rain. Trees and larger shrubs (Acacia spp., Lycium shawii, Ochradenus baccatus, Tamarix spp., etc.) tend to be restricted to wadis.

On the northern and central plains, where our site is located, two main communities can be identified (each with many local variations):
1.- Dwarf shrubland dominated by Rhanterium epapposum with Astragalus spp., Fagonia spp. and Plantago spp. This favours reasonably well-drained soil on shallow sand or amongst rocks in pockets of sand.
2.- Dwarf shrubland dominated by Haloxylon salicornicum prefers deeper sand than the Rhanterium community but is also found on shallow sand, gravel plains and occasionally on rock surfaces. It is frequently associated with other Chenopodiaceae such as Anabasis lachnantha and Agathophora alopecuroides.

The typical vegetation of these rock and gravel deserts are open, xeromorphic dwarf shrublands intermixed, after rain, with perennials and annuals. (dominated by Artemissia sieberi and Achillea fragantissima). Central Arabia is dominated by Haloxylon salicornicum communities. This specie is associates with Astragalus spinosus, Fagonia bruguieri, Farsetia aegyptiaca, Gymnocarpos decandrus, halothamnus bottae, Slasola cyclophylla and stipagrostus spp.

Reference: "Hot Desert Ecology" by Fahad M.A. Al-Hemaid, PhD; "An Agroecological Exploration of the Arabian Peninsula" by Eddy De Pauw; "Vegetation of the Arabian Peninsula" Ghazanfar, Fisher, M. (Eds.)

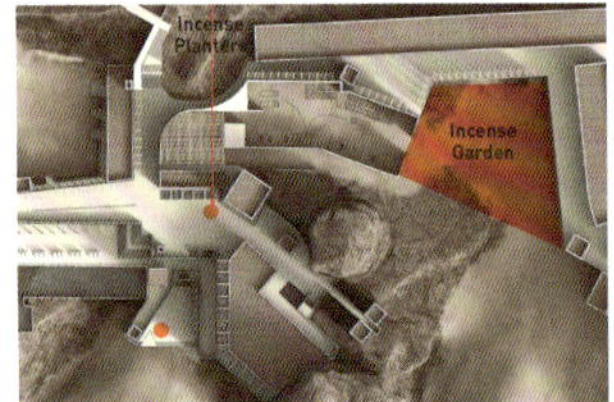

ECOLOGY AND SUSTAINABILITY

Our ecology and landscape proposal, developed with Balmori Associates and Transolar, aimed for the site to become a showcase of sustainable technologies working in concert to produce a building that was net-zero energy use on an annual basis. We proposed a network of strategies including, but not limited to: the smart use of thermal insulation through deep masonry construction; low emissivity glass; radiant cooling; operable natural ventilation; calculated sun shading; night irrigation; rainwater collection using the aforementioned "Nabatean channels" carved into the rock that lead to multiple gray water cisterns; a new "bio-reactor" system located underneath our garden oasis which used the vegetation above to assist in the filtration of water, wind-catching towers; tall gravity-fed water filtration towers; and a singular solar field hidden from the view of guests to generate all resort power.

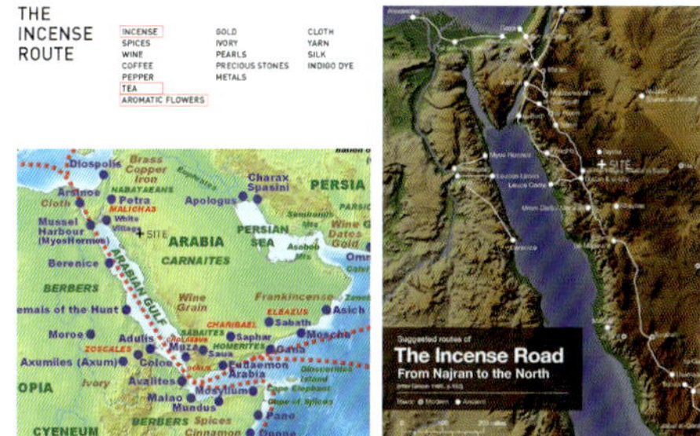

The Incense Route was an important trade route who brought frankincense and myrrh by camel caravan from South Arabia. The demands for scents and incense by the empires of antiquity, such as Egypt, Rome and Babylon, made Arabia one of the oldest trade centers of the world. Cities along these trade routes grew rich providing services to merchants who rested in oasis towns. These centers served as international marketplaces, and areas where knowledge was also exchanged. Cities such as Palmyra, Petra and Al Ula, on the fringes of the Syrian Desert, flourished mainly as centers of trade. They also became cultural and artistic centers, where peoples of different ethnic and cultural backgrounds could meet and intermingle. New inventions, artistic styles, religious faiths, cultures, languages, and social customs, as well as goods, were transported.

Soon after 24 BC, the Incense Road began to be replaced by the Incense Sea Route. As Nabataean dhows carried Incense from ports along the southern coast of Arabia north to Nabataea and Egypt, the inland route slowly passed out of existence.

We are proposing to regenerate an Incense garden within the complex. Plants such as Gum Arabic tree (Senegalia Senegal); Frankincense tree (Boswellia sacra); African Myrrh (Commiphora myrrha) and Wild Rue (Perganum harmala) will be planted scarcely on this grove.

THE INCENSE ROUTE

Frankincense
Boswellia Sacra

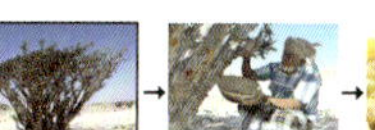

Gum Arabic tree
Senegalia senegal
HEIGHT: 5-12 m
SPREAD: 5-12 m

Frankincense tree
Boswellia sacra
HEIGHT: 3-7 m
SPREAD: 4-8 m

African Myrrh
Commiphora myrrha
HEIGHT: 3-4 m
SPREAD: 3-5 m

Wild Rue
Perganum harmala
HEIGHT: 0.6-0.9 m
SPREAD: 1-1.5 m

85

ORGANIC WATER RECYCLING

While water filtration is a part of everyday 21st century life, it is rarely beautiful to behold. Through working with the company Organica, we proposed that our garden oasis sit above a "bio-reactor" cistern, which used plant roots and bio-films to purify water for resort reuse. This was to provide the resort with, literally, a 21st century oasis that provides the same functions as those of yesteryear, but using the most advanced strategies of ecological engineering available today. Also proposed was the world's largest "lunar canopy"—a giant hollow patterned lattice placed high above the garden oasis that had the function of radiating the heat collected from the resort air conditioning into the night sky after temperatures had dropped.

ACCESS WITHOUT ROADS

Opposite page : This photo was taken from the interior of one of the carved rock tombs of Mada'in Salih. The horizontal carved shelves are where bodies and bones would be placed.

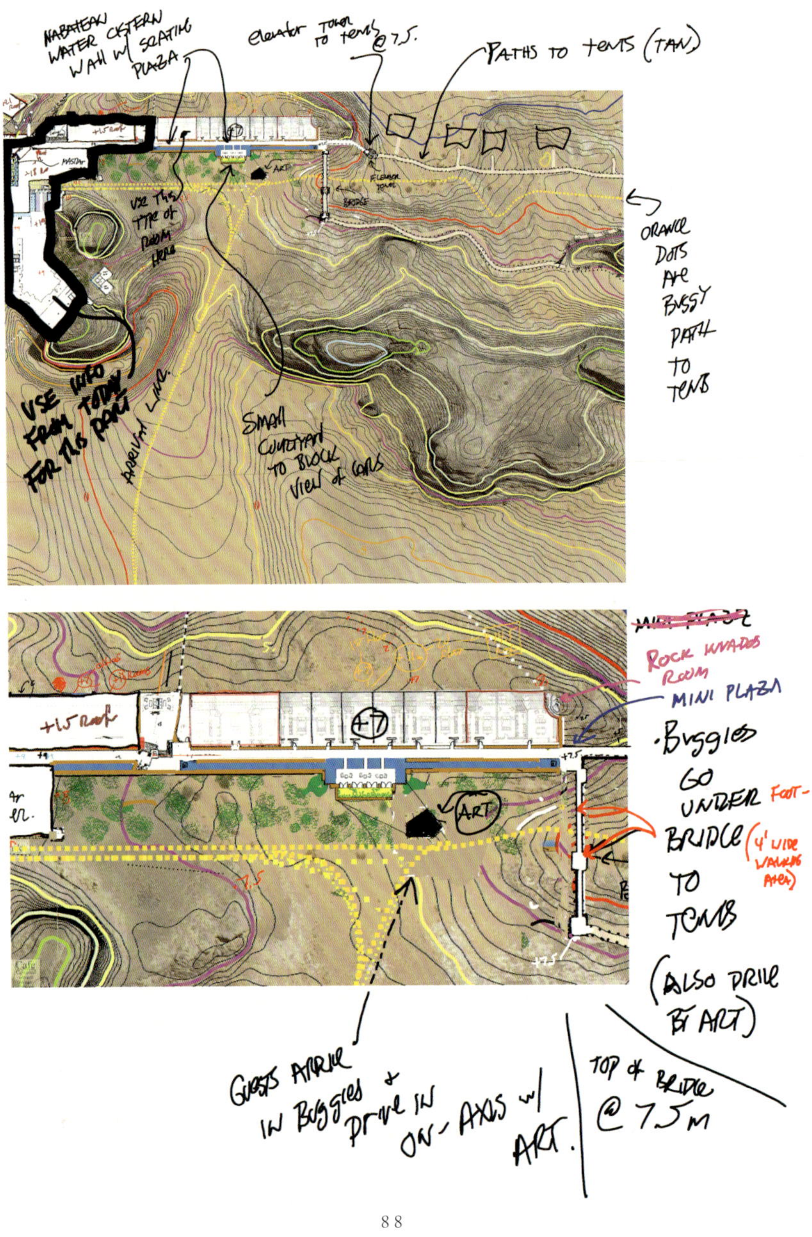

UGLY SKETCHES

One often finds architecture books filled with perfectly manicured sketches that align with the final design. I suspect, however, that most architects, as is the case with our office, generate a lot of sketches that are, 99 percent of the time, rather hideously ugly. Sketches in our office are used to communicate design ideas to each other far more than for presentation purposes. As such, we thought we would include some of our ugly sketches in this book—merely to represent their thousands of brethren that didn't make the cut.

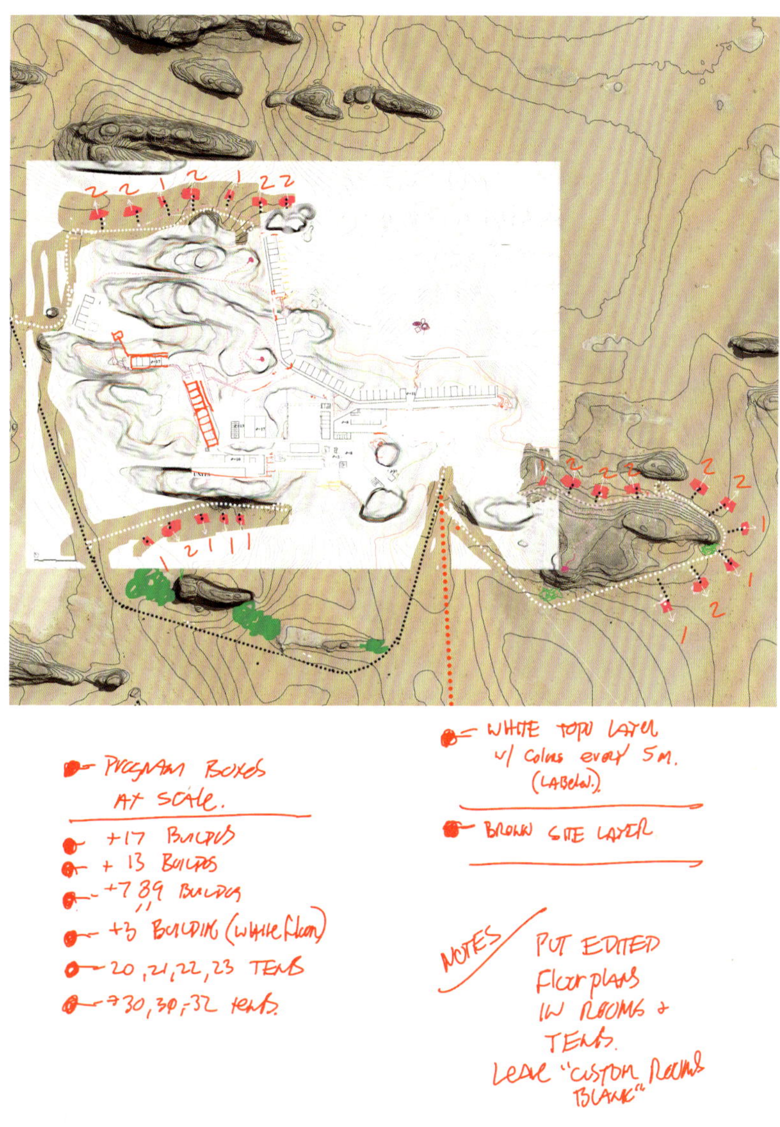

89

MORE UGLY SKETCHES

These sketches show studies of desert vehicle circulation, villa locations, and topographical inclines relative to what vehicles can realistically handle. I have always wished that I was one of those architects with perfectly structured handwriting, however, as you can see, such skills prove elusive. Such "Frankenstein" images are common in our office—in that they fold information and representations from multiple sources and software types into a single document, usually in a digital collage that allows us to see the various design ideas and related data simultaneously.

DIGITAL SCREEN DRAWINGS: VIEW FROM AFAR

Since the early development of Wacom screens that allow for rather precise on-screen hand drawing, one of our favored methods of design is drawing architectural ideas directly into the context using basic perspective and tentative scaling. This is far faster than 3D modeling the context early in the process and often allows us to focus on fewer areas that require modeling rather than modeling the entire site context.

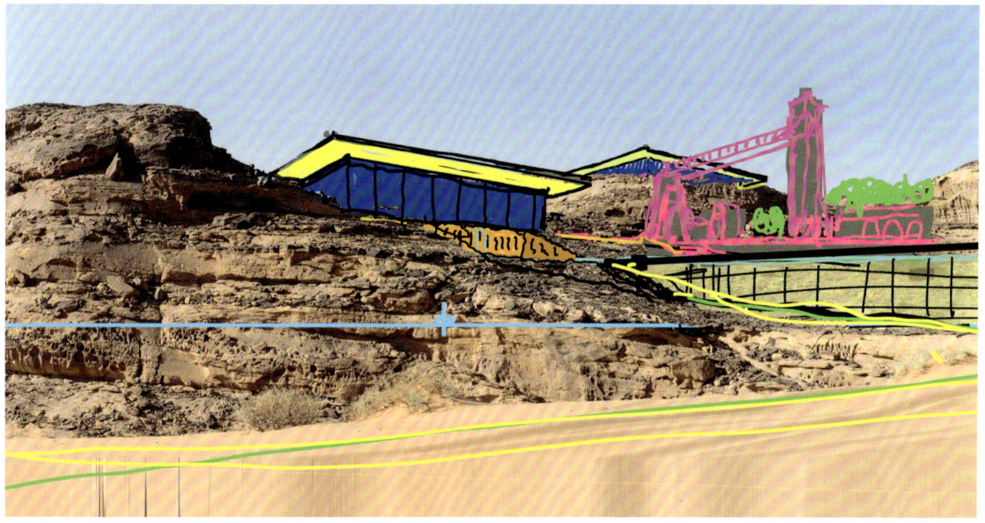

91

DIGITAL SCREEN DRAWINGS: INTERNAL CORE

The sketches presented here are only four of hundreds of similar drawings. In this case, they are illustrating how the main recreation and arrival core could sit next to the rocky basin of the selected site. They were helpful in determining that we were showing too much architecture and needed to tuck it further into the site to allow the geological formations to have more of a visual presence.

POST IPSO FACTO REPRESENTATION

The image on the left shows the central circulation tower via cel shading to flatten the materials and view the composition geometrically rather than perspectivally.

The above image uses the same technique to illustrate the intersection between the ceremonial entrance stair and existing rock formations shown in pink.

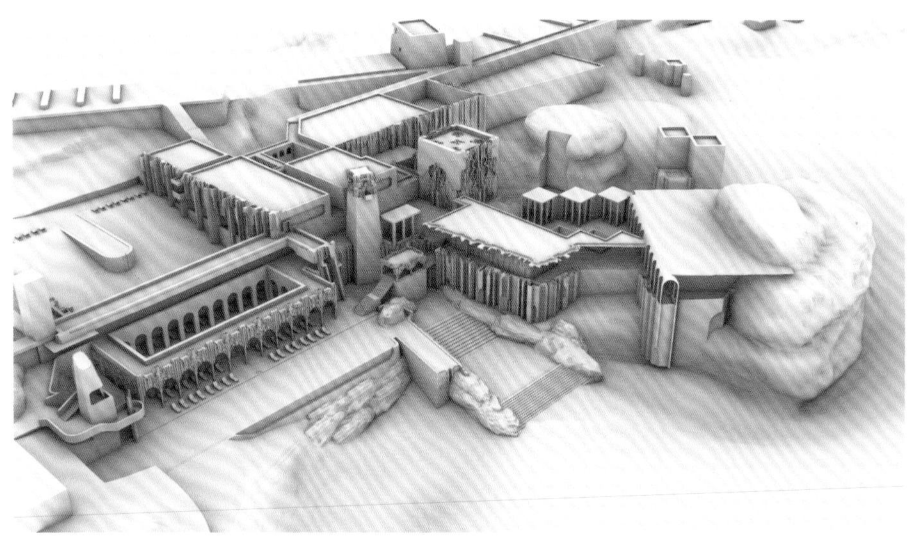

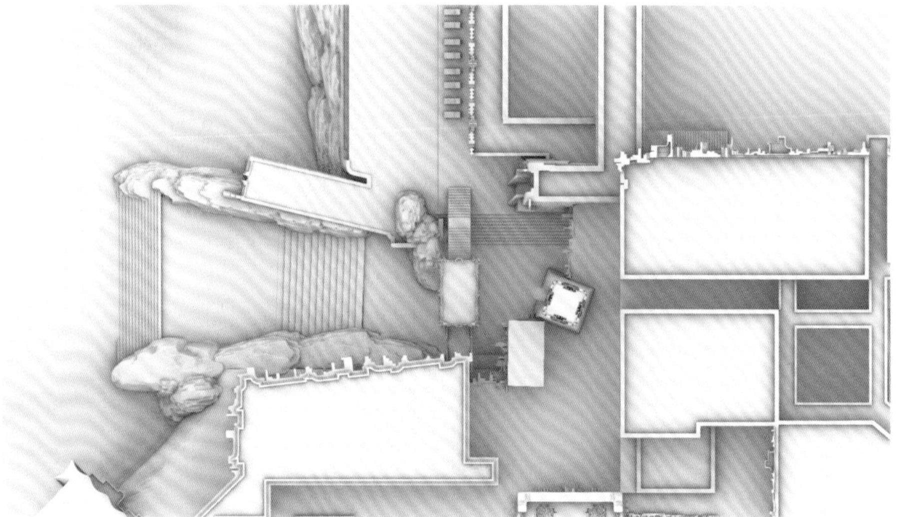

Preceding pages: Guests would arrive in a desert vehicle, the only way to access the site, along a choreographed path that would take them by particularly stunning rock formations and around an escarpment where they would receive their first view of the resort proper. From this vantage point, they could see a distant hidden world framed by the tallest stone promontories in the area. Our intent was that the first glimpse of the resort would allow it to appear as a mythical city deeply embedded into its surrounding site.

DESIGN FAST FORWARD: THE RECEPTION CUBE

Simultaneous with developing overall massing and circulation arrival routes, we also worked on the close-up aesthetic experience of particular areas. Our office has a policy that all design ideas must operate on "multiple ontological levels"—meaning multiple levels of "being." Often this is a question of scale, meaning that a building must be visible in one way from afar, but look different from a middle distance and then look different again when viewed closer up. A building that operates on multiple levels, either through distance or other criteria, engages the human viewer through curiosity and fascination, rather than cheap narrative metaphors that fleetingly disappear or worse, are never known. Architecture doesn't come with instruction booklets, so buildings cannot rely on descriptions of their narratives to make them culturally valuable—this has to be done aesthetically. This image is an etching of our reception cube design showing what it looks like from the moment guests are dropped off.

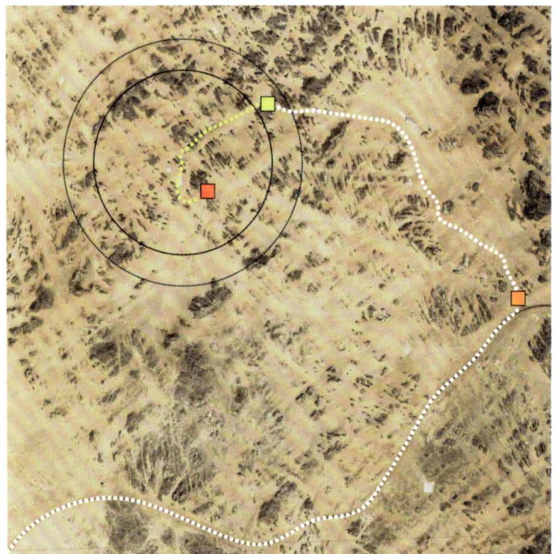

TRANSPORTATION INFRASTRUCTURE

Throughout human history, the desert has always been a place of mystical journey as opposed to one of mundane destination. In order to further accentuate this experience, the process of guests arriving at the resort was choreographed to reveal not only the site's natural beauty, but composed "vignettes," where the resort slowly reveals itself through being seen in smaller glimpses along the way. These diagrams illustrate how the guests would be brought to the site either by helicopter, or by way of cars that would transfer them to self-driving, or chauffeured, desert vehicles for the remainder of their journey. Although services such as restrooms are provided, this switch is intended to be one that takes minimal time—assuring that guests begin their journey to the resort proper as soon as possible and leave their everyday lives behind.

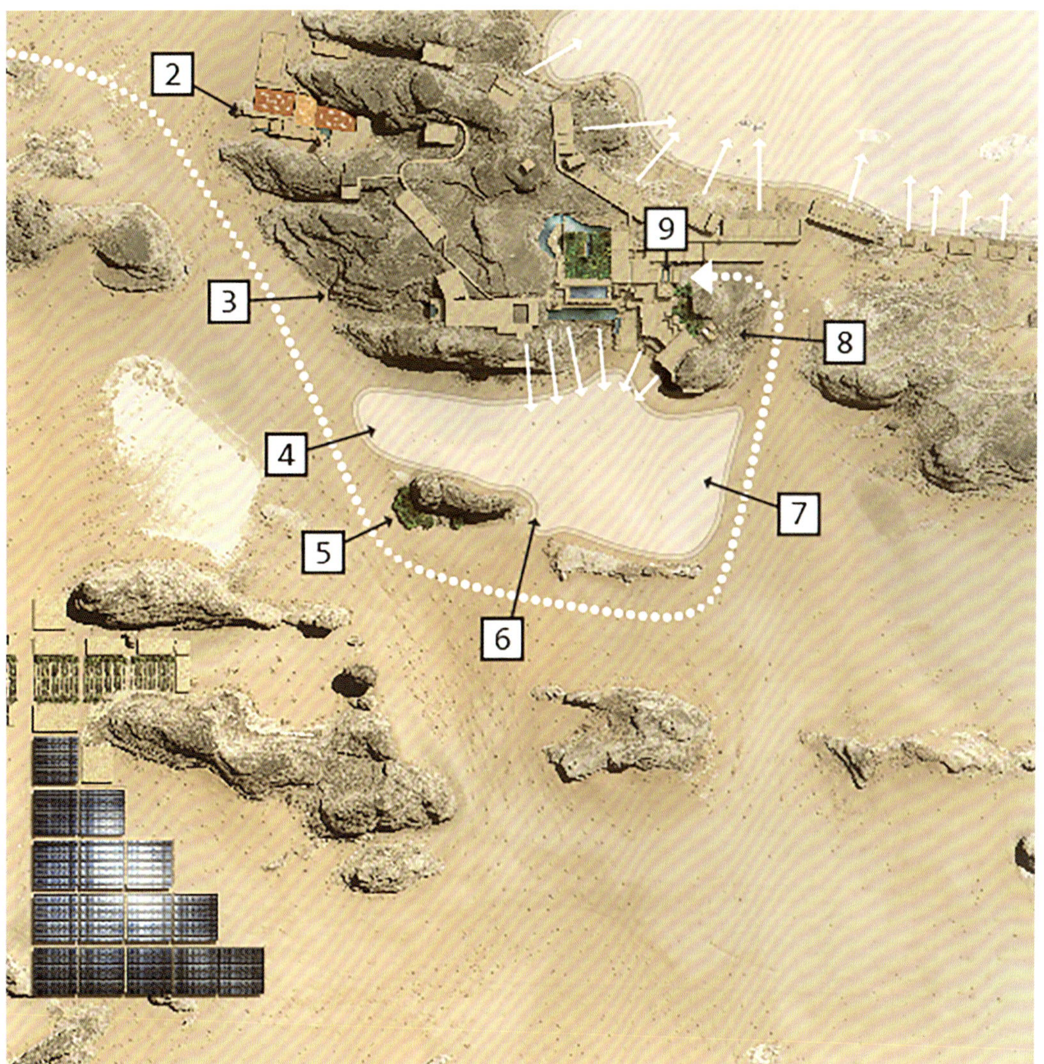

A CHOREOGRAPHY OF VIEWS: SEEN AND HIDDEN

The above image shows numbered key views of special locations composed to be particularly dramatic, providing opportunities for photographs and, as much as we worry about seeing any architecture in this way—"Instagrammable" moments. The lower left quarter of the image shows the "satellite campus" that housed additional resort programs, located within close proximity to the resort, yet visually hidden by large rock formations. The solar field and its equipment center share parking and support services with the staff and plant nursery programs. By integrating these functional programs into a singular, condensed, campus environment, staff and worker vehicular traffic is minimized elsewhere. This allows the 360-degree views from the resort itself to remain almost entirely unobstructed.

Hegra existed largely because of its importance to the incense trade. We proposed to acknowledge this with the cultivation of a small native species incense garden that surrounds the guest prayer towers. This garden includes and protects the Frankincense and Myrrh trees which defined the species of the historic incense trade. Carved deep within an adjacent rock is an incense drying room and gallery where guests can experience the process of incense production and take home the scents of the past. While we proposed the carving in the rock, we chose to leave the façade as a blank canvas for future collaboration with a local sculptor who would develop it further.

101

THE DESERT STILL LIFE PAINTING

Nearly at the end of the guest's arrival journey, visitors would slowly pass by the colorful burst of the framed still life prayer tower situated in the incense garden. Shortly after, they would drive into a protected porte-cochère for their final arrival. The exterior of the structures is fully clad in AI-designed tile that fuses references from multiple historic regional sources. The composition of the complex is intended to expose guests to their first close-up view of the architecture—yet the towers bear no sign of their function, in order to keep the experience mysterious, leaving the guests to wonder about their use and the place they are about to enter. We used historic Dutch still life paintings as a model for the composition of how the prayer tower stands among the sandstone areas and topography.

FRACTAL / AI-GENERATED TILE PATTERNS

The program required separate facilities for prayer—one for men and one for women. In order to treat these equally, we used a conjoined tower mass that is differentiated through the use of fractal and artificial intelligence generated tile patterns that use the DNA of historic patterns without simply reproducing them. This image shows one of the studies that was ultimately used on our design for the prayer towers in different tonal arrangements of blue and copper, and gold and green. The pattern has seeming regularity, but is neither regular nor symmetrical.

THE PRAYER TOWERS

The above image shows the final state of the joined prayer towers. Guests enter the commonly shared glass cube that has washing facilities and from there—and with equal importance—men and women separate into their prayer facilities. *Following pages:* The use of extravagantly colored tiles on the prayer towers was intended to give guests the view of an architectural still life painting, composed and visible from a single view. Unlike the illustrations of fresh fruit, fish, pitchers and cups, as one finds in typical still life paintings, ours was one that composed geology, architectural masses, color and pattern into a dramatic moment of chromatic relief against the monotone desert backdrop.

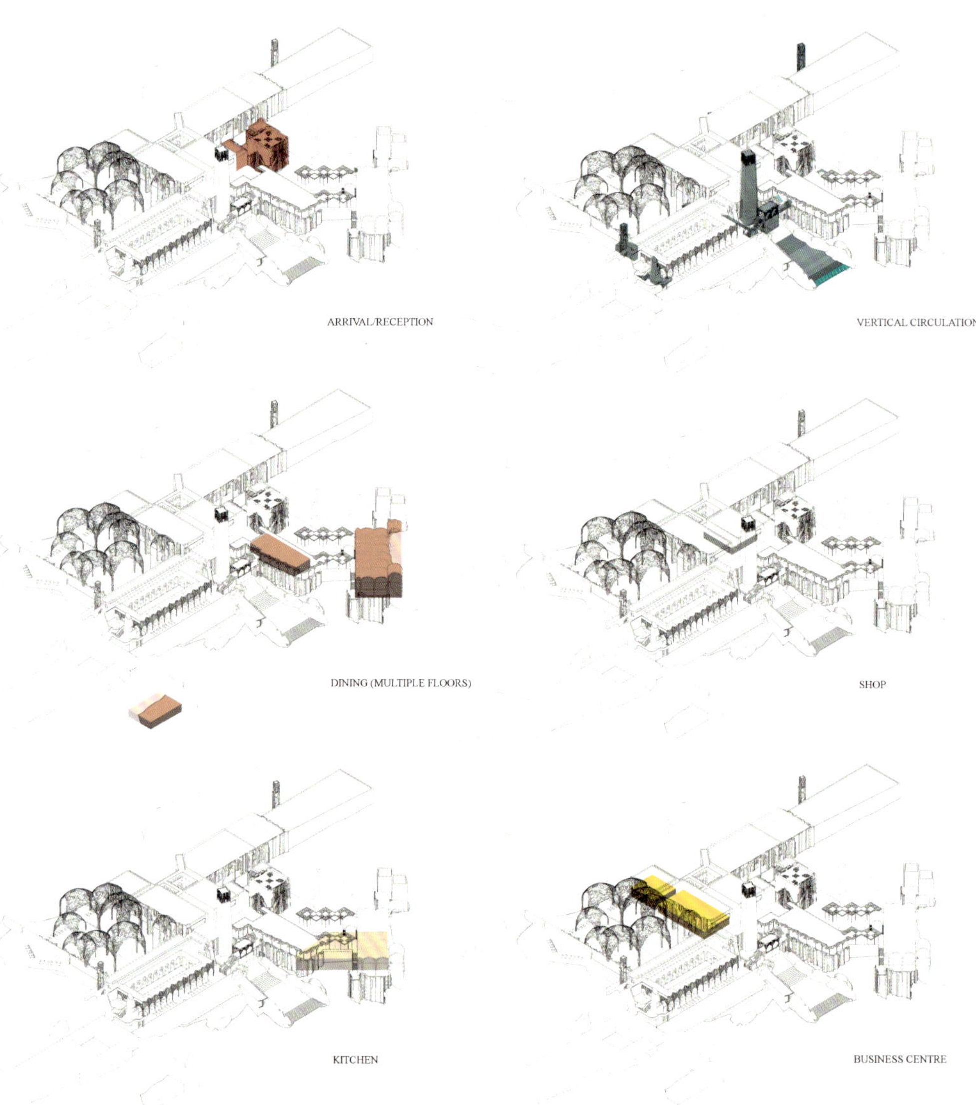

A MENAGERIE OF PROGRAMS

Upon arriving at the "reception cube," guests enter the core of the resort where they become familiar with the communal programs including reception, restaurants, cafes, business center, oasis garden, pools, childcare, and observation platforms. Each of these drawings isolate a distinct element of the program with a specific color. While such drawings convey very little about the architectural experience, they are helpful for both our clients and us in assessing the functionality of certain programmatic proximities and the means of circulation that connect them. *Following pages:* Fast forwards to all of the programmatic elements of the core area combined into the final architectural complex and its relationship to the surrounding geology, as seen in the final physical model.

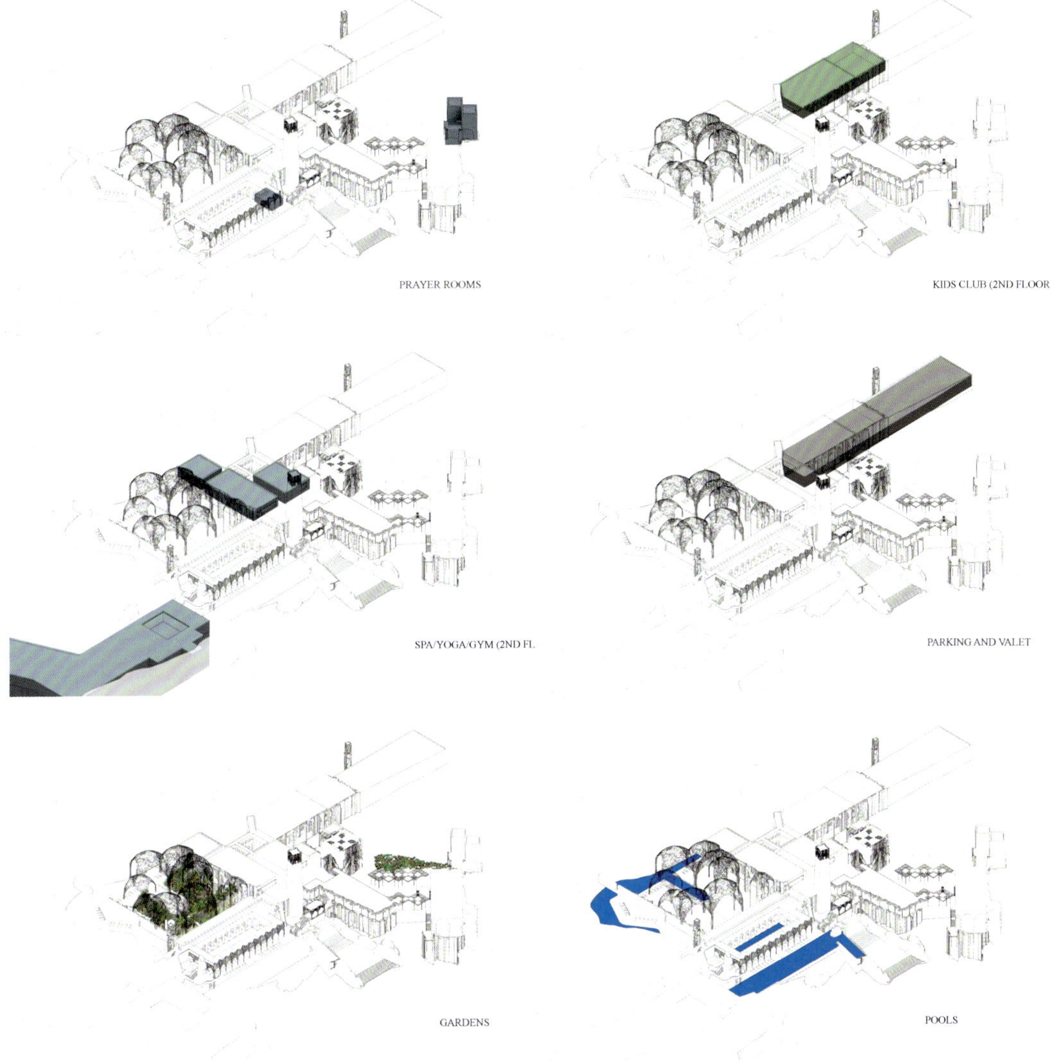
PRAYER ROOMS
KIDS CLUB (2ND FLOOR)
SPA/YOGA/GYM (2ND FL
PARKING AND VALET
GARDENS
POOLS

EVERY ROOM WITH A VIEW

Opposite page : **The** Old Town district in Al Ula is a mud-brick mini-city of nearly 900 interconnected houses that was occupied for nearly 800 years as a key destination for pilgrims traveling from Damascus to Mecca. Residents occupied the town up through the 1980s.

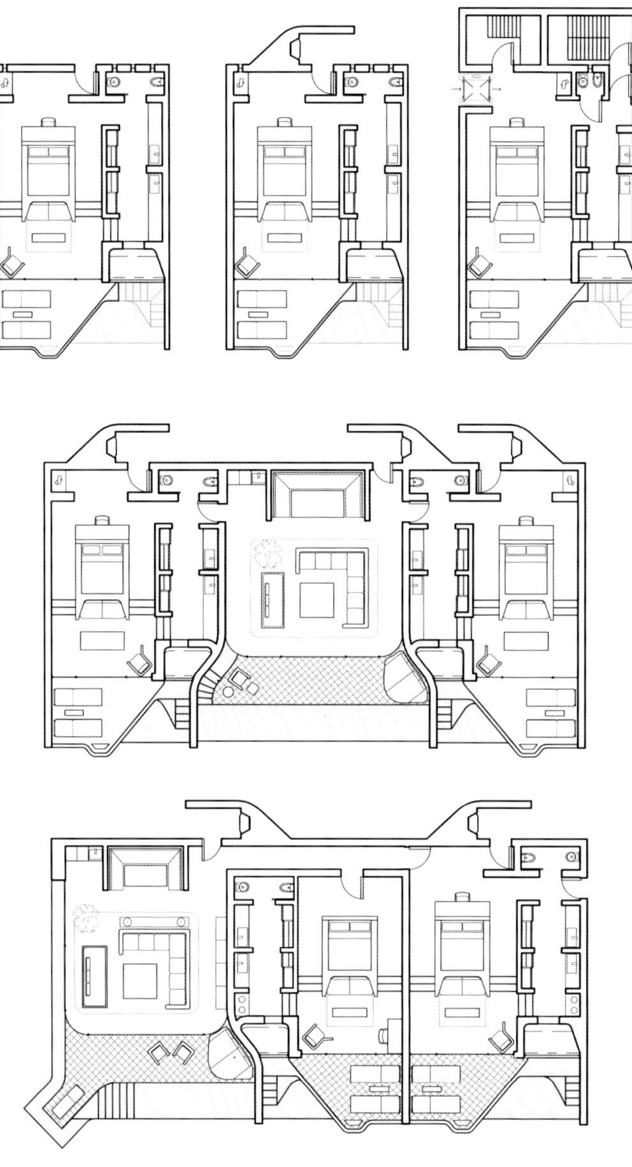

GUEST UNIT TYPES: ROOMS

For the project we developed multiple unit types, ranging from studios to two-bedroom suites. These plan variations show these unit types in row and corner conditions as well as how they would fit into the various building types. All of the guest rooms include a balcony and a plunge pool. Additionally, many of them feature natural rock walls as they are literally built into the surrounding geological formations.

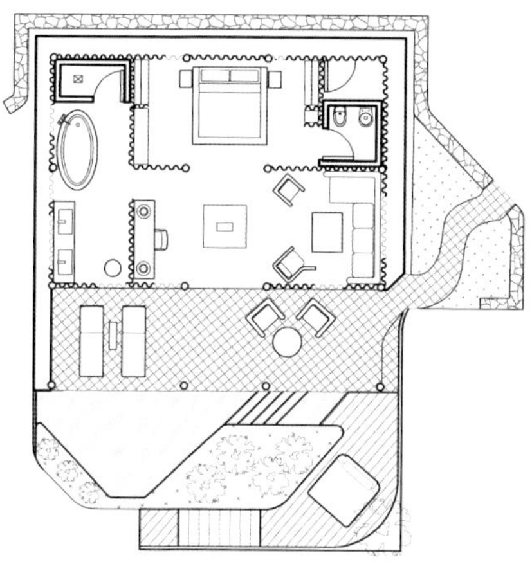

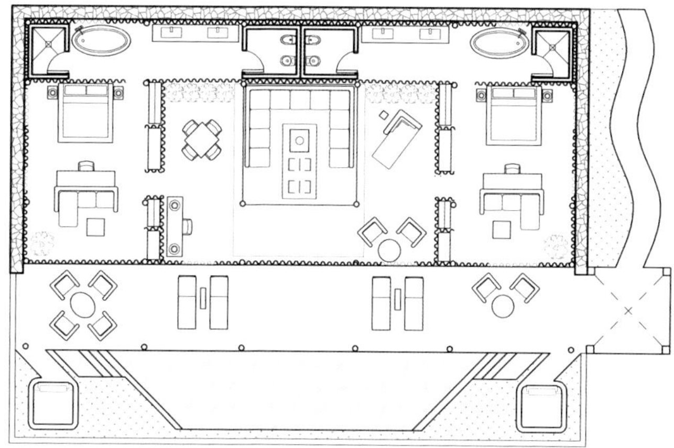

GUEST UNIT TYPES: REMOTE TENTS

In addition to the more standard resort room types, we also designed two sizes of remote guest "luxury tents" that would offer a more isolated and exclusive desert experience. These two plans show the variations—one with one bedroom and the other with multiple bedrooms—all equipped with their own covered outdoor areas, pools and air conditioning powered by the vast solar field located nearby.

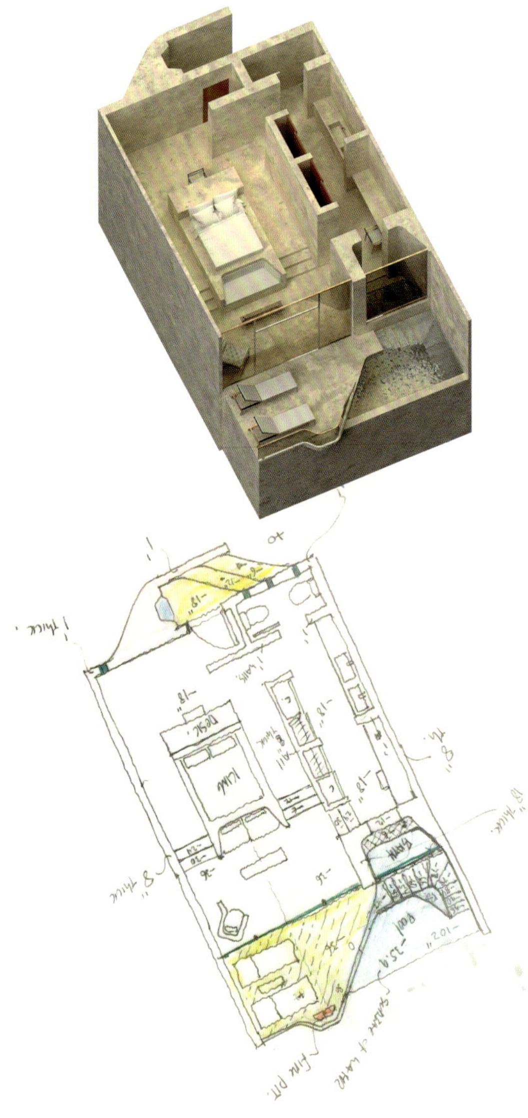

ONE-ROOM GUEST SUITE

This image illustrates a standard studio room, complete with its own living area, outdoor plunge pool, and balcony. All rooms were provided with uninterrupted views toward the distant desert horizon. This particular unit type, through placement of the bath and shower above the plunge pool, gives one the unique experience of showering in a vast and open expanse of desert. The use of lenticular glass prohibits viewers from seeing inside the showers from outside the room.

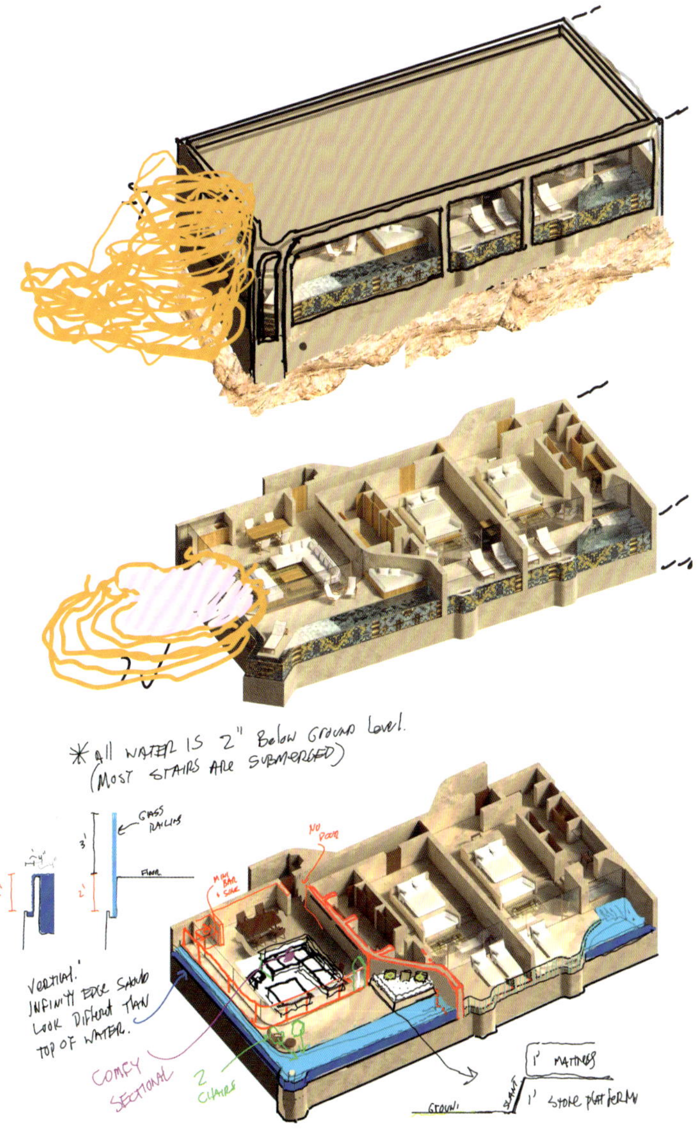

TWO-BEDROOM GUEST SUITE

This sequence shows how one of the two-bedroom suites would engage with a specific natural rock formation on the site in order to become part of the aesthetic experience. There are multiple types of geological formations that entered rooms—some would be sanded and polished to make more visible their intricate and colorful veining, others although cleaned, would maintain their original rusticated aesthetic properties. Images of both types of rooms are illustrated above in these early hand sketches.

SITE-INTEGRATED SUITES: EXTERIOR

Preceding pages: This selected oblique view of a two-bedroom suite shows how it intersects with the existing rock formations of the site. This image also illustrates in more detail, the terrace and small pool—both with a stamped and patterned metallic ceiling that wraps around the corner of the unit and dies into the existing sandstone form.

This page: The roof, while shown as a flat concrete substrate in this image, would be covered with crushed sandstone gravel to better blend-in with the site when viewed from higher locations. The front façade is dominated by AI-generated tile work that forms a horizon band along the pool area.

119

SITE-INTEGRATED SUITES: INTERIOR

The same two-bedroom suite with its roof removed shows the relationship between the living area and the existing rock formations. Wherever possible, guest rooms—of all sizes and types—were integrated into existing sandstone formations to provide a feeling of "embeddedness" with the site itself. The geological features provide visual and tactile interest in the residential interiors.

SKETCHING ARCHITECTURE INTO GEOLOGY

The above images are rather rough sketches that illustrate how the guest rooms, whenever possible, could be gently built into the site so that the sandstone outcroppings could be used as walls—and produce a rustic natural rock feature that would be offset against the otherwise minimal room. The room is designed with little articulation and detail so that their unobstructed views toward the desert horizon remain the guests primary focus.

WHERE ROOMS MEET ROCKS

These images show further-developed process drawings and renderings of the rooms on the adjacent page. In these images the views collaged into the rooms are the actual views those rooms would have of the desert beyond. Ultimately the above direction wasn't used because we decided to design all the furnishings of the room interior to feel as if they were all part of the ground-plane. The goal was to produce an interior that was carved rather than a space with generic objects placed within it.

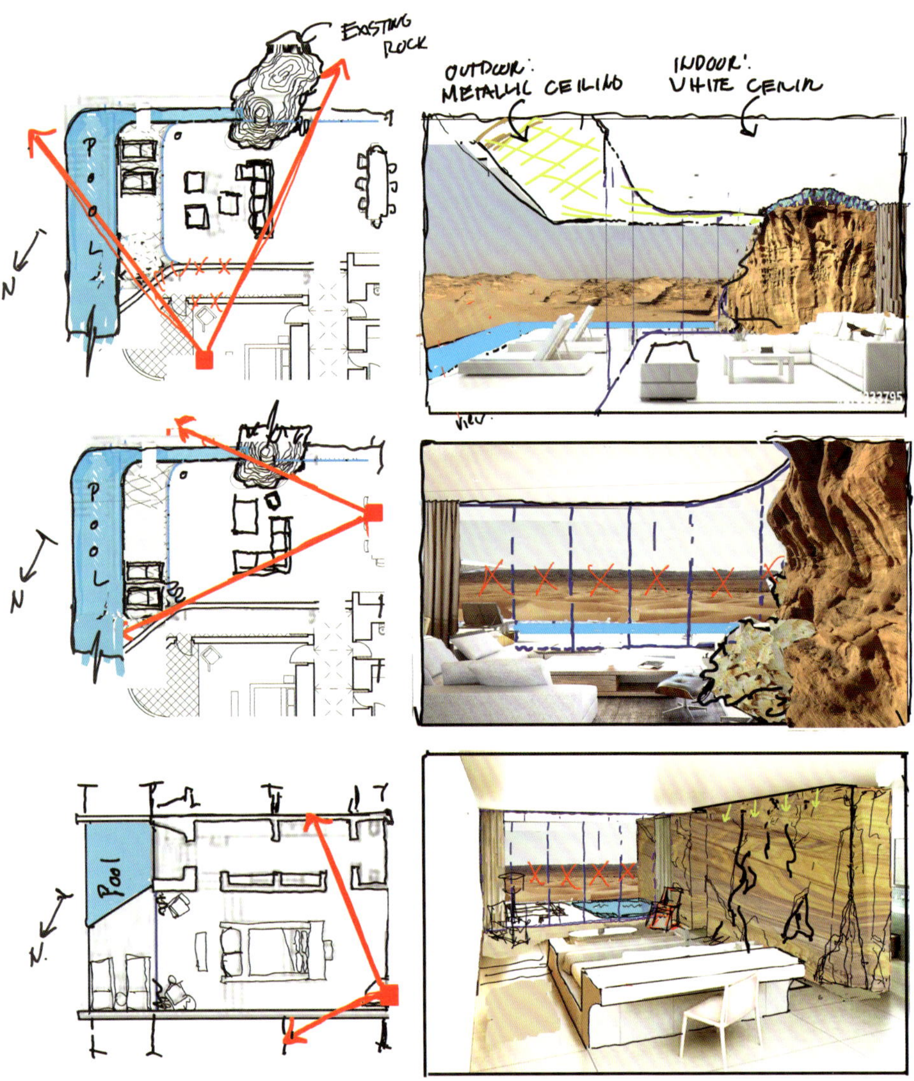

SETTING KEY INTERIOR VIEWS

Once the guest suites had been designed, we wanted to show their interiors photo-realistically in order to capture the aesthetic qualities of the spaces. This requires a time-consuming process of selecting views, modifying camera locations, tweaking the lighting, and material effects and compositing the space with realistic furnishings. This is always a dilemma in our office—how does one show a space photo-realistically when the interiors haven't been fully designed? To do this we typically select limited and neutral furnishings that convey scale and comfort without distracting from the primary focus—the space and views.

SKETCH FURNISHINGS STUDIES

This sequence shows how we typically populate a scene using quicker renderings and collages prior to actually 3D modeling the full interior contents. Such images give us a good idea of what the final image will look like and allow us to make any changes before committing to the final view. The upper view is the collage and lower view the rendered 3D model that emerged from the visual study. *Following pages:* This is a view from the interior of the selected suite over the outdoor pool and terrace, toward the desert sunset. The desert background shown is the actual view one would see from this particular room.

REDISCOVERING ANCIENT DESIGN LANGUAGES

Opposite page : This is a close up image of Bedouin jewelry. The Bedouin people, being nomadic, have no historic architectural heritage to study. Their artistic emphasis tends to be placed into items like woven blankets, rugs, and in particular, intricate jewelry, as shown here. We used these types of crafted items to fold Bedouin reference material into our design language, in particular through patterns shown in weaving and the intricate metalwork visible in pieces such as Bedouin bracelet.

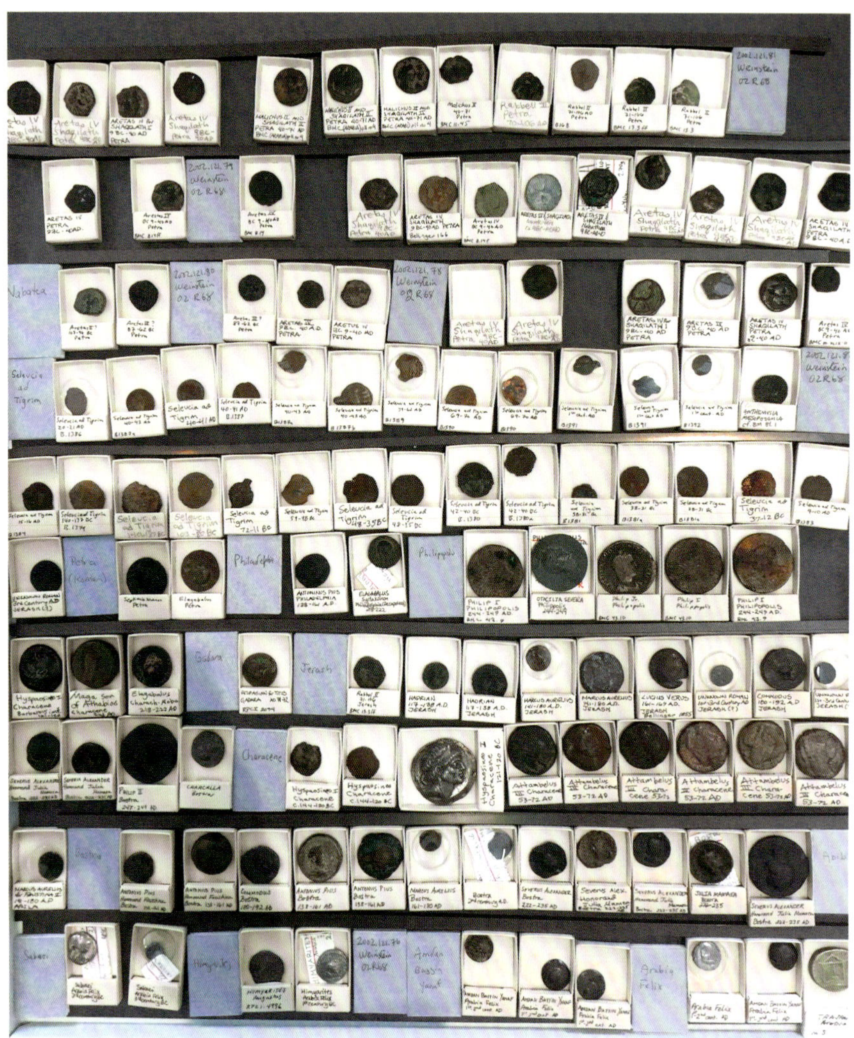

NABATEAN COINS

When I found out our office was selected to be a finalist in the competition, one of the first things I did was to go on a research binge regarding Nabatean civilization. I had been to Petra, in Jordan, so I had some awareness of their ancient carved architecture, but knew very little about their economy, territory, artistic culture, or beliefs. For several weeks, I feasted on Nabatean culture—and having been on the faculty at Yale University since 2001, I used my access to get my hands on some actual artifacts. As it turns out, Yale has an incredible collection of original Nabatean coins, some of which are shown here.

THE VALUE OF HISTORY

In order to help establish the color and material palette for our project, I selected a mix of the available coin types and put them all in my hand for this photograph. You can see that they use different metals and different methods of reproduction—leaving the imprint of the ruler or other cultural message from the era in which they were made.

Nabatean coinage was put into circulation under King Aretas II, 103–96 BCE. The early silver coinage was tagged to the weight of the Roman Denarius, or at times the Greek Drachma, illustrating the interconnected trade of these overlapping ancient civilizations.

THE BEDOUIN TENT

While societies after the Nabateans left less in the way of monumental architecture, this does not indicate that they did not have a fantastically innovative culture in design. One area we researched was that of Bedouin weaving. Shown here are the interior and exterior flooring types for the tent structures which they have used for centuries. In Saudi Arabia, the Bedouin tents were almost always black and made of a variety of materials, but often goat hair that was loosely woven. Weaving in such a way allowed for a constant air flow—even in the absence of any wind or breeze. This was a notable temperature control innovation that we proposed in several of our indoor-outdoor spaces.

131

NABATEAN / BEDOUIN PATTERNING

One of the hundreds of Bedouin weaving patterns and color combinations we researched is photographed above. The forms and colors in this image seemed particularly prevalent in the Al Ula areas—with the horizontal and stepped merlon forms so common to the carved façades of the Nabatean tombs. The colors also seem to reflect the deep rust, orange, and black tones of the surrounding desert. As these woven designs are all pattern-based, they were particularly useful as inputs for the AI design techniques we developed for this project.

A HISTORY OF CUBIC FORMS

One common motif found on the Arabian Peninsula that seemed to span from deep antiquity to the present was the presence of cubic forms in the design of stone architecture and objects. This photograph I took from inside the Saudi National Museum shows a pedestal or altar that dates back to 500–300 BCE, far earlier than the emergence of Nabatean civilization. Such artifacts would likely have been influential on the Nabateans in subsequent generations of design that used similar forms and carving techniques.

NABATEAN INCENSE BURNERS

Seemingly descendants of the previous artifact are these two incense burners from the Nabatean era, which also include cubic forms, topping tapered supports that are carved with various religious inscriptions. These types of forms became a recurring motif that we used in our own architectural design—referencing multiple eras in the deep history of the Arabian Peninsula. *Following pages:* This image illustrates an early sketch of an architecture based on a cubic formal language using contemporary glass and metal materials instead of carved stone.

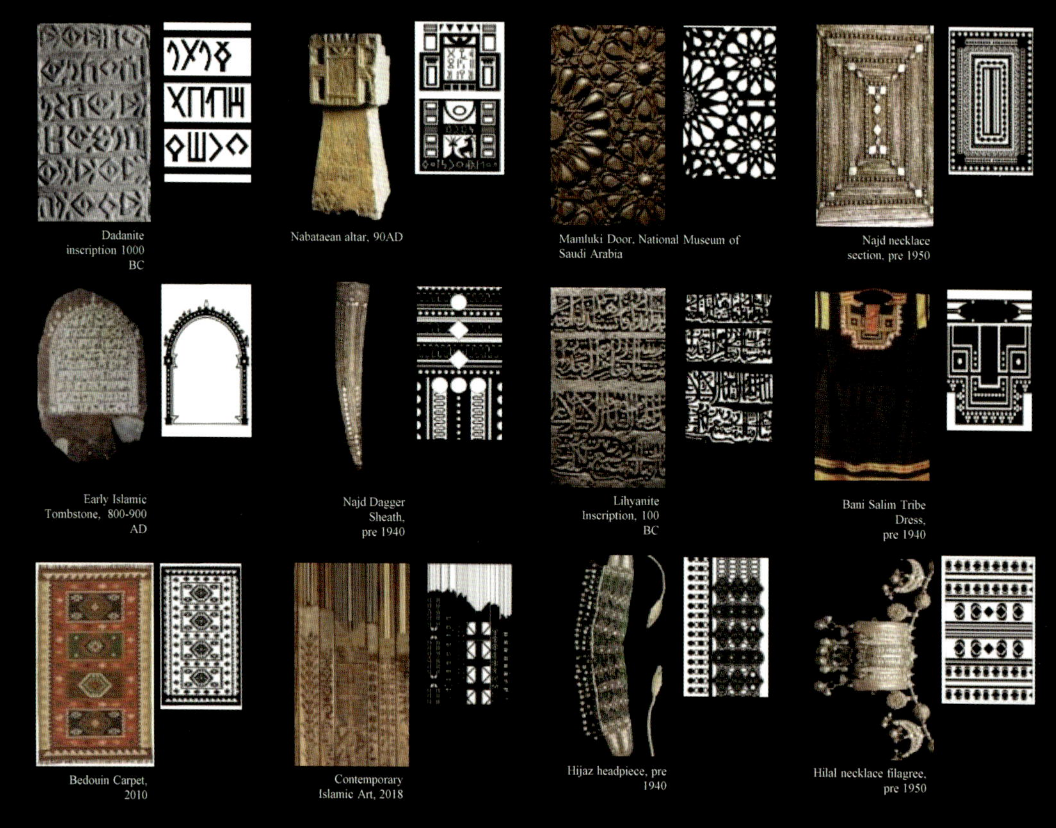

Dadanite inscription 1000 BC

Nabataean altar, 90AD

Mamluki Door, National Museum of Saudi Arabia

Najd necklace section, pre 1950

Early Islamic Tombstone, 800-900 AD

Najd Dagger Sheath, pre 1940

Lihyanite Inscription, 100 BC

Bani Salim Tribe Dress, pre 1940

Bedouin Carpet, 2010

Contemporary Islamic Art, 2018

Hijaz headpiece, pre 1940

Hilal necklace filagree, pre 1950

EXTRACTING PATTERN INFORMATION FROM HISTORY

Above is a collection of design references spanning over two millennia that includes everything from ancient Dadanite stone carved inscriptions to Bedouin jewelry and early twentieth century patterned Saudi clothing. Adjacent to each original artifact is the black and white pattern which was extracted from it. These black and white images were used in the process of designing with artificial intelligence, as it allowed the neural networks of the computer to better focus on the pattern rather than on the material's qualities. Ultimately, this allowed us to fuse even more references regarding material and color information by introducing them from additional sources.

A CULTURE OF ISOLATED ADORNMENT

The architectural language of our resort was contingent on fusing such details, patterns, and geometries from objects such as this highly adorned and segmented Bedouin "hilal" shoulder necklace from the early twentieth century. While there is not a large body of research on Bedouin jewelry, I can say from what I was able to find, that all of it was of incredible intricacy and beauty—some of the most stunning and unusual body adornments I have ever seen. *Following pages:* Fast forwards to the lunar canopy in more detail, which was based on some of these jewelry patterns.

ARTIFICIAL INTELLIGENCE AND FRACTAL RECURSION

Opposite page : **This photograph shows** an intricately carved wooden door of a Saudi house.

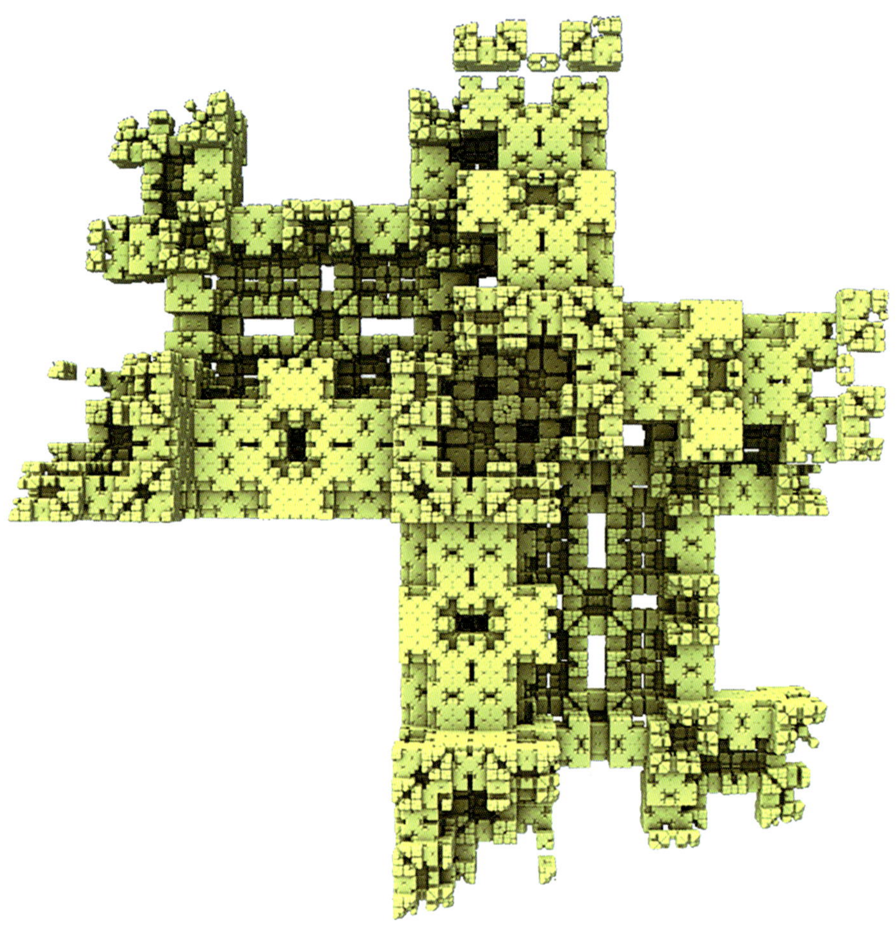

THE 3D MANDELBROT SET

In 2009, a group of programmers from the group "Fractal Forums" developed a way to project the Mandelbrot set into three-dimensional space. The mathematical set was developed by the mathematician Benoit Mandelbrot—who I had multiple discussions with at Yale before he passed away. These previously unknown kind of objects, 3D fractals, are "pure" manifestations of the Mandelbrot equation and often become recursive 3D forms with infinitely scaled self-similar shapes. By controlling various parameters of equations within the Mandelbrot set, our office generated these forms for architectural use. The resulting 3D information was hybridized back and forth with artificial intelligence, sometimes digitally, sometimes optically, to produce the architectural language of some of our most recent projects.

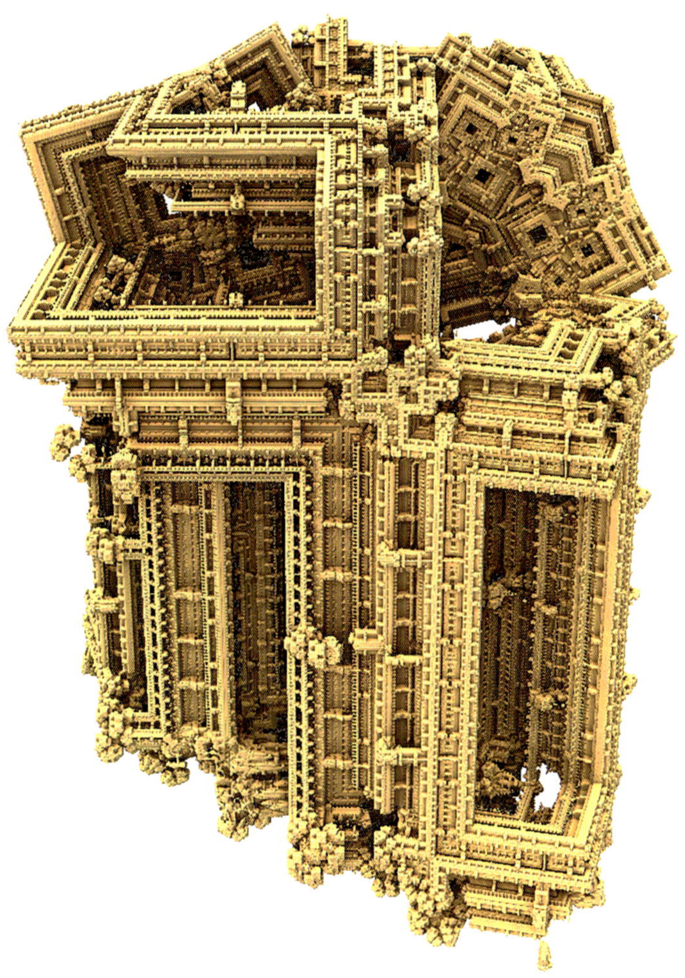

143

3D FRACTAL RECURSION VIA ARTIFICIAL INTELLIGENCE

Our office has a long history of working with recursive fractal geometries as a means to manufacture form and detail at multiple simultaneous scales. For this particular project we used parameters that would produce what we call "3D sponges." Geometries that had aesthetic qualities that didn't mimic, but seemed somehow related to the Nabatean and Bedouin forms and patterns we were studying. This was a tricky territory, as we did not want to mindlessly reuse historic patterns and forms in a post-modernist manner, but rather, wanted to capture some of the geometric rigor and intricacy of the precedents we had been immersing ourselves in researching. Pictured above are two of hundreds of examples of fractal structures generated as we learned to produce a mathematically based architectural formal language that had aesthetic sympathies with historic artifacts from our research.

3D ARCHITECTURAL RECURSION

The next step in translating a 3D fractal, or 3D sponge, into architectural form was to extract a scalar starting point. Our typical start is to search for aspects of the form that have the aesthetic appearance of operating at the scale of an architectural façade. This leaves a lot of leeway, but it allows us to develop a common idea about the next design steps. The façade study shown here could be forty stories tall or four stories tall. What we look for is the presence of a form that operates at multiple ontological levels—for instance, massing, aperture, detail, and texture. Architecture is one of the largest things humanity produces, and therefore has the opportunity to address the largest variation in scale. These fractal forms are starting points for thinking about how our typical idea of scale could be extended into new and higher-resolution languages of architecture.

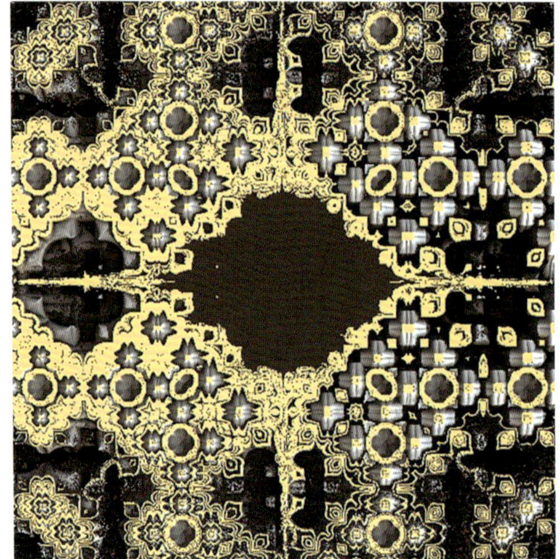

DEEP 2D FAÇADE STUDIES

While our work with fractal generation software from the preceding pages was done in 3D, our use of artificial intelligence systems in the continued design of our project was done primarily in 2D—meaning we were constantly moving between 2D and 3D as we worked in between these technologies. As such we started to develop what we called "deep 2D" patterns, which were two-dimensional, but had three-dimensional visual depth that could be reproduced via additional digital modeling. These could also be varied by altering various parameters.

SHALLOW 3D FAÇADE STUDIES

The result of the previous process was a "shallow 3D" façade language, which used the mathematical source material and fused it via artificial intelligence with more culturally derived patterns, materials and forms—all then 3D modeled with additional depth as shown in the above images. These "shallow 3D" forms became a language of building façades that operated as sunscreens in front of glass, in the tradition of the use of such screens in historic Saudi architecture. While the fractal and artificial intelligence was for aesthetic and cultural reasons, the performance ambitions for these designs were to be sustainable and ultimately ecological.

EXTRACTING ARCHITECTURE FROM ANCIENT SCRIPT

Above is a zoomed in detail of carved historic script from Hijaz found in the Saudi National Museum. Our design process involved abstracting the pattern and form information from artifacts such as this script. By using historic artifacts as source material, we aimed to use artificial intelligence recognition systems as a way to fuse patterns into architectural façades and structures. The use of artificial intelligence in the design of architecture is in its infancy. In response, this project seizes the opportunity to become not only a world class resort project, but also a project of historic and architectural importance through the introduction of pioneering technologies such as AI in built form.

ALMOST-BELIEVABLE ARCHITECTURE

Much of what we produce in our various design experiments is clearly unbuildable, as the detail to scale ratio is simply too delicate or fragile to be made out of anything other than 3D-printed metal—which would be prohibitively expensive. Other designs are clearly buildable, with no obstacle to being CNC carved or cast into high-density CNC foam. In between are structures like the one pictured above that seem possibly, maybe but maybe not, buildable. We wanted to use this as a pavilion inside one of the pools, but determined that the detail was just too out of reach to be realistically proposed.

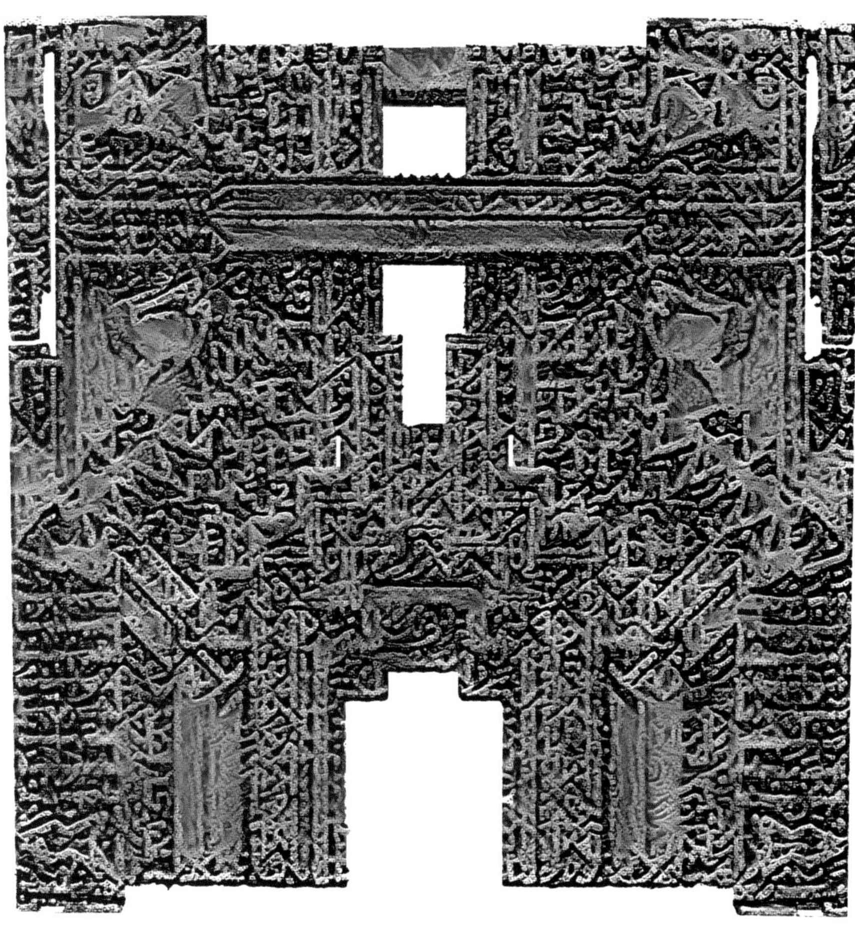

ARTIFICIAL INTELLIGENCE STUDY 020_033_0.4_200

Our office aspires to be on the leading edge of the use of advanced technologies in architectural design. Beginning in 2017, we developed what we believe to be one of the world's first uses of artificial intelligence to assist in the design of architectural form. This technology in this project, however, was not used for the reason of mere novelty, but instead to help us take the many cultural design references we gathered in our growing digital library of forms—from Dadanite, Lihyanite, Nabatean, Islamic, Bedouin, and historic and contemporary Saudi design cultures—and fuse them into singular, intricate and deeply three-dimensional architectural forms and façade structures, such as the one above.

151

ARTIFICIAL INTELLIGENCE STUDY 020_017_0.5_1000

This series of images shows multiple outcomes of artificial intelligence "style transfer" technique, where we selected key patterns, materials, colors, and forms as source material and allow the AI systems to construct new combinations through adversarial networks and pattern recognition. Sometimes these translations involve only form and pattern, but can also involve color as illustrated in the example above.

ARTIFICIAL INTELLIGENCE STUDY 017_050_1.0_3000

At times, the artificial intelligence systems gave us wildly unexpected results, such as this fusion between more regularized Nabatean geometries and the formal and chromatic lusciousness of Bedouin jewelry. The result is a stunningly weird architecture of giant beads, wound wires and hints of geometric rigor. While a great majority of what the AI systems produced was unusable, the ones that we did ultimately use were of patterns, materials, and form fusions that we would not have come up with without the use of such systems. In this way we used AI as a design tool—not a replacement for design. It is merely a step in a much longer process of iterating options looking for what we are trying to produce.

ARTIFICIAL INTELLIGENCE STUDY 040_C21_C22_0.8_3000

The above image uses similar input material to its sister on the opposite page, but with varied parameters. As is visible, very different results emerge from the same ingredients. The AI translation on the right uses Bedouin jewelry forms to match the architectural lines present in a prototype reception pavilion. The above image is another attempt at the same strategy, but with less success as the scale of the parts are not as well aligned, which tends to produce blurry areas with less descriptive and less easily interpreted AI details.

ARTIFICIAL INTELLIGENCE STUDY 044_088_0.9_3000

These images, of the hundreds we produced, became source material for the design of our astronomical observatory—a prototypical test case for our architectural language being applied to a real-world program and constructible form. We used these technologies to generate the exterior formal "shallow 3D" façade ideas as well as the intricate interior tile murals that covered many of the important interior surfaces. The above deeply carved sandstone façade is based on historic forms of script from the region fused into a new language of form.

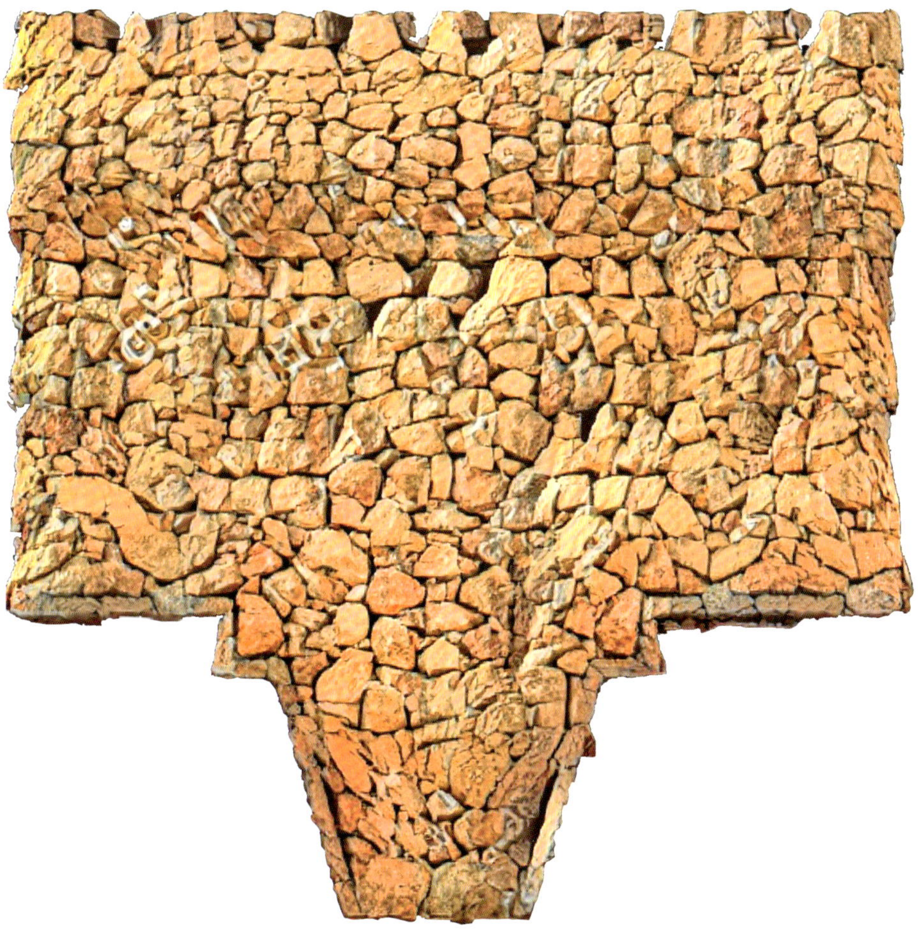

155

ARTIFICIAL INTELLIGENCE STUDY 044_092_1.5_3000

The use of AI technologies also allowed us to reconsider particular materials, such as this reconstruction of our astronomical observatory in interlocking stone chunks. We ended up rejecting this example as it came off more Incan in its shaping of interlocking cyclopean stones. Ultimately, we opted for a mix of CNC carved stone with metal inlays and accents as base materials for the architectural language.

ARTIFICIAL INTELLIGENCE STUDY 005_069_1.5_3000

Despite having similar genetics, the two AI-generated images on these two pages are, as can be seen, quite different, with the orange structural mesh on the right developed more delicately and the recesses having different apparent depths. One, on the left, focuses on color whereas the other, on the right, focuses on formal structure, which was more useful to us in this design instance.

157

ARTIFICIAL INTELLIGENCE STUDY 020_069_0.5_3000

Often, when we input certain parameters we get results that are promising, but not directly useful. When this happens, we often re-run the AI style transfer numerous times with different adjustments given to the inputs, resulting in very different results such as the two variations above. We also sometimes "kitbash" successful areas of multiple AI products together to get a final façade direction.

DESIGN FAST FORWARD INTERIOR: IRIDESCENT PATTERN

The fractal and AI-generated images from previous pages were used in different capacities. One of these was to help generate new tiling patterns for the project's most important interior volumes. These offer wildly unique aesthetic experiences, such as the floral, iridescent and multi-axial symmetry of the image above. This direction was rejected because it was over-articulated in the center. This placed too much emphasis on one particular point that was symmetrical over two of its axis. Moreover, this had the effect of splitting the building not only into left and right sides, but top and bottom—which worked against our immersive ambitions.

159

DESIGN FAST FORWARD INTERIOR: BLACK AND GOLD PATTERN

The interior test above was based on the combination of some of the structural fractal and AI patterns with the cultural precedents of the black loosely woven goat hair used to produce tents throughout Bedouin history—all fused with the metallic patterns and inlays of arabesque metalwork. While dramatic, this direction was abandoned because it too closely resembled, ironically, computer circuitry despite its origin in deeply historic sources. We used a similar, although less circuit-like, strategy for some of our outdoor arcade interiors.

ARTIFICIAL INTELLIGENCE STUDY 005_070_1.5_3000

One of the most interesting features of Islamic architecture is the common use of corbeling, which is far less present in Western architectural traditions. These sequentially cantilevered corbels, almost like mini-domes, often help to construct niches or act like Renaissance pendentives. On a recent trip to Samarkand, Uzbekistan, that I took to document such corbeling, I noticed they were often traced with different colored edges. The AI style-transfer in this above image captures that with the copper-toned mesh that criss-crosses the corbeled façade structure.

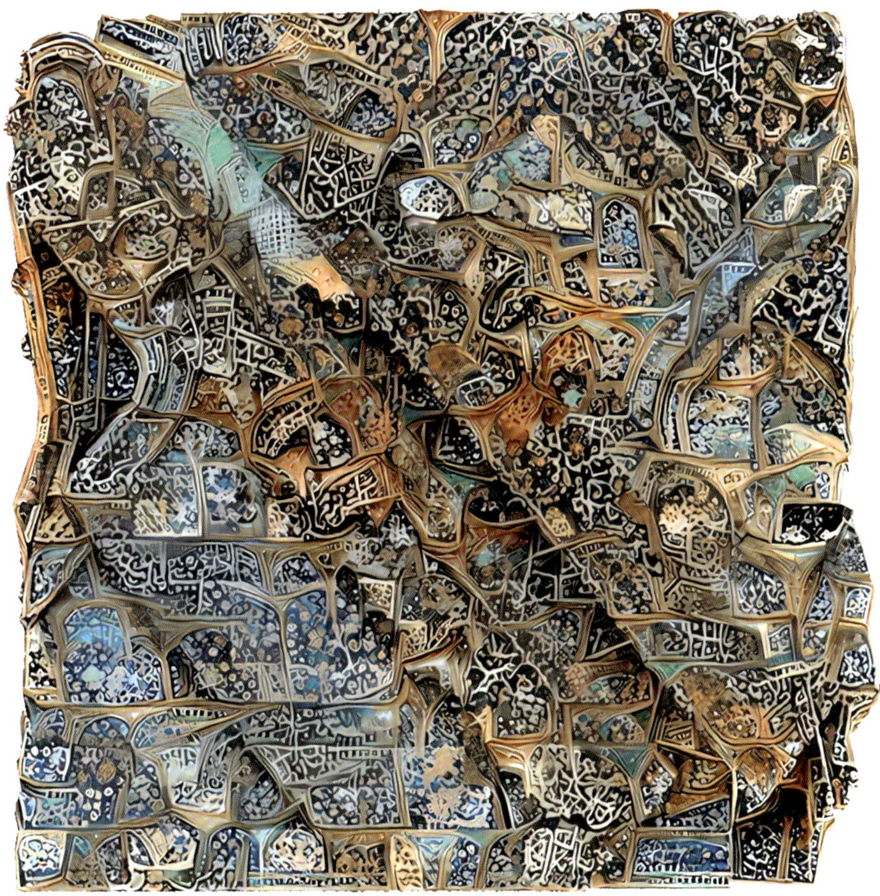

ARTIFICIAL INTELLIGENCE STUDY 038_070_1.2_3000

A variation of its neighbor, this object similarly uses corbeling structures as a basis to form a structural network mesh across a façade with a pre-established geometrical logic, in this case dominated by a large diagonal aperture that runs from the upper left to lower right. While we didn't use this diagonal variation, we found it to be particularly beautiful in how it isolated blue areas where there was less geometric detail—linking the formal, material and color-based aspects of the design composition.

ARTIFICIAL INTELLIGENCE STUDY 028_028_1.0_1000

This AI style transfer was based on a solid, patterned, bronze door held in the Saudi National Museum. The door is dominated by a mesh that contains gem-like features that push through and become raised far above the surface. This translation was particularly interesting as the AI aligned the door mesh with the geometrical direction of the underlying façade language, creating a hybrid structure that looks entirely feasible as an architectural façade. Ultimately, we didn't go in this direction as the language seemed too defensive and armored for the welcoming ambitions of a luxury resort.

ARTIFICIAL INTELLIGENCE STUDY 028_085_0.5_3000

At times, we attempted to use contemporary Arabic script as a basis for pattern generation, as can be seen in the above example. In this case, the AI tried desperately to torque the script forms to align with the lower horizontals and central portal geometries. Nonetheless, the overall effect was far too graphic and to be honest, we had no way of knowing what the AI-generated result said. As this was an international resort, we felt that a reception building that only some visitors could "read" was not ideal. A risky proposition in any competition scenario. Also, it may have said something terrible.

ARTIFICIAL INTELLIGENCE STUDY 024_016_1.0_3000

The above two examples use the same underlying formal basis for the style transfer, as is evident in their shapes. The above example, however, developed into a more graphic, pixelated structure while the version to the right used larger corbel-portions to re-create the overall shapes. The more 2D graphic language was eventually converted into a language of tiles and used to cover the interior surfaces of important resort volumes.

ARTIFICIAL INTELLIGENCE STUDY 024_070_0.8_1500

We liked the capacity for the corbel-based façade to capture light and produce "mini-shadows" on the building itself over the course of the day, but thought the design had a slightly too aggressive appearance. With its sharp edges, points and ragged forms that looked like knapped flint, we felt that the look was more intimidating than welcoming in the context of a luxury resort.

POST IPSO FACTO REPRESENTATION: THE POOL TOWER

This image was done after the project was complete using cel shading techniques. It shows the water filtration and observation tower located nearby the pool area. Closer to the viewer is the more abstracted pool tower that houses a massage room. We left this tower structure relatively under-articulated, according to our standards, as we thought such abstraction produced a nice contrapposto composition effect when compared with other resort areas.

167

POST IPSO FACTO REPRESENTATION; THE RECEPTION CUBE

This image shows the reception cube as visible from a non-existent viewpoint elevated in the desert adjacent to the resort. It is an image of the reception building in its early stage of design, showing an iteration that was more shallow and vertical than the final direction selected.

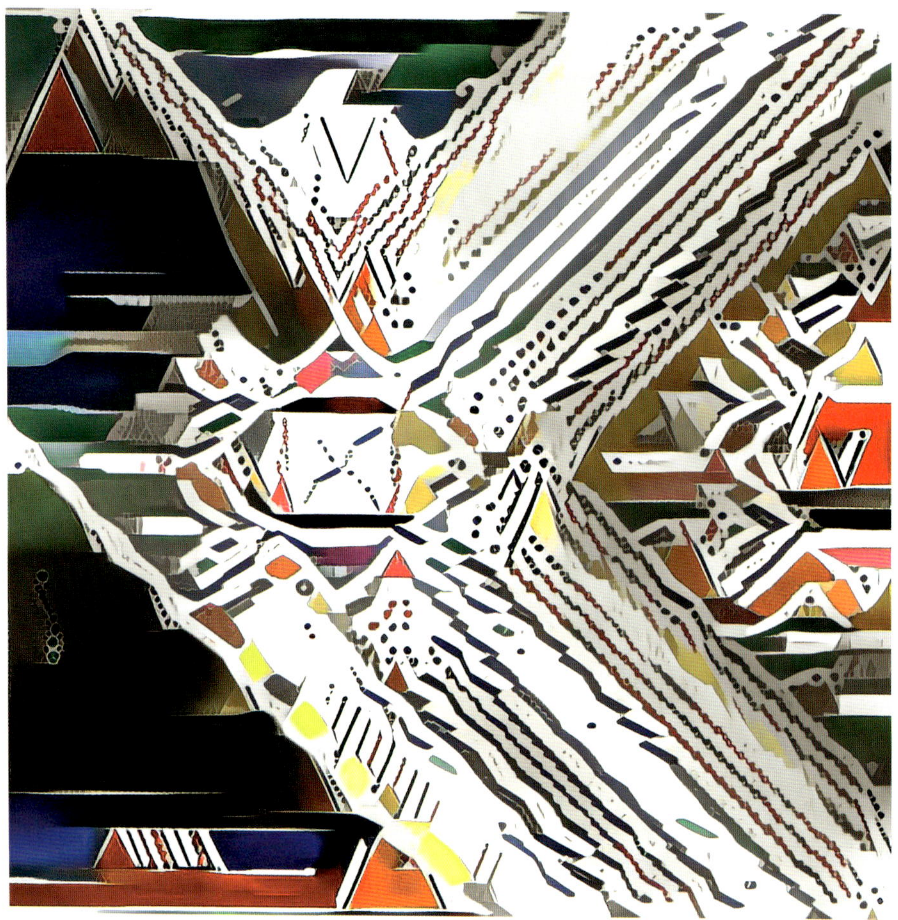

ARTIFICIAL INTELLIGENCE STUDY 034_032_1.0_200

The use of artificial intelligence in this project wasn't limited to its ability to manage forms, patterns, and geometries, but also to its unusual ability to re-arrange colors into new color schemes. The above image uses traditional Saudi colors, but re-arranges them into zigzag forms with wildly different tones and chromatic juxtapositions. Ultimately, we thought this looked too much like a flag—too nationalistic to be used as a basis for an interior or exterior language.

ARTIFICIAL INTELLIGENCE STUDY 029_081_0.8_3000

This image uses Bedouin weaving patterns that are re-arranged by AI into new formal relationships. This is highly unusual as weaving is based on continuity—for example, blue string being threaded along a pattern such that it appears and disappears behind other colored strings at key locations. While the above image appears woven, it's actually impossible to weave in a traditional way as it would require strings of precisely calibrated different colors. While we didn't use it in the design, we thought it was interesting that we had produced a clearly woven form that would be impossible to actually weave out of physical materials.

ARTIFICIAL INTELLIGENCE STUDY 018_017_1.5_3000

This AI style transfer crosses a vertical background façade with the corbeled pattern found in previous iterations resulting in an interconnected web of copper inlays surrounding areas of indecipherable text and tile patterning. While we liked the general look of this one, it failed to communicate the historic aspects of the original artifacts and patterns. Instead of using it as a façade language in any particular building, we opted to use it as custom woven rugs in common lounge areas within the business center.

171

ARTIFICIAL INTELLIGENCE STUDY 038_088_1.0_3000

Melted, drooping, and Gaudi-esque was the general consensus of this particular AI translation, which has an underlying diagonal façade geometry, fused with wood-carved script forms and patterns. What was particularly interesting about this iteration is that the pattern spanned the diagonal divide, attempting to stitch the disparate parts together through connecting strongly visible vertical elements. This had the unintended effect of looking biological, which was further enhanced by its flesh-toned colors. It was rejected primarily for being too creepy.

ARTIFICIAL INTELLIGENCE STUDY 040_024_0.4_3000

When the AI systems we used seemingly didn't know what to do, it blurred areas, as is visible in the image above. This translation attempted to fuse abstract Nabatean step forms with Dadanite script carved into red sandstone. This is an example of two languages being unsympathetic with one another—resulting in the aforementioned blur. While not without interesting visual qualities, this direction was abandoned for being...well, a mess.

ARTIFICIAL INTELLIGENCE STUDY 007_087_1.0_3000

As opposed to the image on the left, this AI fusion used patterns and forms that were entirely sympathetic with one another—resulting in a design that appears as if it has already been 3D modeled in careful detail. The pattern is modulated by the AI to address flat areas with smaller scale and shallower patterns and the deeper 3D areas with more depth and stronger geometries that are deployed at a larger scale. We eventually adopted a more developed iteration of this language in a symmetrical scheme that featured the pattern at a much smaller scale and resolution. *Following page:* This image of a fractal-generated 3D surface features interlocking hexagonal inlays. In laymans terms, a great ceiling.

ARTIFICIAL INTELLIGENCE STUDY 012519_EM_PATTERN1

Preceding pages: This image shows a very early fractal "cave" interior that we explored for a previous underground project, but updated for possible use as a carved resort space. *This page:* A next step in the development of the project was in translating the wealth of 2D design ideas we had generated via fractal recursion and AI into 3D forms. To do this, we typically used high-polygon-count digital management programs and at times, trial versions of medical software programs that took MRI layers of our "3D sponges" that we could then translate into architectural software programs. This 2D image and its 3D translation were among the first to use this process.

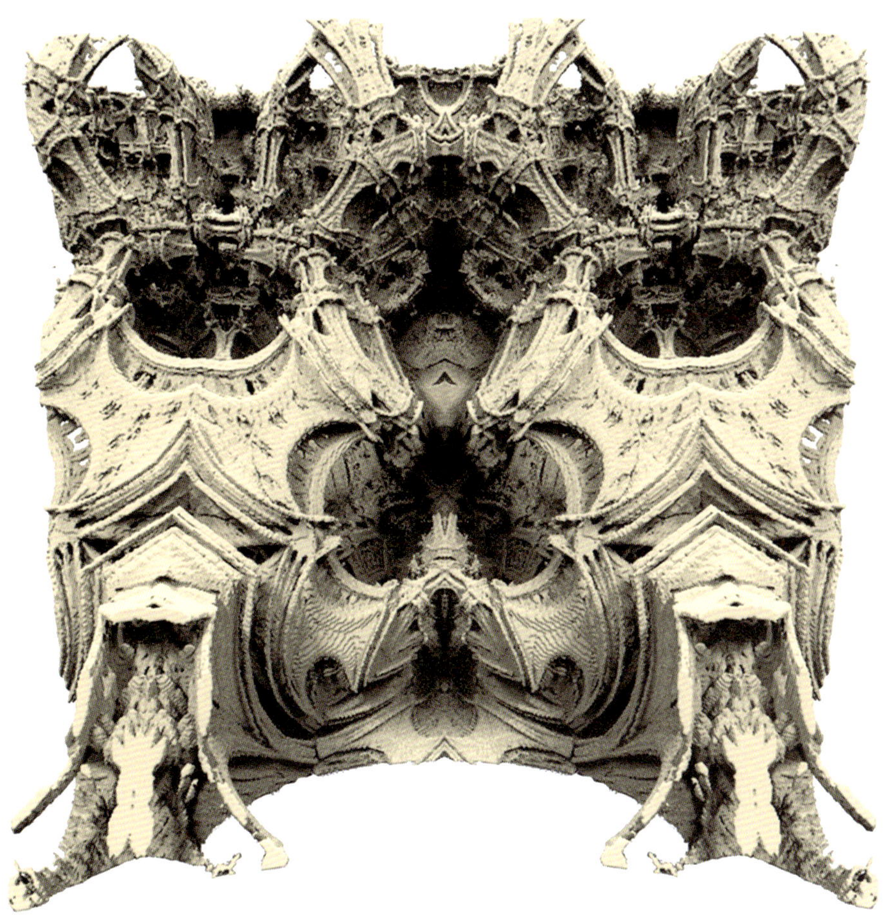

3D EXTRAPOLATION: 2019_110818_KA_FRACTAL_73

Of paramount importance in developing our 2D-3D-conversion process was learning to control the techniques on which we relied. The above image evidences a lack of control, where the 3D extrapolation from the 2D image takes on an uncontrolled and almost evil or wicked aesthetic from a much tamer and more beautiful 2D source. Much of the development on the following pages show such transitions as we gained greater control of this process.

AI + FRACTAL GENERATION: 2019_110218_KA_FRACTAL_44

One of our earlier "successes" in this process was in generating 2D images with multiple organizational structures, in this case multiple fractal grids combined with looser amoeba-like structures. The file that generated this image is three-dimensional which allowed us to excerpt and re-run the fractal generation with new parameters and produce different results. These parameters could be matched to enter information we received from the artificial intelligence pattern fusion process. The two digital techniques were refined against one another as the project progressed.

181

EXTRAPOLATION INTO 3D: TEST 2019_110818_KA_FRACTAL_73

In this 3D translation, the computer interpreted the amoeba shapes as shapes to boolean out—leaving "bites" missing from the cube, however the overall form is still articulated in the same language. Despite architecture being one of the most complex endeavors in which humankind engages, architectural software is among the least capable of managing high-polygon counts, or in other words, complex form. Write your Senator.

EXTRAPOLATION INTO 3D: TEST 2019_110218_MB3D_337

Various attempts were made to translate the fractal/AI information into new three-dimensional forms by using both medical MRI and high-polygon count sculptural software systems. We went through hundreds of iterations and we eventually developed a reasonable degree of control over what was being produced. One welcome surprise was what we refer to a "digital artifacting," which illustrates imperfections on the surface that emerge from different digital workarounds. In this case, the digital artifacting on the above object took on a character uncannily similar to the porous sandstone formations of the site. A welcome ghost in the machine.

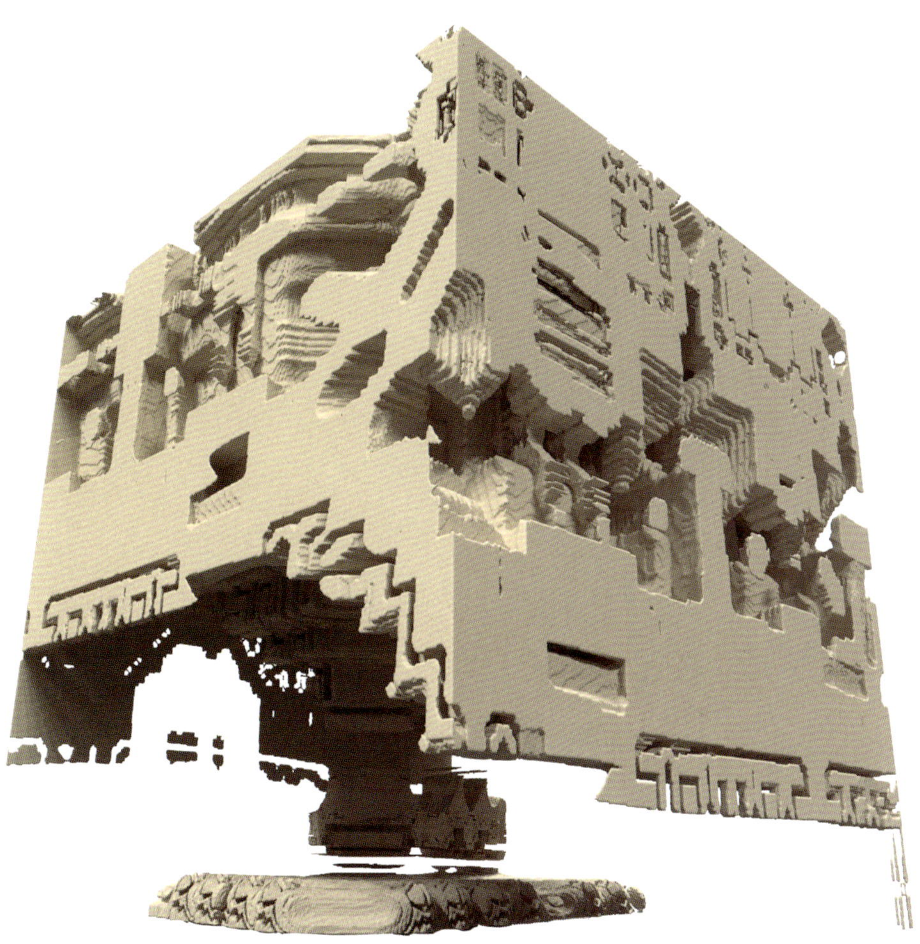

EXTRAPOLATION INTO 3D: TEST2019_110218_MB3D_341

While the image on the left is largely defined by "extrusion" that moves continuously through the original cube, the above image is defined by "embossing" of forms into the surface. Embossing façades is a favorite technique of ours in the office as it gives the appearance of thickness and a certain aesthetic of gravitas. We found this particular iteration interesting because of its combination of exhibiting such thick, heavy form—while technically levitating. As our office has not quite cracked the structural engineering required for levitation of stone, we went in another design direction.

EXTRAPOLATION INTO 3D: TEST 2019_111318_KA_BOX_86_W4INA

Controlling different parameters in the extraction from the AI and fractal materials produced architectural "moves" at varied scales, as illustrated in these two images. The above image uses small deep openings, as can be found in historic Saudi architecture in locations such as Diriyah, all arrayed on a slight diagonal.

185

EXTRAPOLATION INTO 3D: 2019_110218_BB_18_1_W3.3IN

Contrasting with the former image is this example which offers a more porous and open architectural language, but still with historic references we were after, such as the Nabatean "step" motif found at the bottom of the form. At times, one could swear we were using Nabatean computers. While we adored the aesthetic qualities of this particular iteration, it was deemed to be nearly unbuildable at any scale given its interior intricacy.

EXTRAPOLATION INTO 3D: TEST 2019_111318_KA_BOX_86_W4INB

This image illustrates an attempt at maximum detail—to see what level of resolution the software could accommodate. Although visually it was close to being what we wanted, many of these were discarded as the width of the filigree structures was unrealistic given what could be reasonably carved in stone by a robotic CNC system. This provided yet another feedback variable against which we could judge the output of our production. While visually compelling, this is a good example of something that, given the scale at which we were operating, was simply unbuildable.

187

EXTRAPOLATION INTO 3D: TEST 2019_110718_BB_12_W4.3IN

The above iteration ultimately formed the architectural basis for our "transportation switch" building, where guests would be transferred from either helicopter or car to desert vehicle. They would then be driven the remainder of the several-kilometer distance to the resort, where there was no road access. *Following pages:* Fast forwards to the completed version of the reception building—the end result of the trials featured on the previous pages, including the fractal tiled interior.

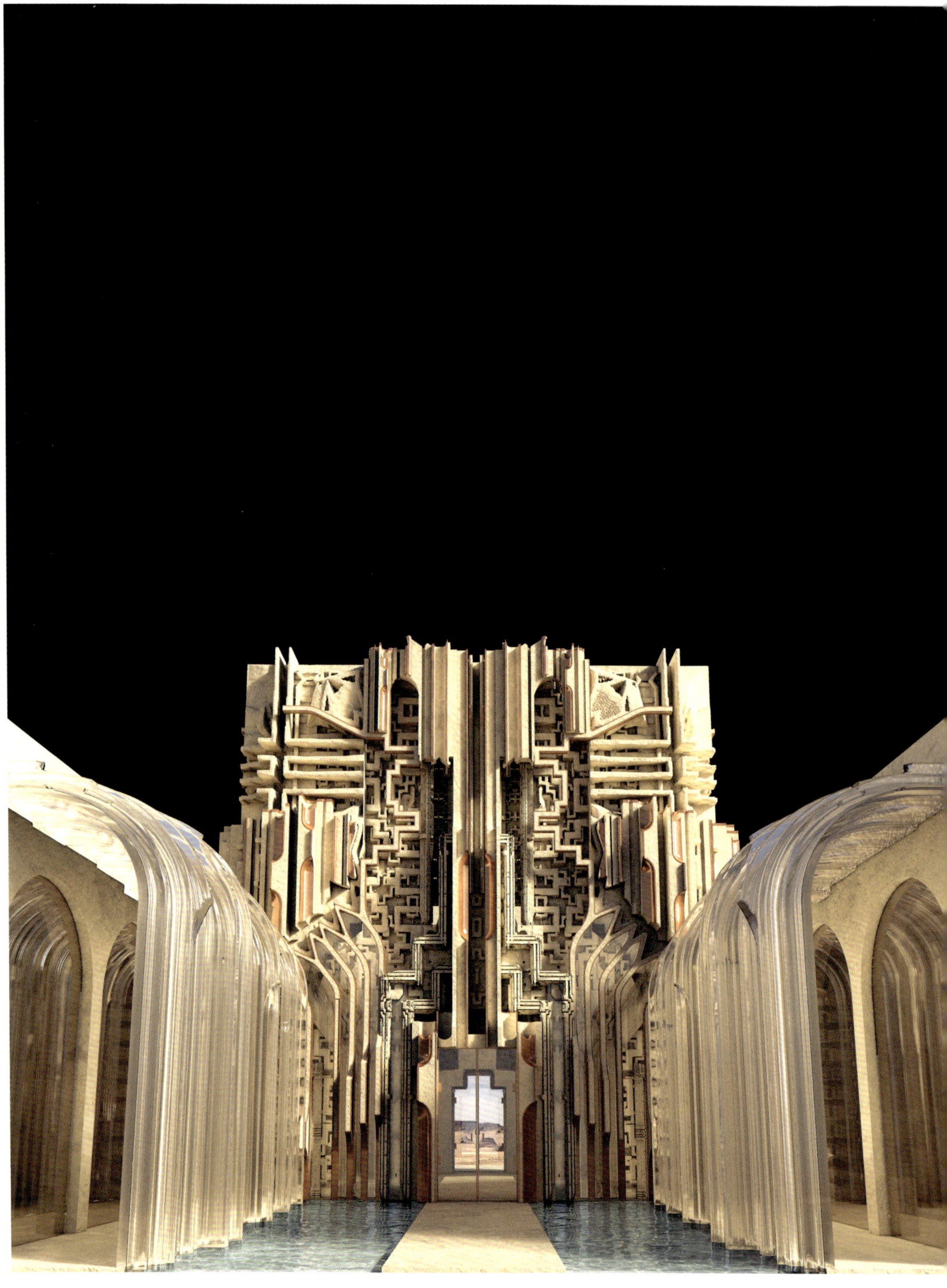

X-RAY IMAGERY

This image shows a unique vantage point in that it is a pure elevation drawing but rendered with an "x-ray" effect. This allows one to see the extent to which the geological formations and architectural structures were embedded into one another. Yellow tones represent geological formations, or sand and red/orange represents built structures.

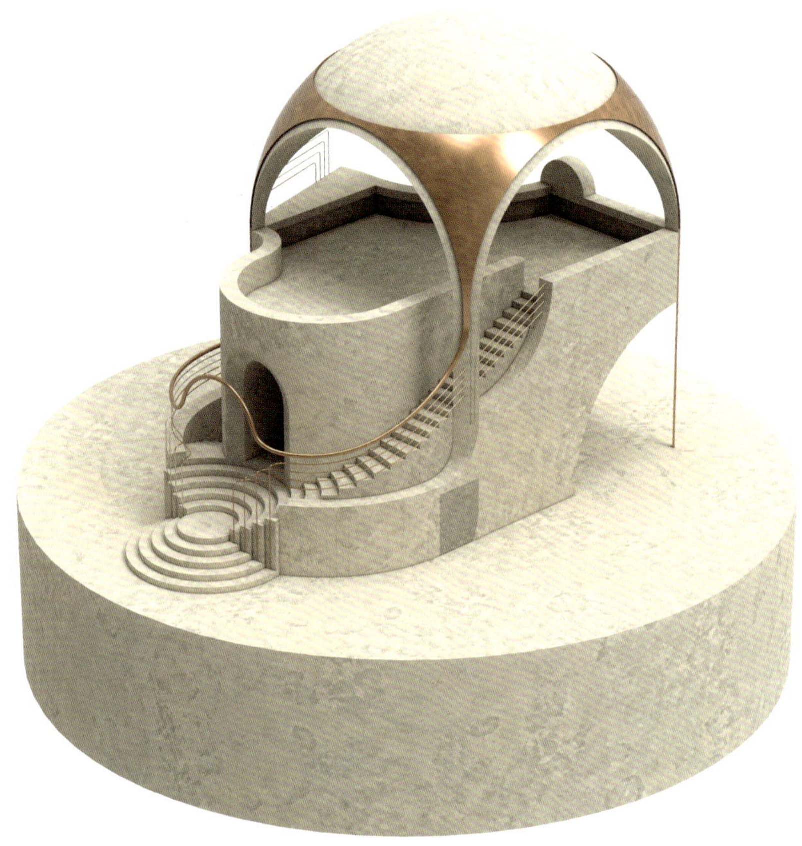

DESIGN FAST FORWARD: MICRO-DOME OBSERVATION PAVILION

While much of the language we developed for the project was highly detailed, we would also later develop a separate design language for tourism infrastructure as part of a related project. The example above is an illustration of this more abstract language, which was used to differentiate public tourist infrastructure from that of the private resort. This language was smoother, cleaner and more aerodynamic, as these pavilions were located in more exposed desert areas with significantly higher wind levels. Additional examples of this will be featured in additional detail later in the book.

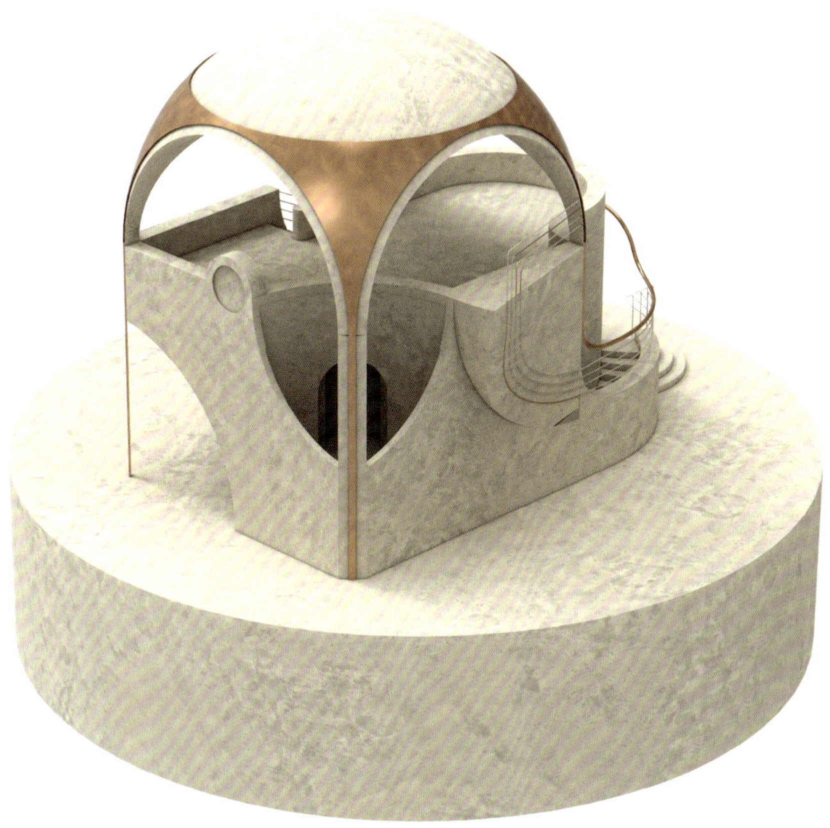

193

MICRO-DOME OBSERVATION PAVILION: BACK SIDE

Some of the tourist infrastructure pavilions would be designed to have temperature-controlled interiors to allow for air conditioning relief from the intense desert temperatures. This pavilion, above, features a lower air-conditioned room with a mini-outdoor courtyard, as well as a shaded upper level for viewing. The form of the pavilion is curved in multiple directions to allow for less wind resistance. This pavilion features a shading dome that is reinforced with a bronze outer shell—an inversion of a vaulting technique frequently used by John Soane.

MULTI-USE TOWERS
194–231

Towers for observation and filtration
Extrusions via AI and FR into vertical forms
Iterations of towers to develop techniques
Rebuilding selected towers in higher resolution
Choreographing circulation knots
Coiling and circulation around towers

Opposite page : This is a tower in Ushaiqer, a small village near Shagra city in Saudi Arabia.

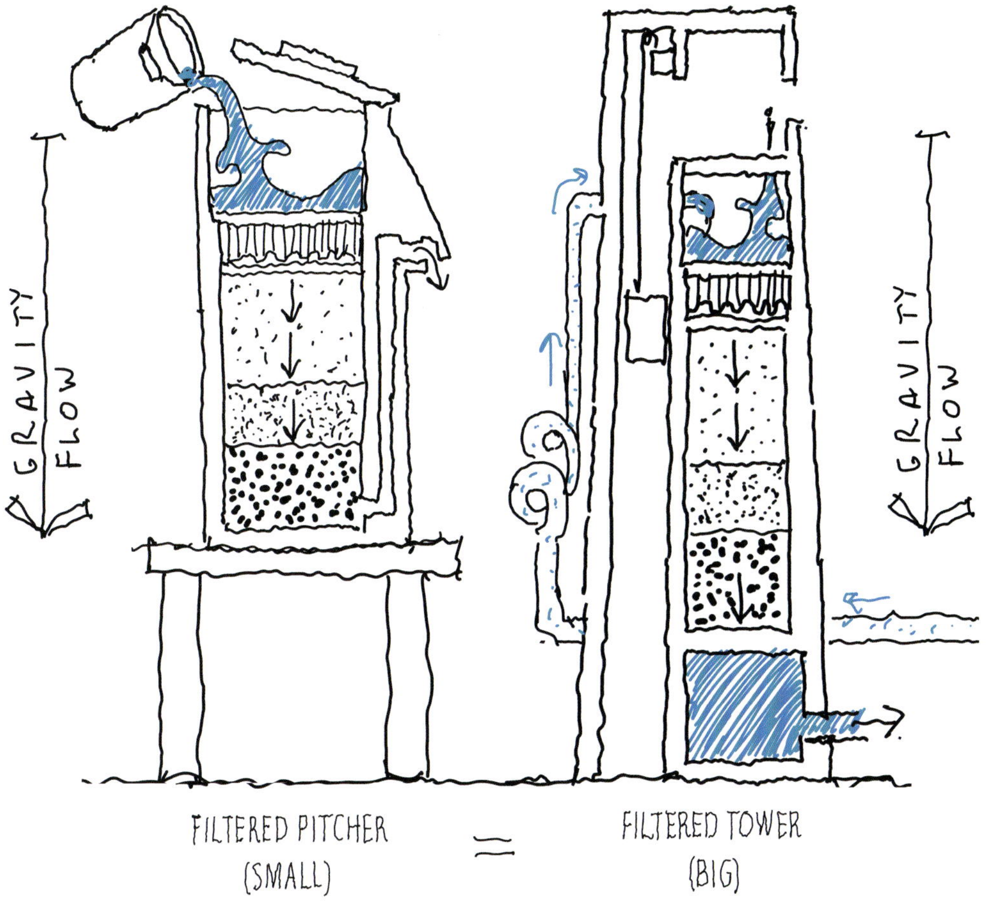

MULTI-USE TOWER STRUCTURES

Preceding pages: These images illustrate how tower structures were composed relative to the final context. *This page:* Very early on in the project, in collaboration with our sustainability consultants and landscape architects, Transolar and Balmori Associates, respectively, we developed a strategy to use a series of tower structures around the resort. This was not only for vertical circulation and observation, but also as giant gravity-fed water filtration systems that would recycle used resort water. In essence, the tower structures were giant "Brita-like" pitchers of the type one might find in their kitchen refrigerator—with layers of sand, charcoal, and other filtering materials. This was extremely efficient in that it relied significantly on gravity rather than constant pumping to move the water through the various layers.

201

VERTICAL FORMS IN HIGH RESOLUTION

Above is an alternate test of the language with less surface detail and cleaner, more legible, massing.

THE PERSISTENCE OF HAND DRAWING

In order to develop the vertical structure language, we went back to hand drawing, as sketches can frequently tell us how our design ideas might appear and be used far more quickly than 3d models. Our design process is rarely linear. Instead, we often rely on shifting between ideas and means of studying them. In these shifts, we use hand sketches, digital 3D models, clay models, Photoshop collages, and verbal descriptions in equal measure. We've also been known to gyrate and gesture wildly to get our ideas across when the above strategies prove ineffective.

TOWER ITERATION: 2020_011019_KM_TOWER_W1.68IN

In order to be able to use a network of filtration towers around the site, we realized we needed a vertical architectural language that differentiated them from the architectural language being used to design the other resort structures. This particular example was a design of a lower, fatter tower, with a sheared wall carved with fractal patterning. *Opposite page:* This example is a test 3D model of a fused tower structure that placed circulation and water filtration side-by-side. This produced structures that were too squat, so this particular direction was abandoned.

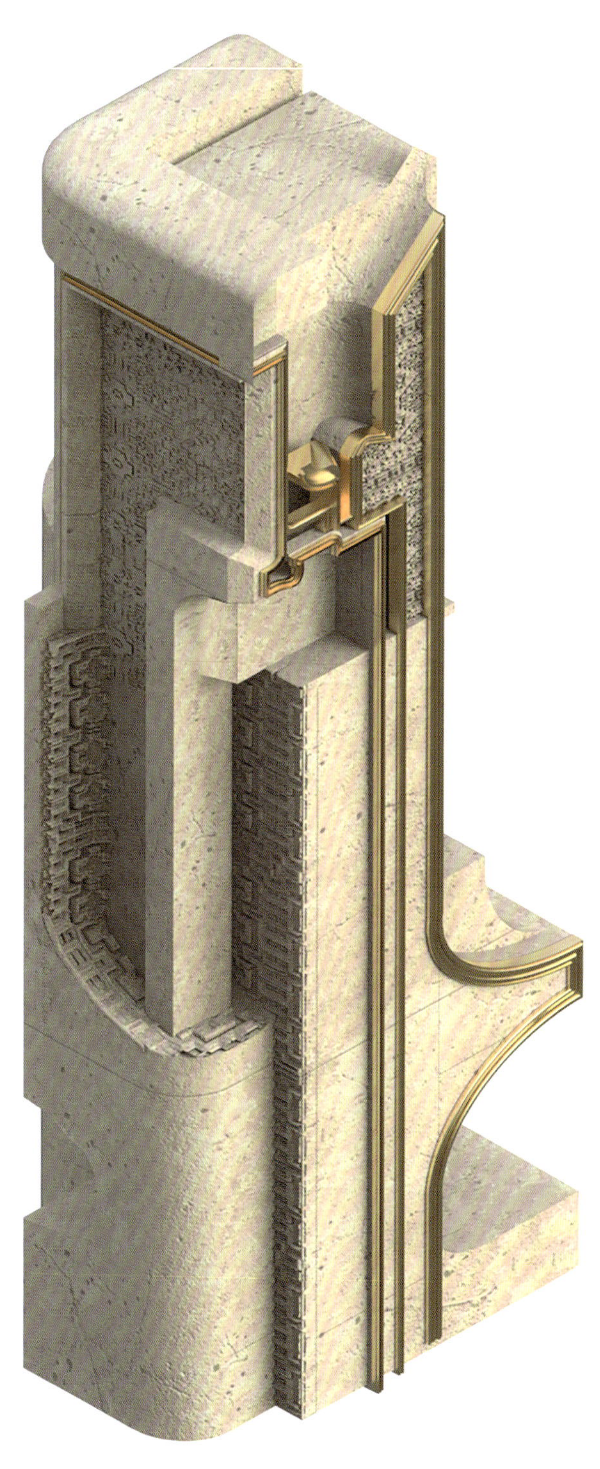

TITLE ITERATION: 2020_010819_ZH_5_W1.53IN

This image shows a test at integrating metallic inlays of bronze into the bodies of the tower forms. The inlays traced patterns generated from the fractal/AI language at a dramatically increased scale. *Opposite page:* This is the back side of the above study, which looked at introducing curvature and radiused filleting to the language to differentiate it from the non-tower building language.

DESIGN FAST FORWARD: THE PRESENTATION MODEL

This is an image that fast forwards to the end of the project by showing our final presentation model. It is shown here to illustrate the important role the tower structures played in the composition of the project. This image focuses more specifically on the pool arcade and central "circulation knot" areas. The difference in materials more vividly illustrate the intricate relationships between forms, especially where the towers and buildings meet the rocky sandstone ground.

THE PRESENTATION MODEL: THE CONJOINED TOWERS

This image shows a close up view of the presentation model focusing on the observation, water filtration and vertical circulation tower adjacent to the recreational complex. The thick, conjoined-tower form was required to contain all of the tower programs yet maintain the vertical emphasis we thought important for the aesthetic relationship to the site.

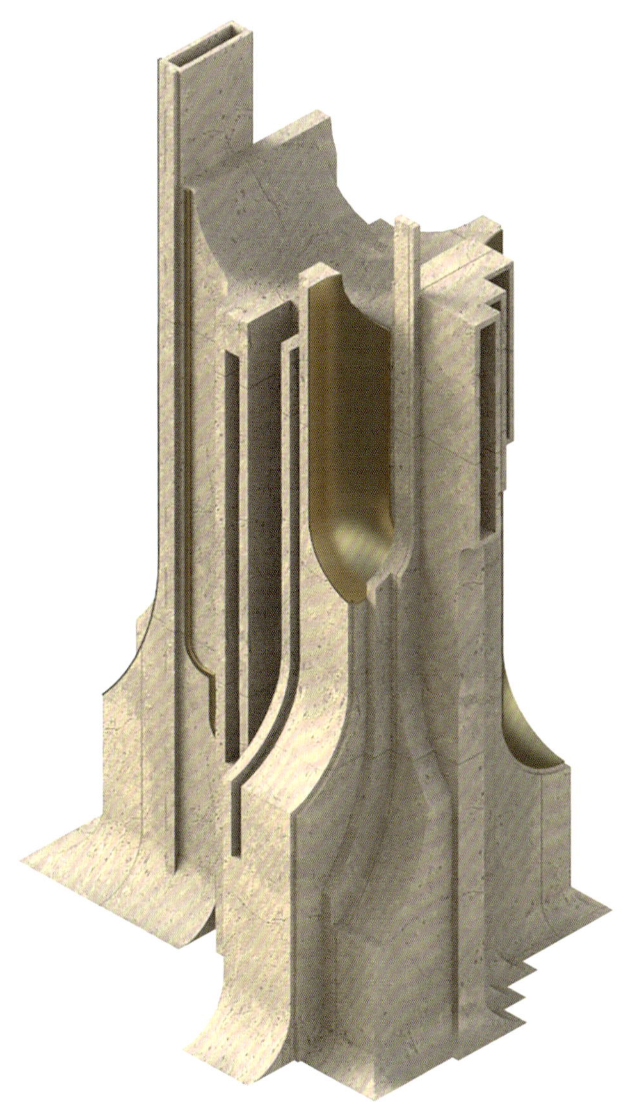

TOWER ITERATION: 2020_010819_KM_TOWER_01B_W1.91IN

While this design direction began as a tower exploration, it eventually became the language we used for the retaining walls, and walls that lined the most important outdoor public spaces. It was too squat to produce viable towers, but was repeatable in a way that made it ideal for long stretches of horizontal surface, as seen in subsequent images.

POST IPSO FACTO REPRESENTATION: WALL ARTICULATION

This image was done after the project was complete and shows the horizontal wall language presented on the previous page. This façade language was repeated at varied scales from the smallest, as shown in this arcade adjacent to the pool area, as well as in its larger form in the background of the adjacent image where it forms the side wall of the ceremonial stair entrance.

TOWER ITERATION: 2020_010819_CC_10_W2.82IN

At one point we tried to salvage previous tower attempts by extruding them further, but found the language was too attention-seeking and detracted from the natural geological formations. *Opposite page:* This is an alternate iteration of this language that uses classical fluting, arabesque patterning, Nabatean stepping and the radiused corners of contemporary design objects like iPhones.

TOWER ITERATION: 2020_011019_ZZ_TOWER1_W2.14IN

Saudi architectural history is filled with towers, windcatchers, turrets, and other vertical forms. We included multiple vertical structures in our proposal to reflect this heritage—several based on this particular study shown above. *Opposite page:* This is a zoomed-in detail of balconies, cantilevers, etched patterns and metal inlays of the previous image. Working at such high resolution is much easier than may have been possible in the past, as architects are now able to "zoom in and out" of a single representational that contains both detail and massing. Historically, larger-scale design ideas such as building massing were conveyed in drawings separate from the detail that they may have contained or supported. One rarely thinks of the effect of simple actions that we take for granted such as "zoom"—but such abilities offer new ways to think about architectural form as multi-scalar, rather than boxes clad with bland corporate products.

TOWER ROOF STUDY: 2020_010819_ZZ_TOWER3_W3.72IN

Several of the water-filtration towers doubled as structures for vertical circulation and guest observation. The above image shows how the internal stair might emerge onto the observation roof. Ultimately, it was decided that we wanted to include elevator access for all aspects of the towers—including the roofs. The final design all had additional masses toward their tops to accommodate the associated elevator equipment required. As such, this design direction was not used in the final project.

219

TOWER ROOF STUDY: 2020_010819_ZZ_TOWER4_W4.22IN

We had also decided that in these "open air" observation roofs, there was too much exposure to the desert sun—and although the height would produce a more temperate experience, it would simply be too bright to produce a comfortable observation environment. The thinness of this particular tower also left very little room for emerging from the interior circulation, as evidenced by the precariously small square footage dedicated to actual observation platform adjacent to the stairs.

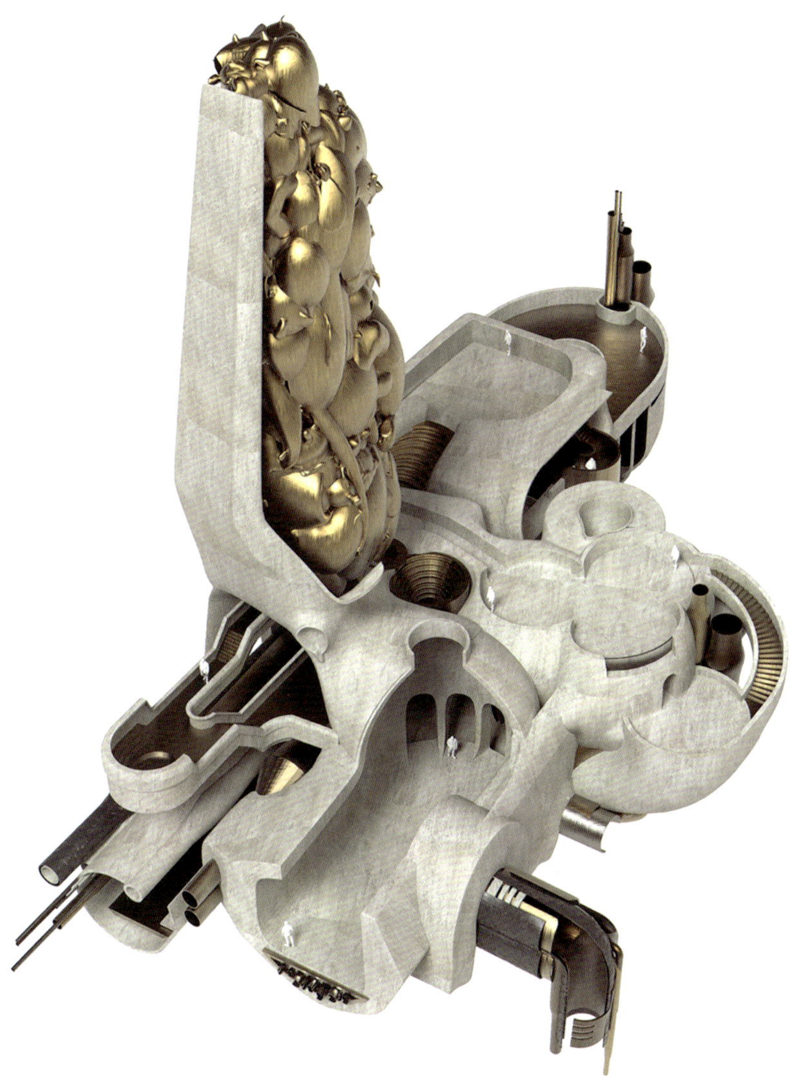

VERTICAL PARKS

In 2017, New York Magazine commissioned our office to imagine the fifty-year future of New York City. Our proposal included draining the East River and producing a fertile urban valley. To access this lower valley, we developed "vertical parks" shown here, that allow visitors to descend through a wide variety of stair types, outdoor rooms, and view platforms. In the absence of parks, several of our projects have converted these languages into "circulation knots" that allow circulation to become a circuitous and volumetric architectural experience rather than merely being limited to generic stair and elevator cores.

REVENGE OF THE ÉCOLE DES BEAUX-ARTS

This iteration was for a "winter park" in the aforementioned project where flowing water would form a solid column of ice, which would function as a sculpture that visitors would circulate around as they moved downwards. For our desert resort proposal, we revived this idea into "circulation knots"—choreographies of vertical and horizontal circulations which mixed shaded areas, viewing platforms and different spatial experiences in order to create what the architects of the École des Beaux-Arts called a "marche." This is a circulation path designed to not only move one from place to place, but to entertain the eyes with aesthetic experiences along the way. We included these two designs from 2017 in order to show the roots of the "circulation knots" we used extensively in our resort design.

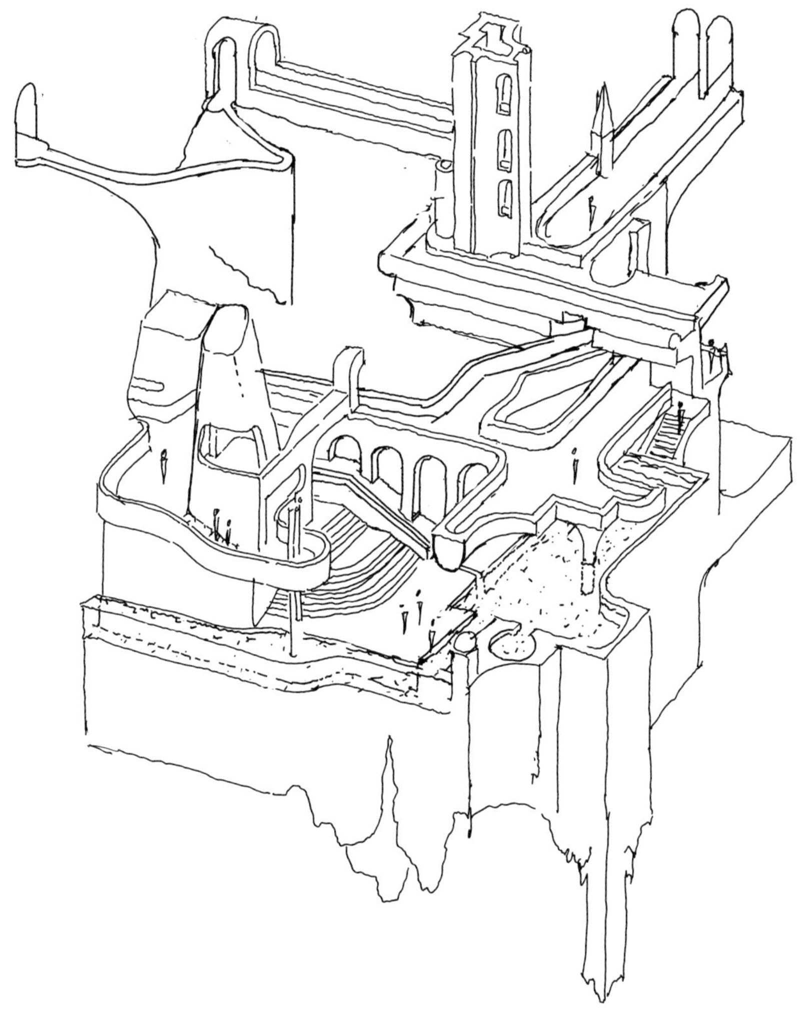

NORTHWEST CIRCULATION KNOT

Above are hand sketches of "circulation knot" ideas that turn resort guest circulation areas into elongated aesthetic experiences of multiple spatial arrangement and views. These interconnected forms typically engage one of the observation or water filtration towers so that they can house elevators for accessibility. This sketch shows the early development of a circulation knot that connected the elevated spa, lower pool areas, and garden oasis. The paths disappear into mysterious inter-dimensional arches, mostly because we didn't yet have enough of the design figured out to know where they would lead. That, and we—as a firm—do actually have special abilities to control multi-dimensional reality. However, we do bill extra for this.

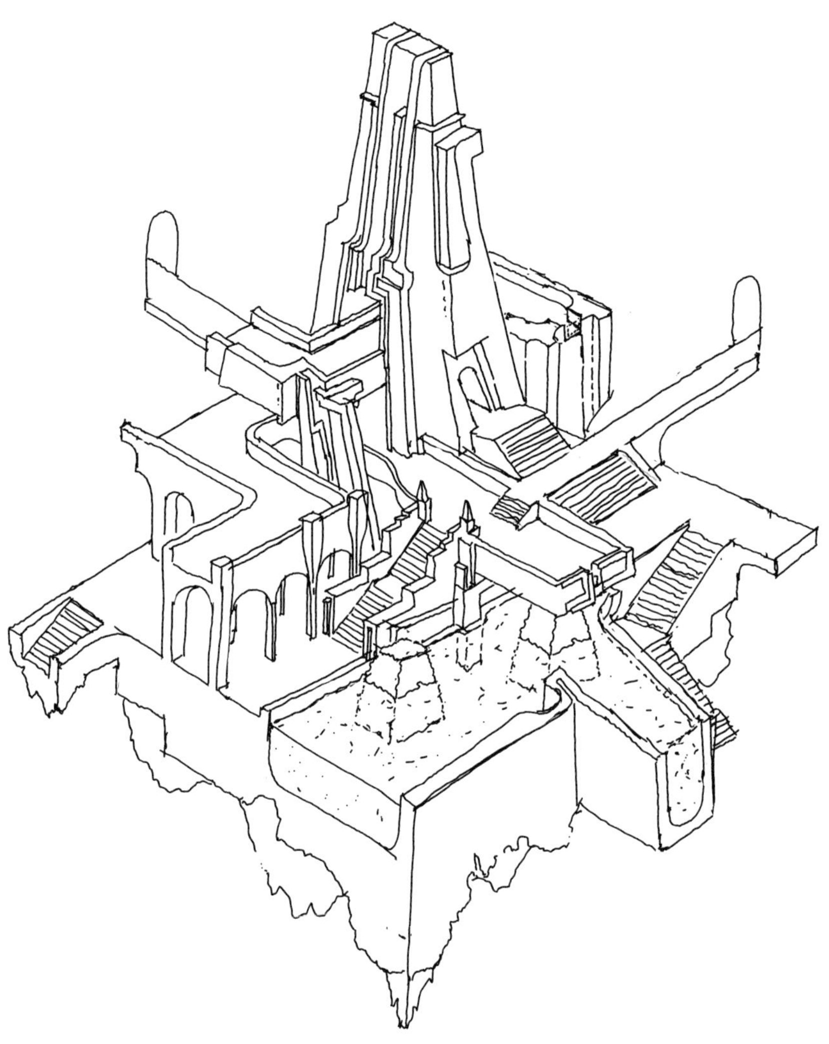

223

CENTRAL CIRCULATION KNOT

This drawing shows a circulation knot that connects the reception, restaurant, business center, and lower pool areas.

CIRCULATION KNOT ITERATION: 2020_012219_BB_3

Above is an early digital model of a circulation knot that connected multiple residential levels distant from the primary resort's central core. The project ultimately contained four major circulation knots that connected various programs and all circulation in vertical and horizontal directions. Almost all of the circulation knot structures contained vertical circulation, observatory, gravity-fed water filtration, and operated as wayfinding markers visible from specific resort locations. While much of the complex was nestled into the rocky sandstone outcroppings and ravines, the towers formed a subtle trace of identity emerging from above the site and visible from a distance.

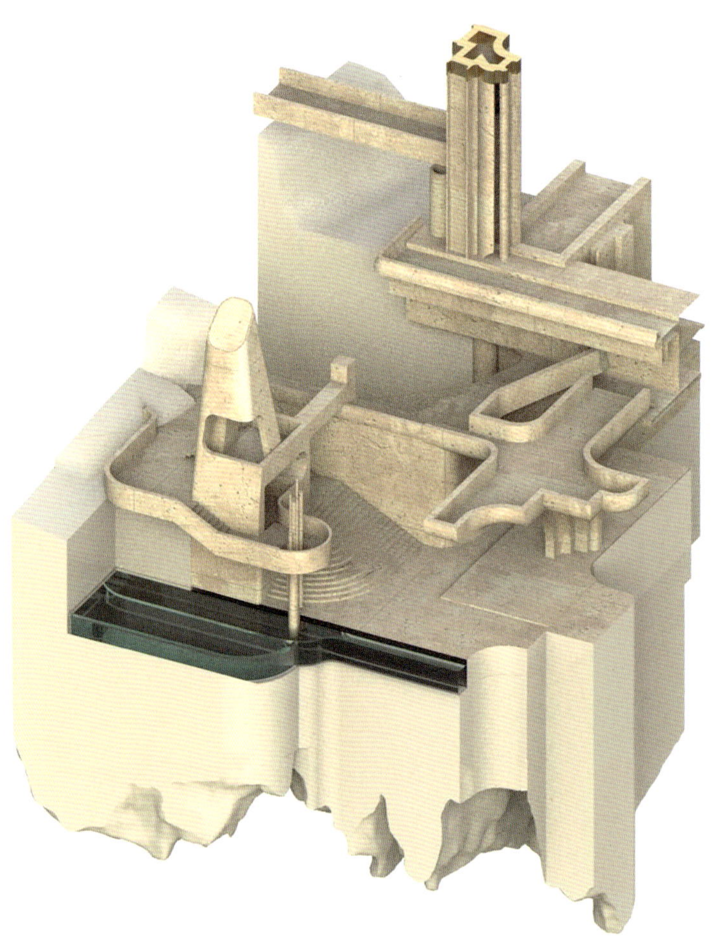

225

CIRCULATION KNOT ITERATION: 2020_012219_BB_2

This image is a near-final iteration of the northeast pool circulation knot.

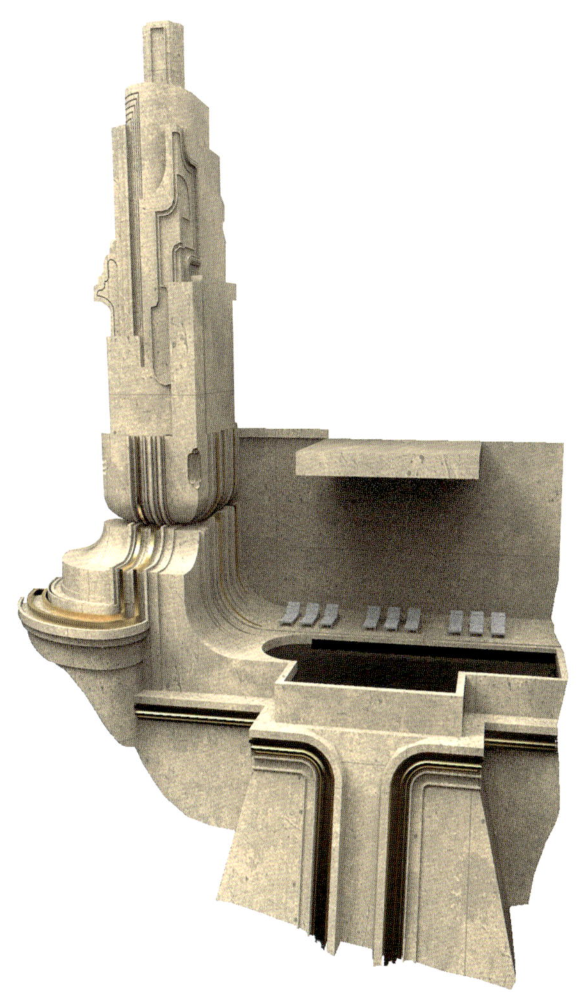

226

THE PRIVATE SPA BUILDING

For our proposal, we designed a day spa with multiple indoor and outdoor pools. Our spa design was built into a ravine that stepped down to the lowest level where we located the largest of the outdoor pools. This image shows that particular pool level with the associated tower that held the stairs and elevators for its access. In this design we treated the tower as an "object" that seemed to rest on a related plinth—providing a focal point for the spa guests and marker from those viewing the nestled building from farther away.

RUSTICATION AS DETAIL

Some of our early tower designs used highly rusticated sandstone that was to be taken from the site itself, as reflected in this early rendering. As is visible, the tower combines the rustic stone areas with more highly refined glass and carved rock features. Such rustication effects work best when able to be carved from solid rock as the Nabateans did, or when constructed from large, cyclopean masonry blocks. We abandoned this particular direction because the local sandstone was too brittle and porous to be able to be cut and transported in such large-scale blocks.

THE CONJOINED TOWERS

On the opposite end of the site from the primary core of activities was the recreational complex, where guests could enjoy everything from tennis to falconry. The playing fields, being large, needed to be located on the desert floor and be accessed from the resort level far above—as such the design required a particularly tall tower. This tower combined vertical circulation, observation, and water filtration, which required additional thickness. We camouflaged this by pairing two towers together as a conjoined double-vertical form. *Opposite page:* This more-developed image shows the tower in the actual context of the site, as opposed to a placeholder, rocky 3D-modeled version, above, that is produced by Hollywood special effects software on low-resolution settings.

إياك نعبد
وإياك نستعين
صنعت هذه الستارة في مكة المكرمة
وأهداها إلى الكعبة المشرفة
خادم الحرمين الشريفين سلمان بن
عبد العزيز آل سعود تقبل الله منه

ARCHITECTURE IN ITS HIGHEST RESOLUTION
232–277

Tennis exchanges between 2D and 3D
High resolution 2D to 3D conversion techniques
Architectural language prototypes
The reception cube test
Iterations to develop formal control
3D printing in metal to study intricacy
Material Research
Next-generation stone carving

Preceding pages : **This is the final image of the** recreational sports complex with the associated tower, shown from neighboring sandstone escarpments. The small building nestled in the left part of the image is a mini-tower containing multiple guest suites.

Opposite page : **This image shows a** close up view of the gorgeously detailed "Kiswah," the fabric cloth that covers the Kaaba in Mecca—an inspiration for some of our more intricately detailed, albeit secular. resort areas.

NABATEAN FLAVORED 3D MANDELBROT SETS

As we further developed the architectural forms in our project, we refined new techniques that used varying combinations of artificial intelligence and fractal recursion software techniques. Eight of the hundreds of variations we produced are represented here. At this point in the design process, we had further mastered the tricky art of generating three-dimensional patterns that conformed to complex architectural forms—so they were no longer flat patterns applied to flat boxes, but rather torqued, curved, inhaled, bulging and stepped for greater formal variety.

The goal of this process was to create a formal language where the patterns and forms were inseparable. If you removed the pattern from these images, you would have nothing, as there is actually no "blank form" lying behind them. We referred to this particular quality of a pattern with depth as "deep 2D," which was developed into the primary façade strategy of the resort proposal. The above images were all translated into full 3D "façade forms" on the subsequent pages.

DEEP 2D PATTERN: TEST 2019_110718_ZH_ITERATION7_W1.7IN

Above is an image illustrating one of the fractal/AI-generated "Saudi flavored" Mandelbrot sets as a deep 2D pattern.

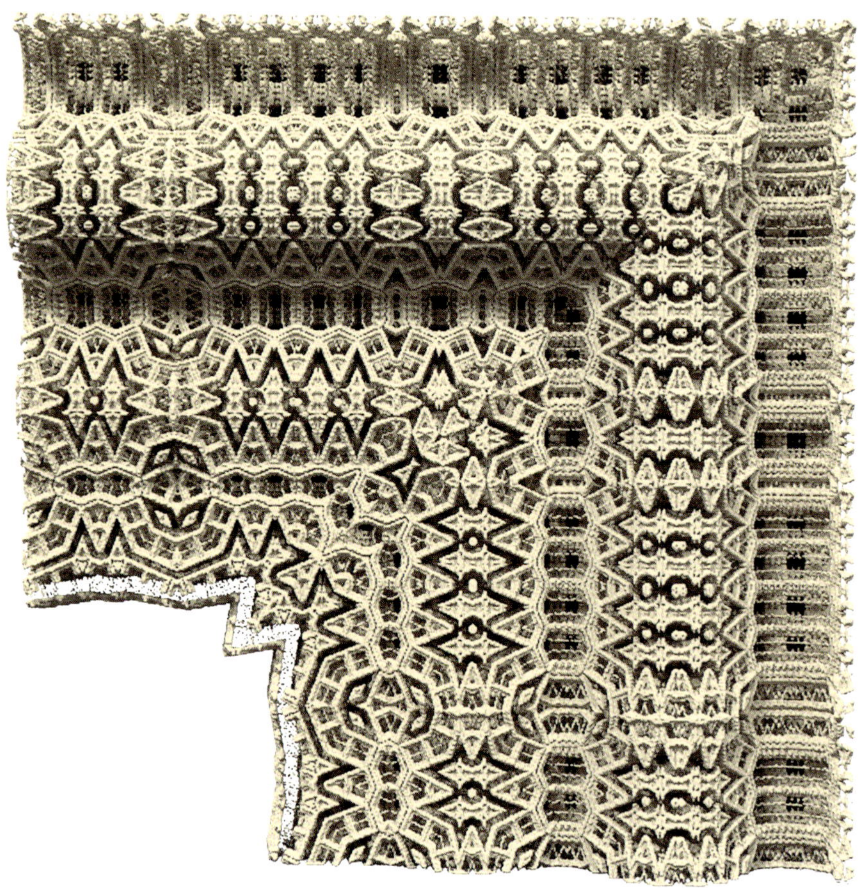

237

FULL 3D EXTRAPOLATION: TEST 2019_110718_ZH_ITERATION7_W1.7IN

By using a suite of digital techniques, we were eventually able to translate AI and fractal data into three-dimensional forms that could be imported into standard architectural software packages. This is an image of such a 3D model, capable of being manipulated in architectural design programs—although it took months to fully develop the techniques that made this possible.

DEEP 2D PATTERN: TEST 2019_110718_ZH_PARAMETER14

The above image shows one of the fractal/AI-generated 3D patterns that was made using classical torus forms placed at orthogonal angles to one another. All of this is etched with voids that use the zig-zag and stepped motifs of Bedouin and Nabatean patterns, respectively. The gold tone was accidental, but seemed to work within the general architectural materials palette and later prompted some literal translations where we proposed special gold leaf areas in important tiled interiors. *Opposite page:* Three-dimensional translation of the original fractal/AI pattern using diagonal torus forms.

FULL 3D EXTRAPOLATION: TEST 2019_110718_ZH_PARAMETER14

2020_030719_ DEEP 2D PATTERN: TEST 110918_ZH_BOX4A_W4.62IN

FULL 3D EXTRAPOLATION: TEST 2020_030719_110918_ZH_BOX4A_W4.62IN

This is an image of a 3D translation of the original fractal/AI pattern on the opposite page, with over-articulated "void" pattern areas removed. Often, these removed areas were too intricate to be produced in real materials, so we simply deleted them and made use of the missing areas as apertures. This technique therefore gave us a logic for locating windows and doors. Apertures simply became the parts of the formal data that could not be produced and were therefore removed using boolean operations to produce voids within the porous solids of the 3D forms. *Opposite Page:* This enlarged image of one of the fractal/AI-generated 3D patterns focuses on radial organizational structures.

242

DEEP 2D PATTERN: TEST 2019_110918_ZH_BOX3A_W4.1IN

243

FULL 3D EXTRAPOLATION: TEST 2019_110918_ZH_BOX3A_W4.1IN

The translation of this particular fractal form from deep 2D into a cubic 3D form was "clean," requiring less excising of overly detailed areas. One such area, however, is visible as the center-occupied column pictured in the pattern version that is not present in the right image. Ironically, I love center-occupied columns in architecture, in particular their use by Joze Plecnik in his numerous early twentieth-century buildings in Ljubliana, Slovenia. Unfortunately, this detail couldn't be kept as it would need to be constructed out of infinitesimally small materials. We found it frequently interesting that the fractal/AI strategies we were using sometimes automatically took on recognizable architectural forms such as arches, lintels, and in this case, the rare use of the center occupied column.

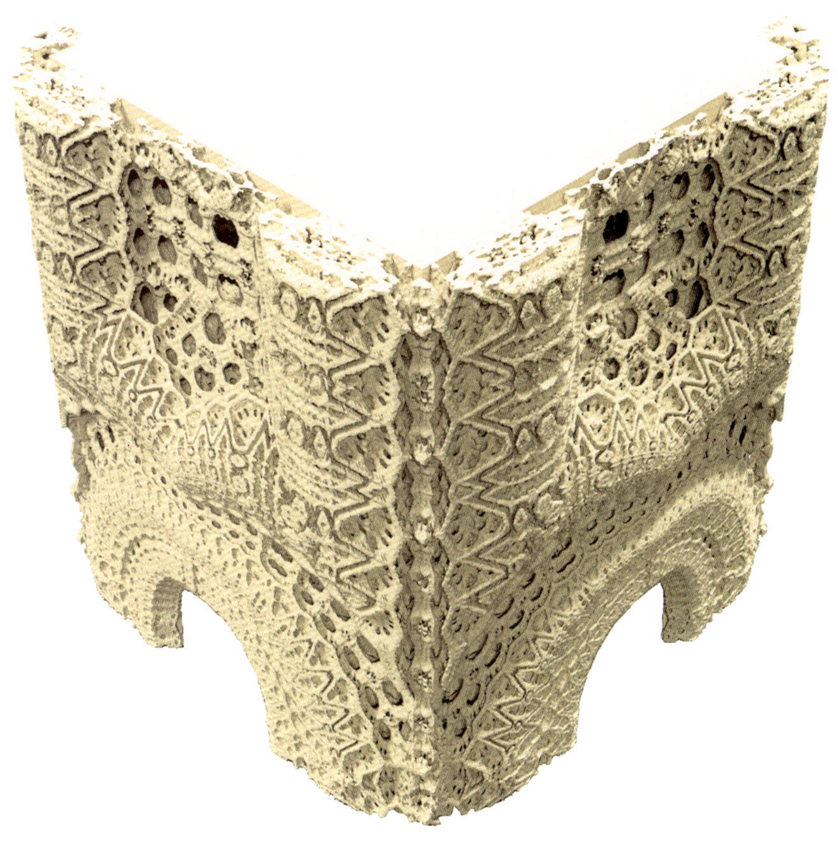

FULL 3D EXTRAPOLATION: TEST 2019_110918_ZH_BOX3B

These are images of the digital models from the preceding pages shown in full 3D. While I'm naturally drawn to symmetry, it was somewhat of a necessity in this project because often a single façade was taxing for our already robust computers—meaning that a non-symmetrical façade would inherently be using twice as much information. The use of symmetry was a cultural aspect of our historic research, and fortunately aligned with the limits of what our technologies were capable of managing in terms of detail and very high polygon counts. We took these views from an aerial perspective in order to convey the thickness of the structures. *Opposite page*: This is a rotated axonometric from the previously illustrated 2D to 3D transition.

245

FULL 3D EXTRAPOLATION: TEST 2019_110918_ZH_BOX4B

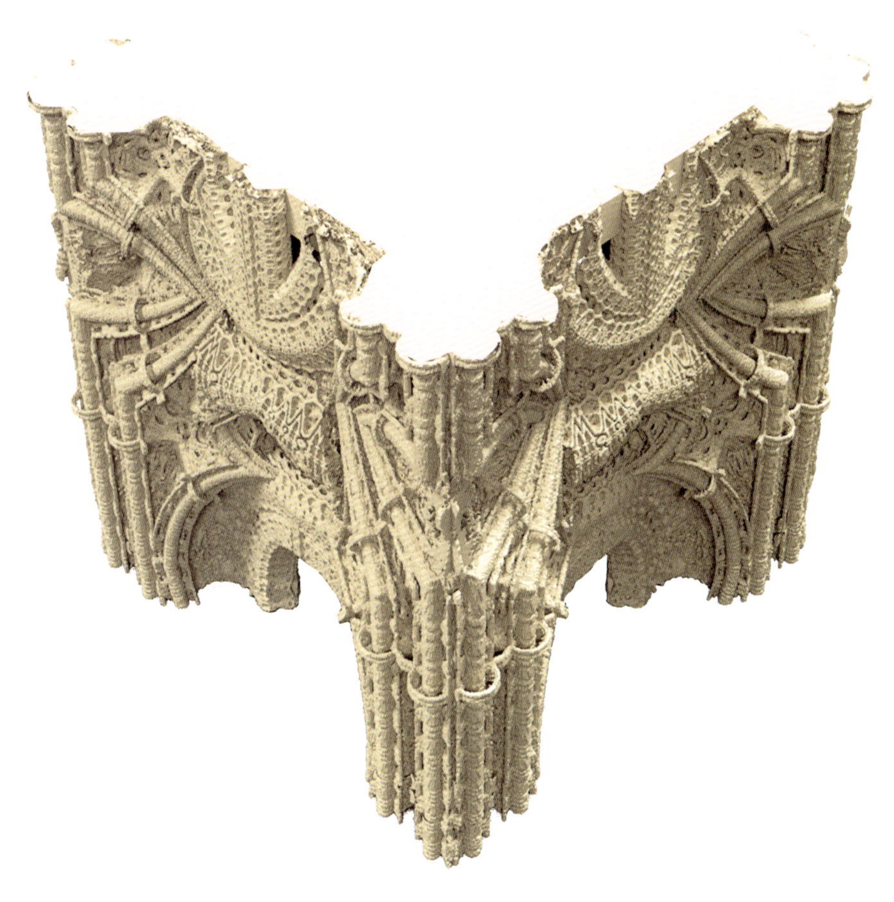

FULL 3D EXTRAPOLATION: TEST 2019_111218_ZH_1B

247

FULL 3D EXTRAPOLATION: TEST 2019_111218_ZH_3B

As is rather common when learning how to use new and complex languages of form, the above two translations took on a rather alien "Giger-esque" quality that we try to avoid at all costs. When geometries become overly voluptuous and complex, they tend to take on the appearance of an alien or biological presence—while a productive territory for architecture, in this case, we felt that it was not appropriate for a region with such incredible formal depth within its cultural traditions. Although they look a bit creepy, we thought we would show these two examples to illustrate this effect. Of the hundreds of 2D to 3D translations we rejected, a significant percentage, such as these, were rejected simply because they looked too biological, or as if Sigourney Weaver was about to tumble out of one with a flamethrower and a cat running for her life.

FULL 3D EXTRAPOLATION: TEST 2019_110718_ZH_PARAMETER14

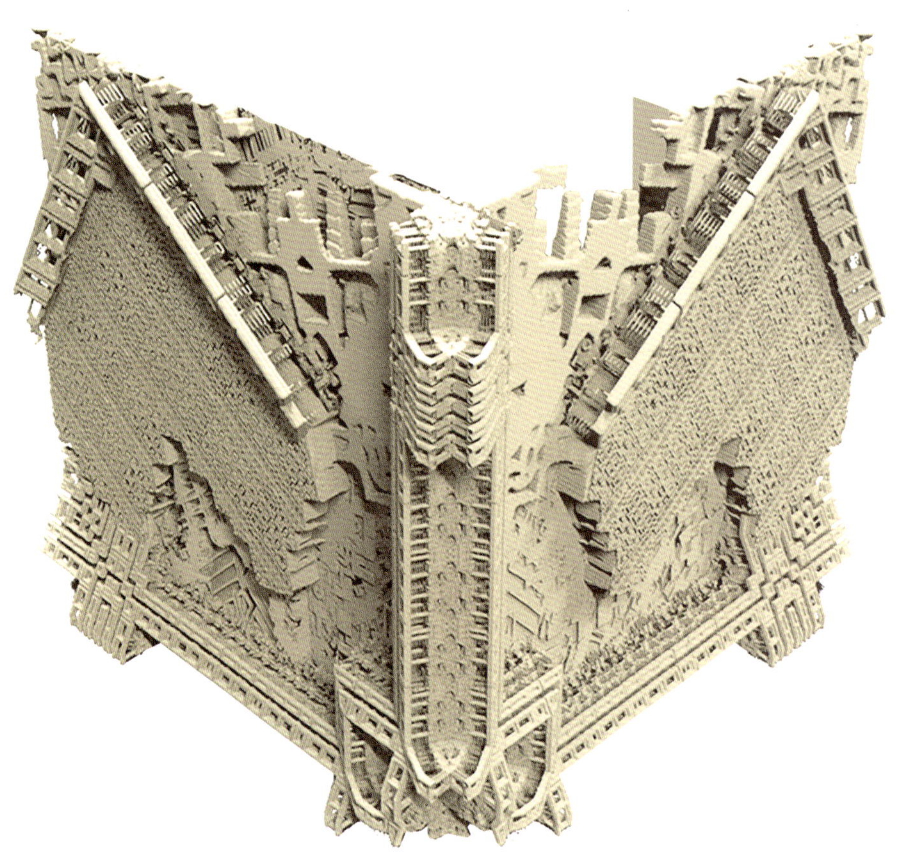

2019 FULL 3D EXTRAPOLATION: TEST_110918_ZH_BOX2B

This shows a rotated axonometric from a previously undocumented 2D to 3D translation. We included this one as it was an early attempt to use a different architectural language we developed in our office, referred to as "kitbashing." Kitbashing refers to the assembly of unrelated digital objects for the purpose of producing high-resolution form. This particular example was an example of kitbashing multiple of our fractal/AI-generated forms together—just to see what would happen in such pattern collisions. As the use of artificial intelligence was used to seamlessly fuse together pattern and form information, the use of kitbashing in this project made little sense as the two languages capitalize on very different digital strategies—collision vs. fusion. *Opposite page:* This image is a rotated axonometric from previously documented 2D to 3D translation.

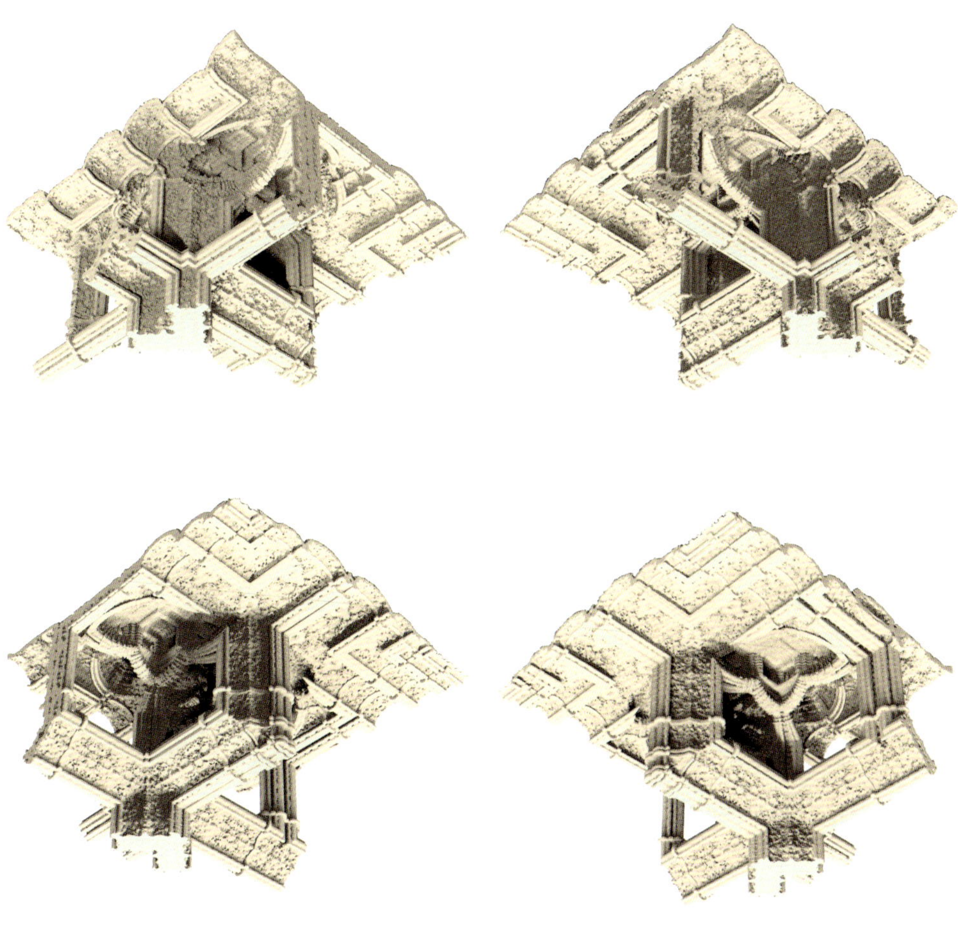

FULL 3D EXTRAPOLATION: TEST 2019_110518_FRACTAL_48

In the process of designing larger building masses, we also used the techniques we had developed to design smaller architectural structures, such as these cantilevered shading pavilions to produce cooling effects in more remote resort locations. This one uses deeply carved recesses to shift between legibility as a pattern and a form, all supported by a single center occupied structural stalk that branches out several feet above ground level.

251

FULL 3D EXTRAPOLATION: TEST 2019_110818_KA_FRACTAL_60

One of the components we wanted to produce for the "neo-Nabatean" architectural language of this project was a column capital. Architectural modernism eschews the use of classical elements—eschewing bases and columns, yet in their absence the transition of forces from beam or ceiling to the floor seems static. Classical columns use components such as capitals to give the aesthetic appearances of "squishing," because of the weight placed upon them. One direction I wanted to research was to find a column capital language that conveyed the same transition of forces, but did so with a more contemporary Arabic sensibility. One of the results of this is above, which would be located on structural elements in the reception courtyard leading to the guest rooms.

FINAL TRANSLATED 3D FORM FOR THE CENTRAL TOWER CAP

This particular design variation is one we worked on extensively to translate into a top for the resort's central observation, water filtration, and circulation tower. The form fuses together multiple geometric systems from Dadanite, Nabatean, and Bedouin sources in order to produce a contemporary artifact that, for us, seemed to hover on the cusp of both ancient and contemporary. The central opening is repeated on each bilaterally symmetrical façade and is the viewing frame from which observers would be able to see distant desert views in the four cardinal directions.

CENTRAL TOWER CAP IN PURE ELEVATION

Above is a rotated view of the same tower top. We thought this design was so successful according to our design goal that it became one of the most visible aspects of our project. References to the various civilizations are not only clear, but also accompanied by multiple changes in scale and detail. *Following pages:* "Grand opening day" image from ceremonial entrance, showing centralized tower structure and fractal/AI designed top as presented on these pages.

REJECTED FORMAL DIRECTION

One of our first test cases for using our custom fractal/AI systems was on the "reception cube," which is the first building experienced by the guests upon arriving from their desert vehicles. In this design, artifacts from Dadanite, Nabatean, Bedouin, and Saudi culture are transformed into a contemporary architectural language. This image shows one of tens of variations that we took through the full 3D modeling phase to test it in the context of the site. These represent directions that were being developed in conjunction with the previously featured translations, using different variations on the digital techniques and source materials. *Opposite page:* Rejected variation of the reception building's formal language.

THE ASTRONOMICAL OBSERVATORY

The above image is the final façade study for the observation pavilion, illustrating the previously described fused-script carving pattern. *Opposite page:* Our design proposal added to the program a multi-function guest "observatory" pavilion located at the highest point on our selected site. This observatory is used during the day as a relaxing, but remote lounge with sweeping 360-degree views of the surrounding desert. At night, the observatory becomes a place where telescopes are set up for guest's use within an outdoor "telescope pit" carved into the stone floor outside the observatory structure—which is designed to protect stargazers from wind.

REJECTED STUDY FOR A DOORWAY

Our design tests spanned scales from building massing to small details. In between are architectural structures such as doorways, a study of which is seen above. This one was rejected for seeming too "sci-fi" and not referencing the historic source material in a convincing way, although it did emerge from it. *Opposite page:* This design was selected for use as it combines multiple historic and cultural references—from Nabatean "merlon" stepping to subtle arabesque patterns occurring at a smaller scale in the deeper recesses of the frames.

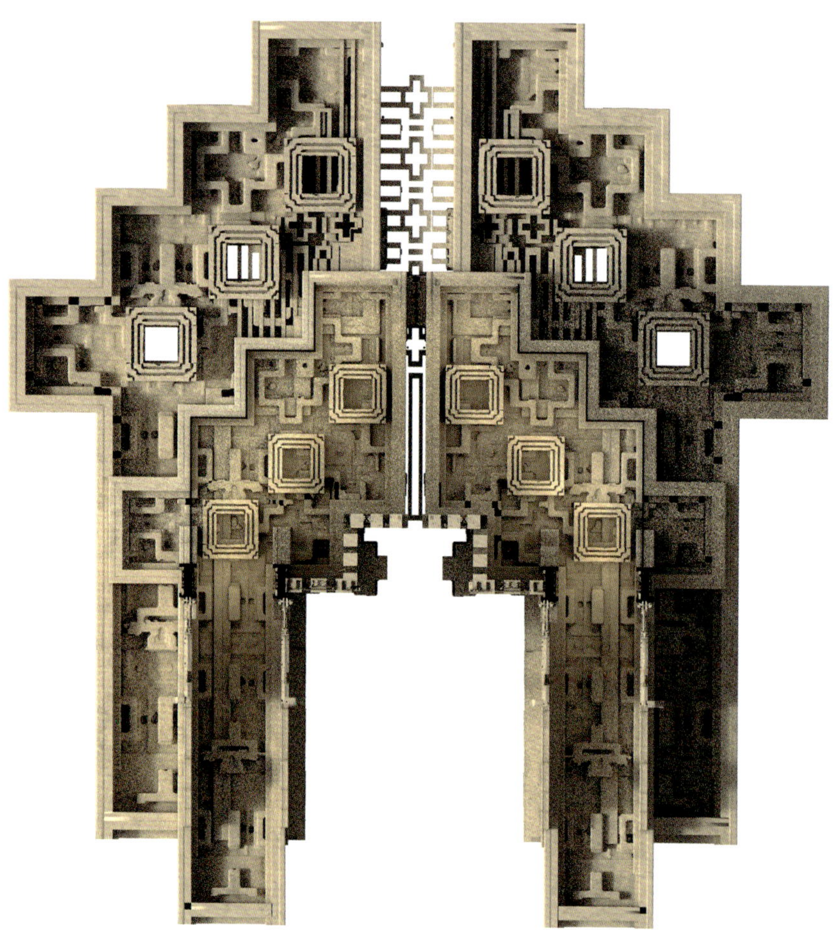

PATTERNS AND MATERIALS: FUSED

In certain cases we used historic source material both within our artificial intelligence design process and after 3D modeling it into architectural form. At times, it produced unusual surprises, such as this façade which seemingly fuses the flatness and pattern of the previous image into a single architectural form. This direction, after numerous additional iterations, became the basis for what would ultimately become our final reception building as illustrated on subsequent pages. *Opposite image:* This is a photograph of a simple Saudi rug thrown over a blank and weathered mud-brick wall.

AESTHETIC ITERATION

Design iterations of the reception building are illustrated above, all using different source material from the fractal/AI design process. While it seems increasingly uncommon to do this in schools and offices, we design multiple versions of our design ideas and select the one that best fits the criteria for the project—even aesthetically. Once we've selected one or a few, we usually do more iterations, then select one, then do more iterations, and so on. We develop hundreds of iterations on each project until it looks the way it should. You may want to ask us how we know? The same way you know when a pot of chili is done—but instead of using our tongue to taste, we use our eyes to see. For some reason, this baffles architects who seem unable to discuss aesthetics as a subject—an issue which I've written on extensively elsewhere.

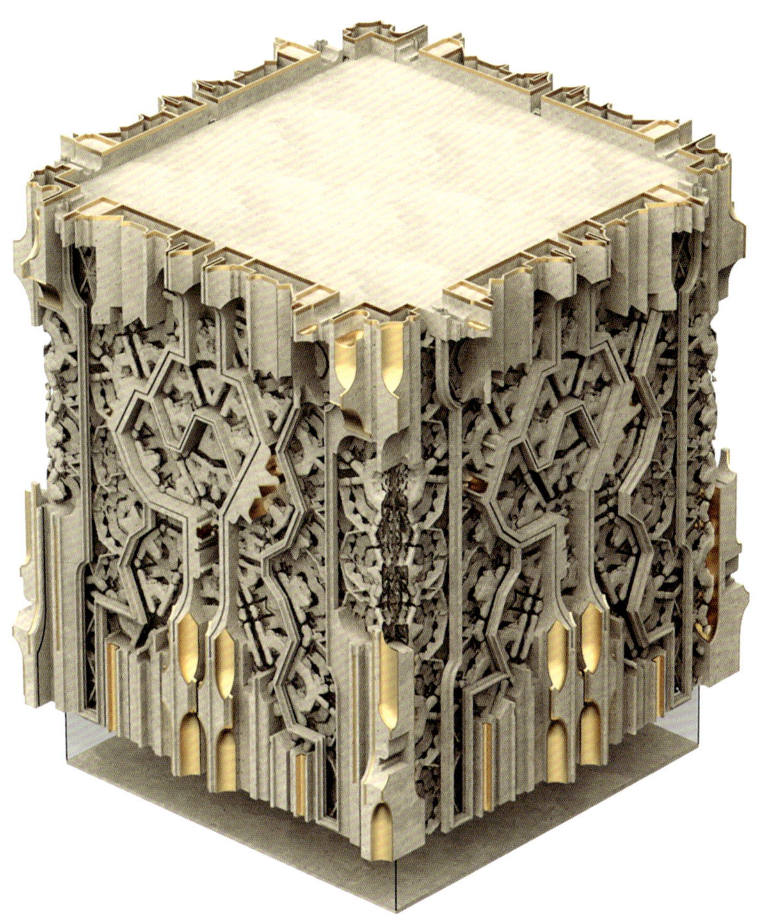

98TH-YARD LINE REJECTION

The above and opposite image show iterations from the previous studies that were taken all they way into 3D form and rendered with photo-realistic materiality. At this point in the design process. we had only a limited number of design candidates, which often indicates that we're close to our final version. These two images show the use of similar fractal/AI-generated patterns in the background with a vertical language used as either a base, framing device, or both.

99TH-YARD LINE REJECTION

The above options were ultimately rejected because they had too clear of a boundary between what was pattern and what was not. That is to say, they seemed separate and not "fused," which was the effect we were trying to achieve. Most of our final iterations contained a mix of fractal/ or AI-generated forms and hand modeling. It's never the case that the computer produces something that we can use without further brute-force design. These rejected examples illustrate the completeness with which we have to develop some options in order to understand why they should not be used. This is a terrible business model.

The final design direction for the reception building is illustrated above. This iteration was selected because it successfully combined multiple historic design references, all of which were used in the fractal/AI design process in a way that was unabashedly contemporary, yet emerged strangely through historic references. It also better fused the patterning and larger scale architectural language in a way where the two could not be easily separated. This form has no entry, but instead had a natural door frame that we used once some of the adjacent wall area was extracted from the design to produce an opening. The thin vertical "fingers" also became windows to allow filtered light into the colorful, tiled interior.

ON RUSTICATION

Throughout the entire design project, we frequently combined high-resolution fractal/AI forms with primitive rusticated areas of raw stone, such as this variation of the reception building. The mix of raw and highly intricate stone was a particular feature of Nabatean architecture that we wanted to emulate in a contemporary way. Strangely, rustication is something in architecture that used to be inexpensive, as it simply meant less finishing required on stone blocks. However, today, as most materials come flat-packed and are shipped all over the world, rustication has largely disappeared from architecture. We want to bring it back.

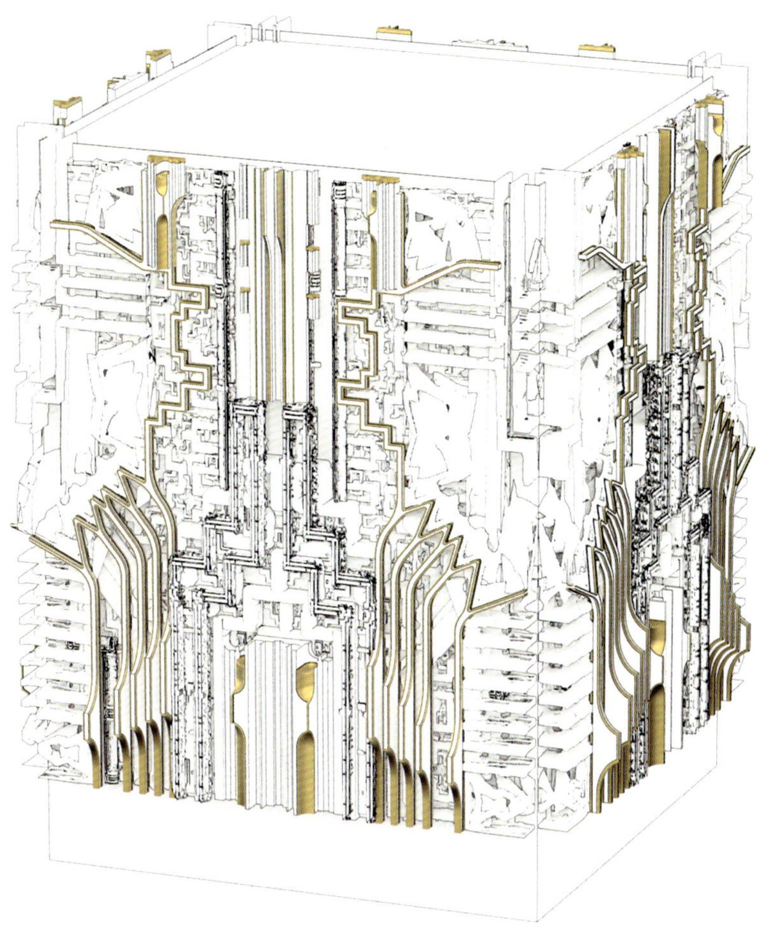

VARIABLE VARIATIONS

Once selected as the final design direction for the reception building, we studied and modified the form using numerous techniques and representational processes, sometimes viewing the form of the building without material, as shown in this shaded-line drawing, above. The computer is not only used to generate form, but to visualize it in different ways, thereby allowing us to further refine it along performative and aesthetic lines. This particular image was used to imagine how the inside of certain tracery forms could be lined in a gold-colored alloy. This gold-inlay direction was abandoned because of weathering concerns.

3D PRINTING IN METAL

In order to fully verify the visual properties of the form in the real world, we commissioned 3D prints in solid metal such as this bronze version of the reception building, which I am holding for scale. The 3D print was roughly a six inch cube, but had such extensive detail that we used the model to test the effect of patina on the delicate patterns—ultimately finding that some of our patterns were too small. Real world testing, as the above model illustrates, is periodically important for a digitally heavy design processes as it forces the forms being studied into the real world where materiality, lighting, reflection, and other aesthetic qualities have to be confronted without digital tweaking. We did take this model to the final presentation, where it ultimately disappeared, likely becoming a paperweight for some intrepid interloper. If you see it, please let us know.

THE ÉCOLE DES BEAUX-ARTS ELEVATION

Over the extent of the project there were multiple areas where very high-resolution design strategies were used to produce signature, impactful architectural moments unlike anything, anywhere,—but were still mysteriously familiar. This was the design goal and why we used the region's historic design DNA as the origin of all of our formal languages. While drawing elevations fell out of favor with the rise of modernism, where façade design largely disappeared from architecture, we use them extensively. A pure elevation, when shaded according to the methods taught at the École des Beaux-Arts, can reveal composition, depth, detail, and proportion in a way that isn't always visible in a constantly rotating, 3D digital model.

CNC MILLED STONE TRACERY

While the observation tower top and multiple other high-resolution areas of the project were proposed in various metals to allow for the realistic capture of their detail, the reception building was large enough that it could be made in stone—with the smallest details well within the tolerances of the proposed CNC carving machines and the strength of the stone itself. The above image shows a near-final rendering of the reception building using a mix of carved and highly rusticated areas.

PAUL RUDOLPH, NABATEAN

One aspect of Nabatean architecture is its rugged, worn, stone edges. However, typical stone construction today is completed with razor-edge cuts and perfectly fitting geometries. This is why the stone buildings of today often look less solid than the stone buildings of yesterday—they are simply too perfectly constructed. We wanted our stone to be a little more "banged up," and proposed brush hammering the edges to produce a more rugged aesthetic appearance, a similar strategy to that of Paul Rudolph, former Dean of the Yale School of Architecture when he designed the building that houses the school, now named Rudolph Hall (where I have taught continuously since 2001, ruining quite a few sweaters). This image captures the roughened edge quality we wanted in the final building.

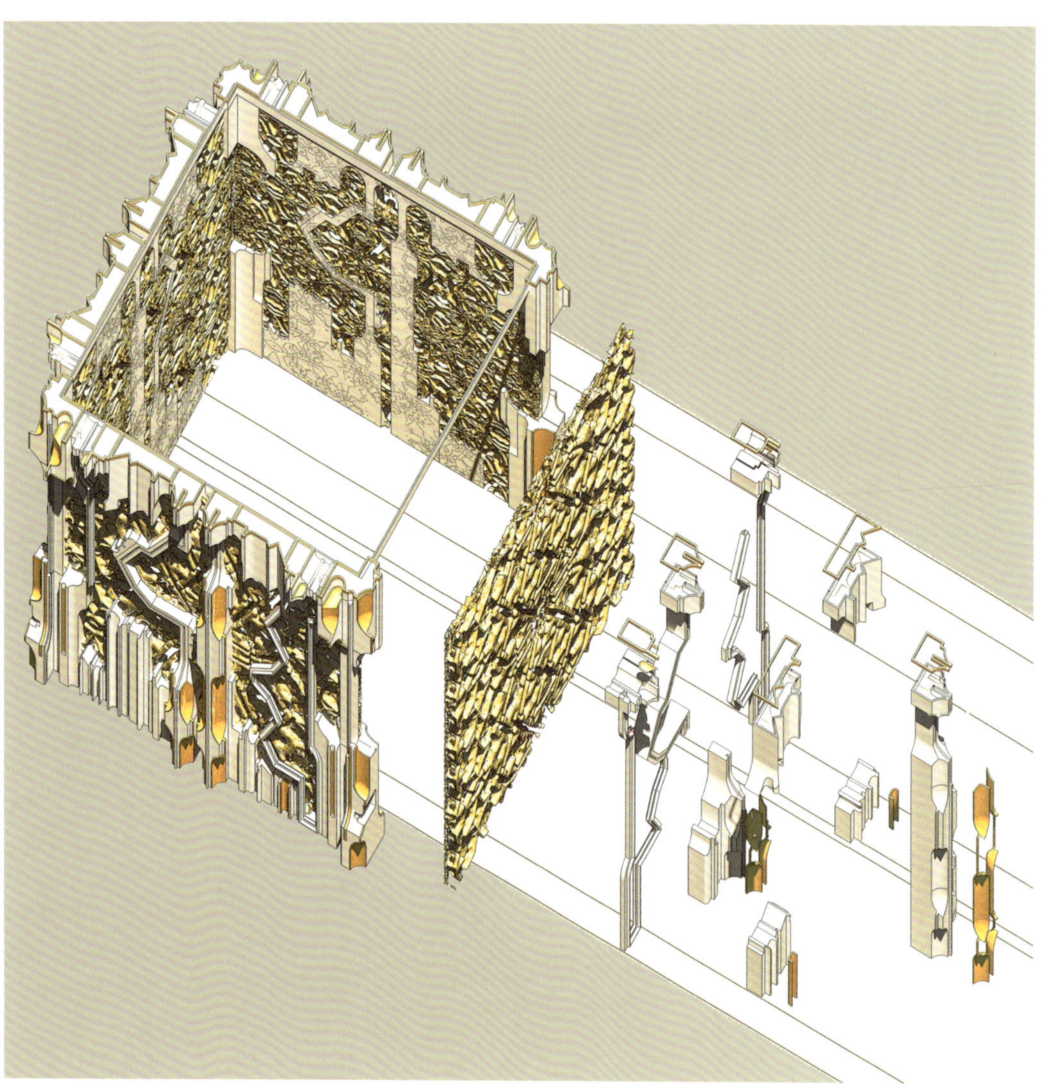

CONCEPTUAL ASSEMBLY

This exploded axonometric shows the conceptual assembly of the various project components. Although the project would not actually be built this way, this image is useful in illustrating the various design layers which are fused to produce the final façade. This image illustrates an earlier version of the reception building. Following pages: This is the final rendering of the reception building with its entrance court that is largely defined by slump-formed, arched glass with water trickling down its surfaces into a shallow pool.

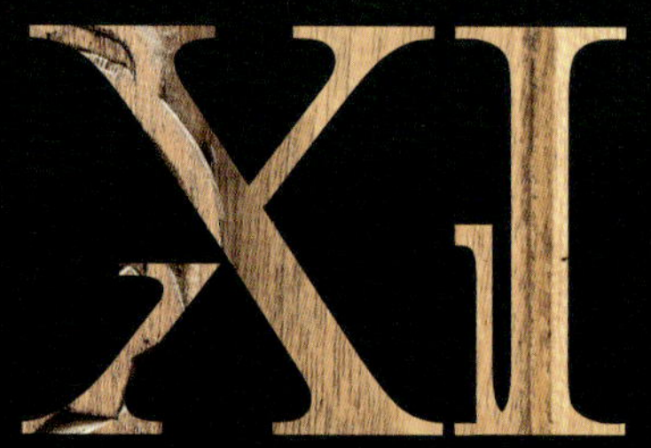

CORE WORKOUT

***Opposite page :* This is a photo of a** carved door handle at the front of a Saudi Arabian house.

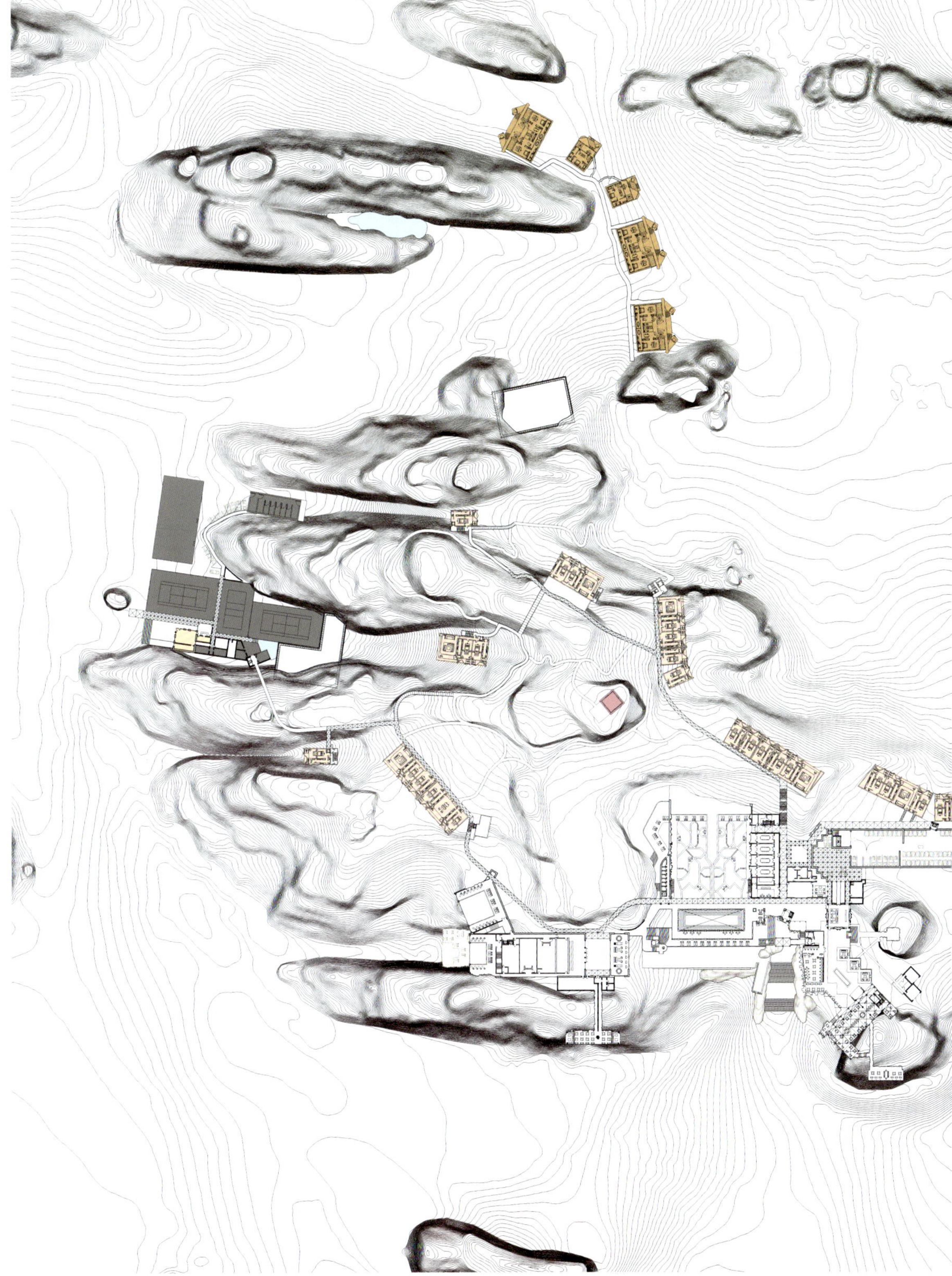

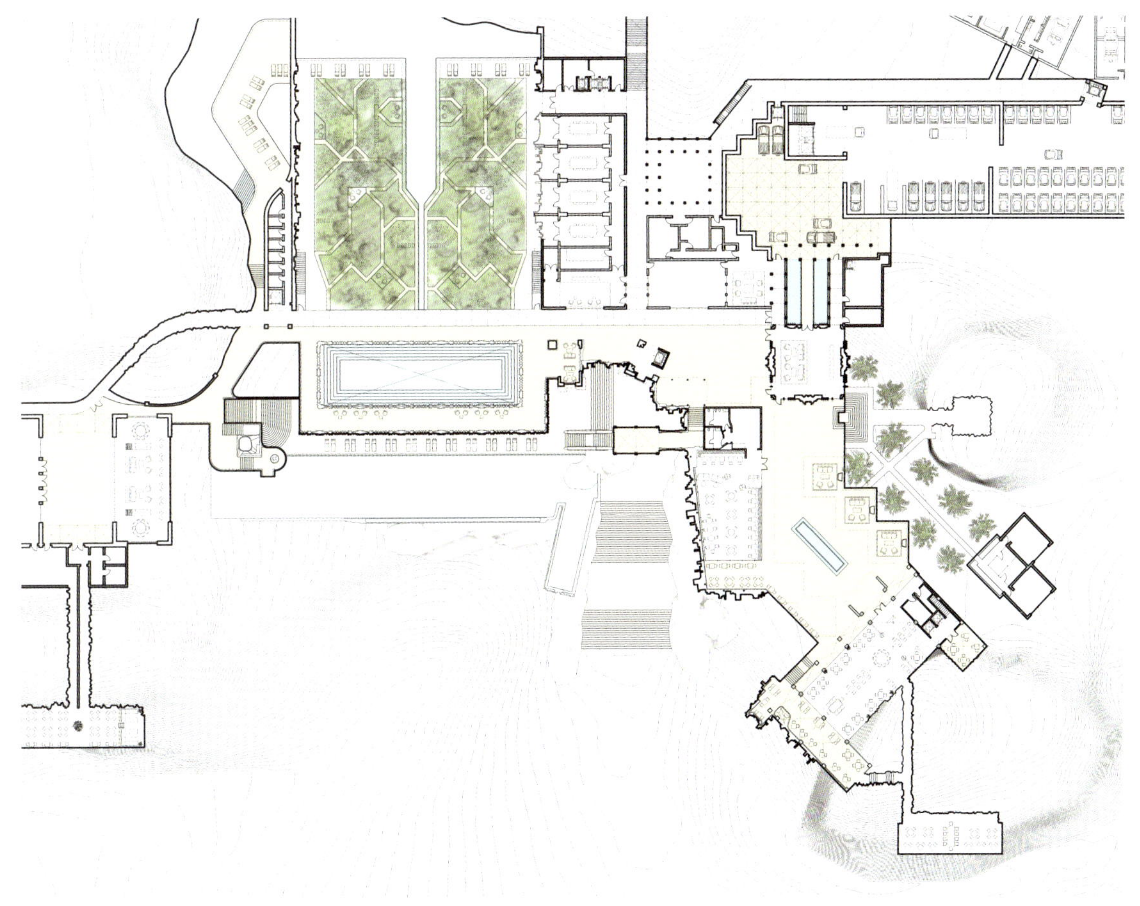

THE DRY LEVEL

Preceding pages: This drawing is the final master plan minus the satellite campus. *This page:* Above is the upper level of the resort's core area showing, in yellow, the primary guest circulation between the reception, restaurants, cafe, business center, and garden areas. The lower level of the resort's core, in white, shows circulation between the ceremonial entrance, shading pool arcades, and pools at multiple temperatures. This project had extensive sectional interconnections between programs. Thus, we found ourselves working in detailed plan layers rather frequently, as more isolated building sections became useless. This was simply because at any given point in the complex, the section would change dramatically, leaving no unifying conditions that represented the project as a whole.

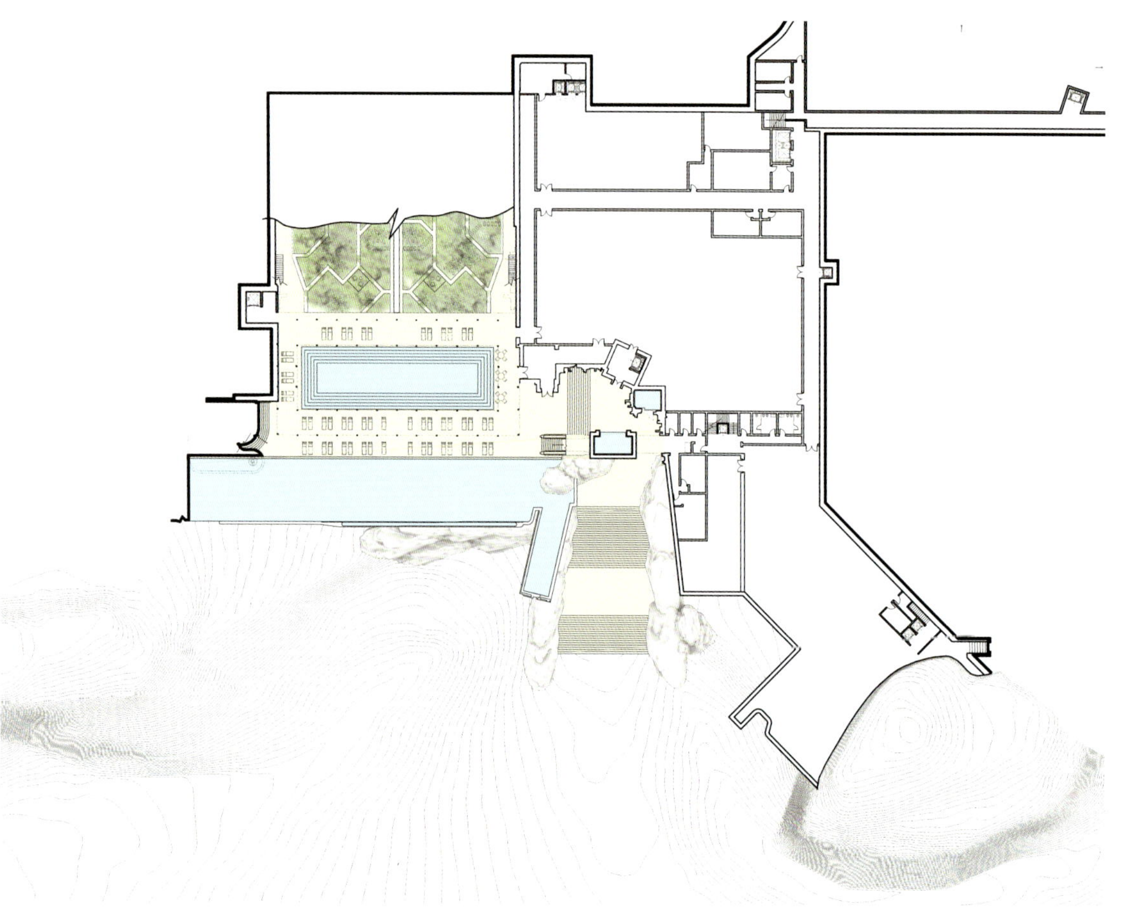

THE WET LEVEL

We divided the building into dry and wet functions such resort/spa combinations. The lower wet level, pictured above, houses multiple swimming pools including an air-temperature pool that would be slightly cooled in extreme temperatures (the horizon pool), a chilled outdoor pool protected by an arcaded courtyard, and two plunge pools at temperatures of 42 and 52 degrees Fahrenheit. These pool areas are directly accessible from the kitchen which resides on the same level, to the right. Also included on this floor was the garden oasis, a collection of native plant species adjacent to the chilled pool. The roots of this oasis would be used as part of a water recovery system proposed by the organic filtration company Organica.

REJECTED CENTRAL CORE STUDIES

Towerless studies of the central core "circulation knots" were abandoned, for various reasons. The top image seemed too much like a 1970s shopping mall, with the swooping forms common to the brutalism of that particular era. The lower iteration was rejected as it was too opaque—producing spaces that were both too dark and blocked the views of the desert horizon at too many locations.

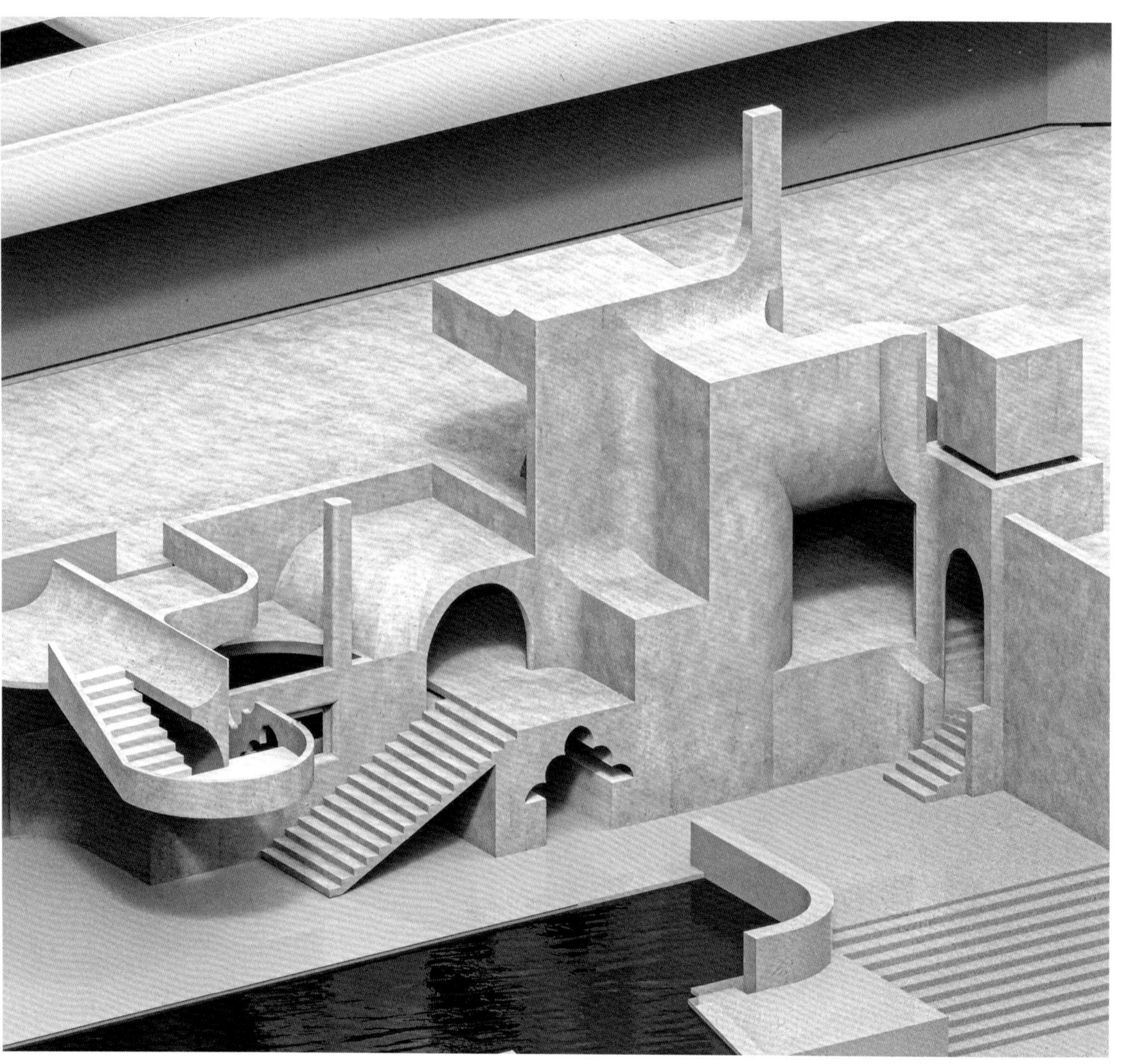

We briefly liked this central circulation core as it had a lively, interactive, and interconnected cave-like quality that fused forms and surfaces. While we appreciated the porous carved cave aesthetic that was reminiscent of some spaces of the Nabateans, it was decided that this language was too playful for the feeling of ancient gravitas we wanted to produce at the resort. We did, however, keep the strategy of the primary circulation stair intertwining between multiple interior and exterior spaces that were clearly defined. This offered a choreographed series of spatial experiences in what would normally be a simple stair and elevator in a hotel lobby.

FIRST TOPOGRAPHICAL RENDERINGS: CORE AND RECREATION

Once we have the general program arrangement of our design idea, we fold it into a context file that has been modeled with as much topographical and textural accuracy as our computers can handle. As our work is often centered around the aesthetic effects of high-resolution detail and textures, it's important for us to at least approximate the context in a way that's as close to reality as we can achieve. The result is images such as those featured above—views of the rocky terrain as generated by the computer. Peter Eisenman once called these textures we use "elephant skin"—which is probably more accurate than we'd care to admit, but it's better than smooth uniform gray with no textural or rocky qualities. The above views show the restaurant area from a distance and the tower that leads to the sports complex.

FIRST TOPOGRAPHICAL RENDERINGS: CARVED CIRCULATION

In certain areas of our resort design, we proposed carving into the sandstone context to produce corridors and programmed spaces. The top image shows the view from such a carved circulation path leading back toward the center of the resort. This carved path led to a specialty restaurant carved into the nearby sandstone escarpment. The lower image shows an early concept of elevated rooms that are connected by towers to lower common-use areas. This strategy was ultimately abandoned as we found it too disturbing to the local context.

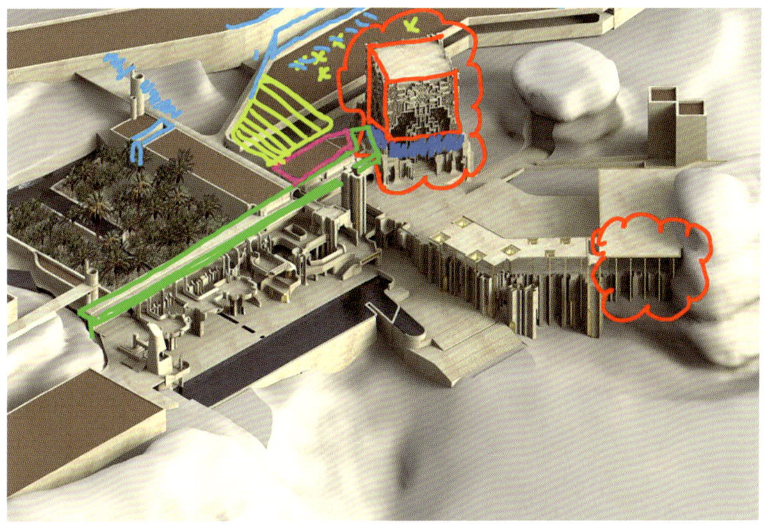

UGLY SKETCHES

While many of the representations we produce in our office are of professional quality—and we think rather beautiful— the truth of our day-to-day operations is that we live in a world of ugly sketches. Hand sketching on top of our Wacom screens has proven to be an incredibly effective tool for communicating internally—the perfect combination of old-school hand drawing and high technology. The above sketches of mine, perhaps embarrassingly, show changes I wanted made to certain resort center areas.

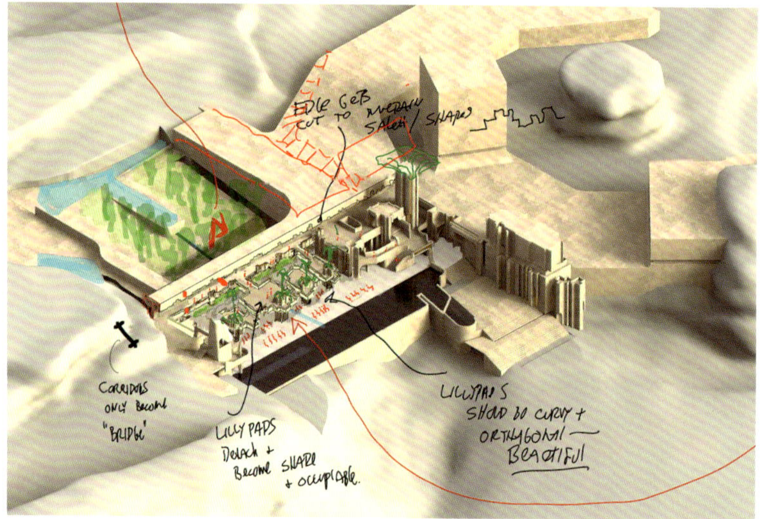

MORE UGLY SKETCHES

The above sketches show revisions I made to the reception building and its adjacent covered circulation (top) and the relationship between the garden oasis and pool areas (bottom). In both areas we were trying to better protect exterior areas with shading devices such as the roof on the exterior hallway that takes guests alongside the garden oasis, and the elevated observation platforms hovering in between the garden oasis and pool. Both directions would ultimately be rejected for better solutions we developed later.

290

DIGITAL SCREEN DRAWINGS: POOL LEVEL

Additional hand drawn sketches done on our Wacom computer screens are shown above. These show revisions I made to the circulation knot adjacent to the main pool and the pool location itself. These sketches are a combination of digital screen captures of 3D models, site photographs, and hand drawn lines and fills. These type of sketches are only for internal use and are never shown to the client as they tend to have an infantalizing, cartoonish aesthetic that doesn't carry any gravitas. They are incredibly effective at conveying ideas between our team members, however, likely saving hundreds of hours of digital modeling—as we could review ideas before any 3D modeling investment was made on them.

DIGITAL SCREEN DRAWINGS: REJECTED ROOM ARRAY SKETCHES

There are also bad sketches of bad designs made in our office. These drawings of mine imagine very long, linear buildings in prominent locations—abandoned almost immediately because they looked like abandoned Holiday Inn's in the remote reaches of rural Nevada.

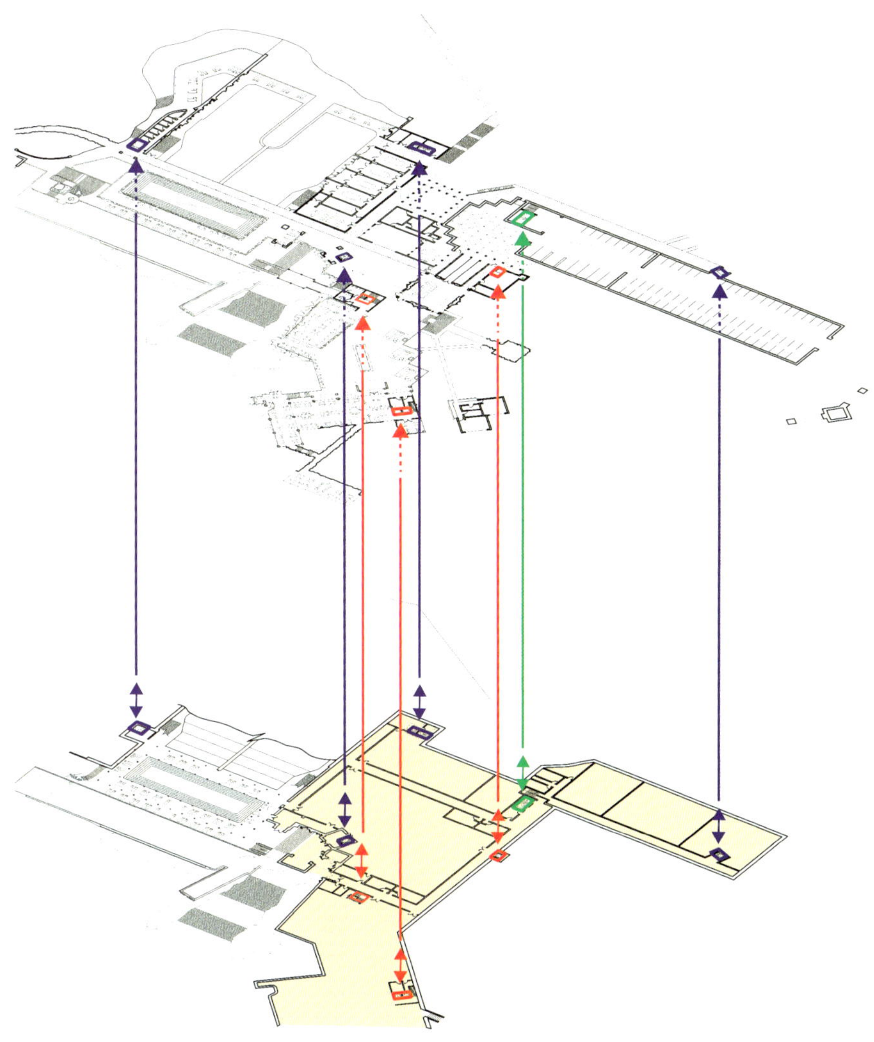

VERTICAL CIRCULATION

The above image is a back-of-house diagram illustrating how the vertical circulation of guests is separate from that of housekeeping, food delivery, and valet. Less exciting work, but key to a program such as a luxury resort where success is contingent on hiding the aspects of everyday life one is trying to, for a time, escape. *Opposite page:* The complex topography of our site required a complex web of interactions across multiple levels in order to give access to guests by hotel staff, but in a nearly completely hidden manner. The images show these levels, each subsequently removed to show the level underneath. While the upper two images show the public areas, the lower image shows the location of the primary kitchens, service areas, and cleaning facilities. This arrangement allowed staff the ability to access guests vertically on the upper levels and horizontally toward the pool areas—meaning there only had to be a single kitchen for the entire resort.

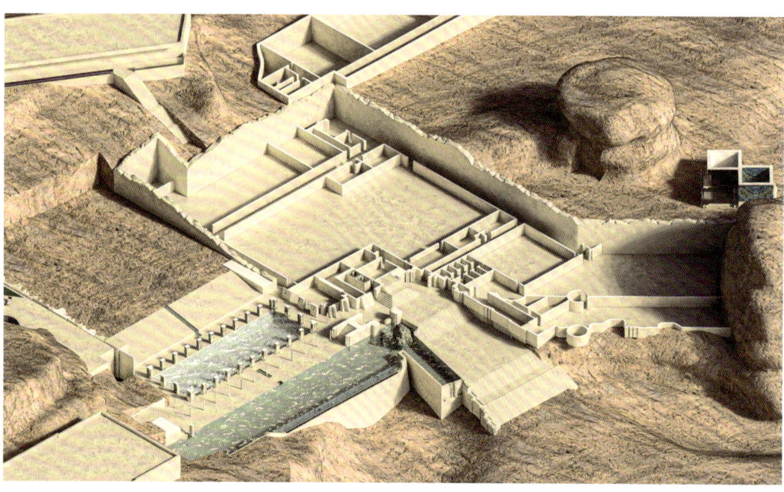

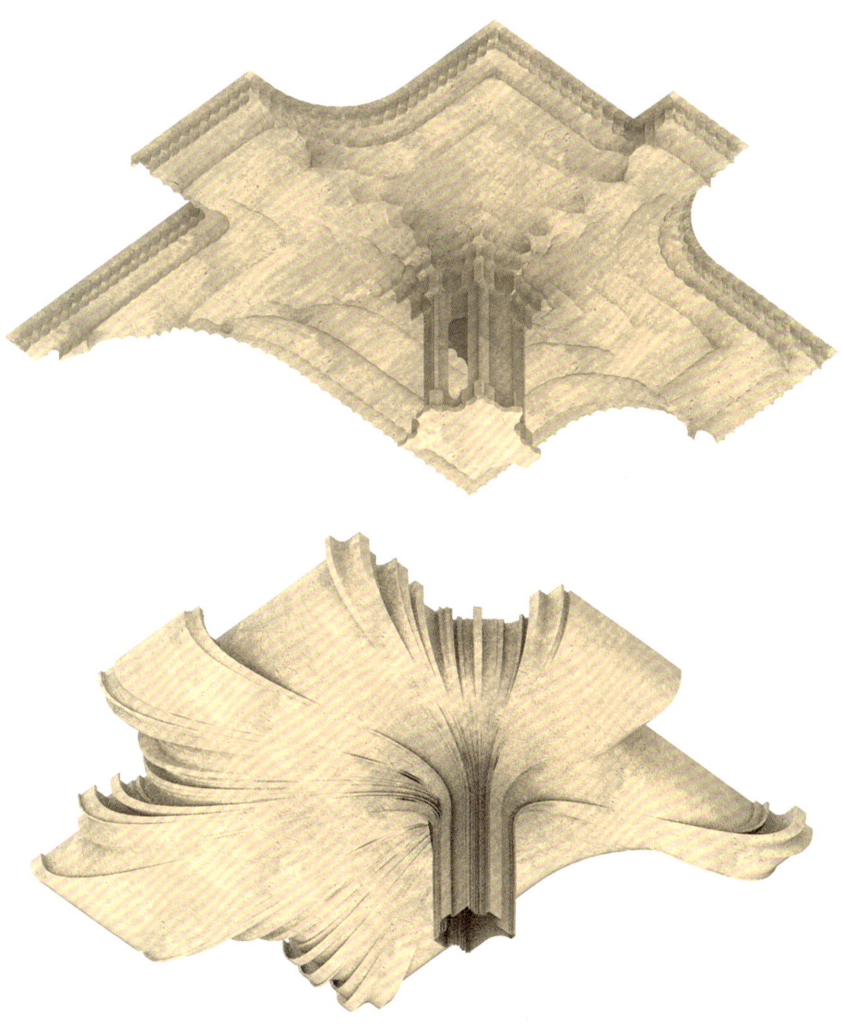

294

DENDRIFORM COLUMNS 1-2

These images show structural columns that flare at the top to provide shade and produce ceilings for the outdoor pool areas. We considered these to be distant descendants of the flared columns that Frank Lloyd Wright used in his Johnson Wax building—his finest work in my opinion. Ultimately, this direction was rejected because they had no regional cultural reference and looked too much like the truly fantastic "little island" that Thomas Heatherwick was designing in New York City, since completed.

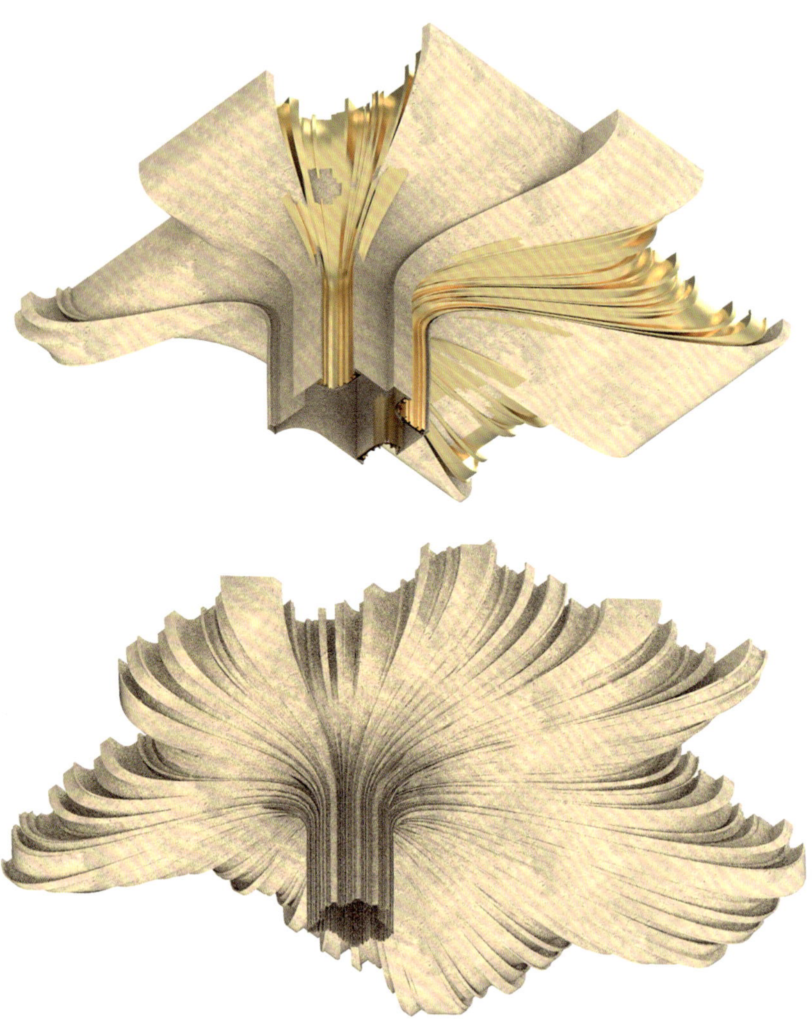

DENDRIFORM COLUMNS 3-4

Above are additional variations of the structural columns with new materials and additional detail. Ultimately, we transitioned from these forms to more traditional arcades as an architectural form with more cultural resonance. This better achieved our desire for spaces that, while exterior, felt more like enclosed and protected rooms or defined volumes. The forms above tend to produce "spaces" rather than "rooms"—and we're far more interested in the latter, in general. The arcade ceiling, being more predictably geometric, allowed us to apply more complex vaults using AI fusions of Dadanite and Nabatean script patterns.

DENDRIFORM SPACES 1-2

In our studies of how to produce a series of outdoor "shaded rooms" for the multiple pools on the lower level, we went through numerous design ideas. The top image shows a "corbeled" system, which has heavy roots in Middle East mosque structures, but is less used in Saudi Arabia than other locations such as Uzbekistan and Iran. The lower image shows "lily pad" like structures in metal that were more randomly dispersed. Neither direction was pursued.

297

DENDRIFORM SPACES 3-4

Following pages: This image is an aerial rendering of the resort showing an earlier rustic tower design and the incorporation of solar panels on the larger roof planes. We ultimately decided against placing solar panels on the roofs, in favor of consolidating all of them in a single massive solar field, secured to the ground and hidden from the resort. This proved far more efficient, as maintenance and cleaning of the solar cells is an important concern in the desert and is better done without workers climbing on buildings while being visible to resort guests.

THE DIGITAL WOOD MODEL

This is an image of the 3D digital terrain models of the site arrayed to study building placement from multiple views. We frequently show our digital terrain models as if they were physically created in wood. This has the effect of descaling the renderings so that they do not look like small versions of a real building, but rather look like small images of a physical model. Jumping between scales and studying the building in multiple ways is important in allowing us to understand aspects of the project that only certain representational explorations reveal.

THE HIDDEN LANGUAGE OF WALLS

These images show early studies of the wall language used to define outdoor public spaces and were based on the chiseled arch structures found in some Saudi religious structures, as well as enlarged corbeling shapes common to mosque architecture. This latter reason is why we abandoned the extensive use of this language, as we decided that using such obvious religious references in a secular space may have not been appropriate for the global and commercial context of the project. This image also shows early ideas of how the site topography was frequently exposed to allow the building and rocky outcroppings to interact aesthetically.

TO FUSE OR NOT TO FUSE

The above image shows an early study of the reception building being placed into a "nest" that rises from the main public plaza. We discarded the idea of "fusing" too many architectural components together in favor of allowing each to retain a stronger individual identity that could be articulated through variations of their architectural language. This latter attitude is one that has emerged in my continued engagement with philosophy and moving beyond the Deleuzian tendency toward single surface modeling techniques—in particular as outlined by Patrik Schumacher, with whom I have had a friendly public disagreement regarding his theories of "parametricism" for years.

A NOTE ON MEANINGLESS DETAIL

Presented here is an early study of the restaurant courtyard and structures. This design direction was rejected for appearing way too science fiction-like, somehow looking like spaceships would emerge from the large end openings at the first sign of alien presence in Saudi airspace. When 3D patterns and textures lose their cultural resonance, they often start to resemble "greebles," which are meaningless detailed textures used in the film industry—originally used in movies such as "Star Wars" as a way to make small models of spaceships appear much larger by encrusting them with micro-details.

THERMAL MASSES AND DECOYS

These renderings show further development of the restaurant building and how it was partially built into the adjacent sandstone rock formations—using a corrugated wall structure which hides the kitchen beyond and allows the building to stay cooler as heat is absorbed in locations far from human occupation. The extended fins cast shadows on the wall to which they are attached, thereby providing a self-shading technique of cooling. The carved rooms of the Nabatean tombs tend to be rather cool as they are protected by the thermal dispersion of the large masses they are part of. This strategy was used in our project where we find "decoy" heat sinks, located to protect nearby occupied spaces from heat gain.

307

ARCHITECTURE AS ENGLISH MUFFIN

This is a more detailed rendering of the edge of the restaurant courtyard showing smaller, more private and shaded dining "nooks" nestled into the retaining walls of the site. Privacy was of significant importance in the program and this extended to our attitude toward hidden and secret outdoor discoveries. Like Thomas' English muffins, the project aspires to have "nooks and crannies," albeit to catch people rather than butter. *Following pages:* This image shows the final rendering of the restaurant courtyard with chilled central pool. The vertical supports and ceiling tracery were hollow pipes in which chilled water could be circulated to provide cooling effects in the immediate vicinity at night when there was less wind and more of a radiant cooling effect.

CIRCULATION KNOT STUDIES

These renderings show early iterations of the primary circulation knots weaving around the main observation and water filtration tower. This direction was abandoned as the tower seemed to have too strong a reference to religious structures. *Opposite page:* This iteration uses a highly rusticated and raw texture for the stone, but was seen as too "science fictiony" and without clear historic precedents for the formal language.

FINAL CIRCULATION KNOT: POOL ACCESS

The final rendering of the pool circulation knot and filtration tower clearly shows the interconnections, both vertical and horizontal, between the main horizon pool, chilled interior pool, shaded arcade, garden oasis, and spa. For a sense of scale, the reclining lounge chairs are visible at the base of the arcade that separates the pools. The depth of the chilled pool is a maximum of four feet to minimize the quantities of water required to be cooled, whereas the horizon pool, where it is carved directly into the stone of the site, reaches depths of fifteen feet in order to create larger thermal mass that can combat heat gain and allows the pool to stay warmer, longer, in the cooler nights.

FINAL CIRCULATION KNOT: CENTRAL CORE ACCESS

The final rendering of the main observation tower and related circulation knot shows the multiple means of circulation between levels and their choreographed views—where a guest would be sequentially reoriented toward the garden oasis, pools and observation and water filtration tower. Both the horizon pools and ceremonial entrance stairs are located to intersect with an existing massive boulder that can be seen in the above image. Also visible is the existing rock formation toward the right of the stairs, at the intersection with the adjacent wall. Wherever possible we used existing geological structures to interrupt the man-made aspects of the project to continually remind visitors of the natural aesthetic qualities of the desert site.

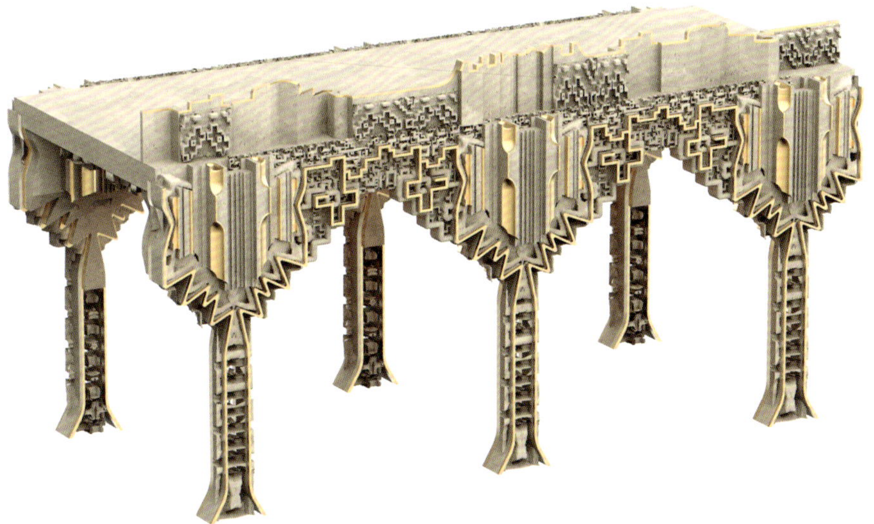

314

THE COUNTERFACTUAL ARCADE

Saudi Arabia is filled with arcades of different geometries and proportions, but we had not seen any that might have had any relationships to the formal language of the Nabatean civilization. Always up for a challenge, we designed this pavilion/arcade at the top of a flight of stairs using the stepped motif used in almost all of the carved stone structures in Mada'in Salih. In essence we imagined what a Nabatean stone arcade might look like if they had ever designed one, which they hadn't. This creative use of counterfactual ideas is a strategy we often find ourselves using as a way to shift outside of our standard design mindset.

We set the arcade structure on a rusticated base of cyclopean sandstone that echoed the patterns found in the pavilion/arcade, but at a significantly increased scale. The lower image shows the flight of stairs leading to the structure and better illustrates the carved stone ceiling. While it is not shown in the renderings, all of the lighting is hidden to illuminate the carved ceilings with a warm beautiful glow. A particular goal of the project was that no light sources, other than strategically located torches and flames, would be directly visible. While architects often associate the future with uninterrupted strips of lighting embedded into everything, we imagine the opposite, where lighting is delicate, glowing, efficient, but ultimately invisible.

Our material studies extended to some of the suite structures where we studied multiple metal mesh patterns in gold tones, eventually—even if briefly—holding the idea that the entire resort complex would be sheathed in gold mesh. We finally decided that the residential buildings would be made from massive cyclopean sandstone blocks taken from the cut-and-fill excavation of the site itself. This has the benefit of being more sustainable and allows the buildings to blend into their rocky surroundings in a more restrained way. *Opposite page:* A cel-shaded image of one of the guest suite mini-towers embedded in its small ravine.

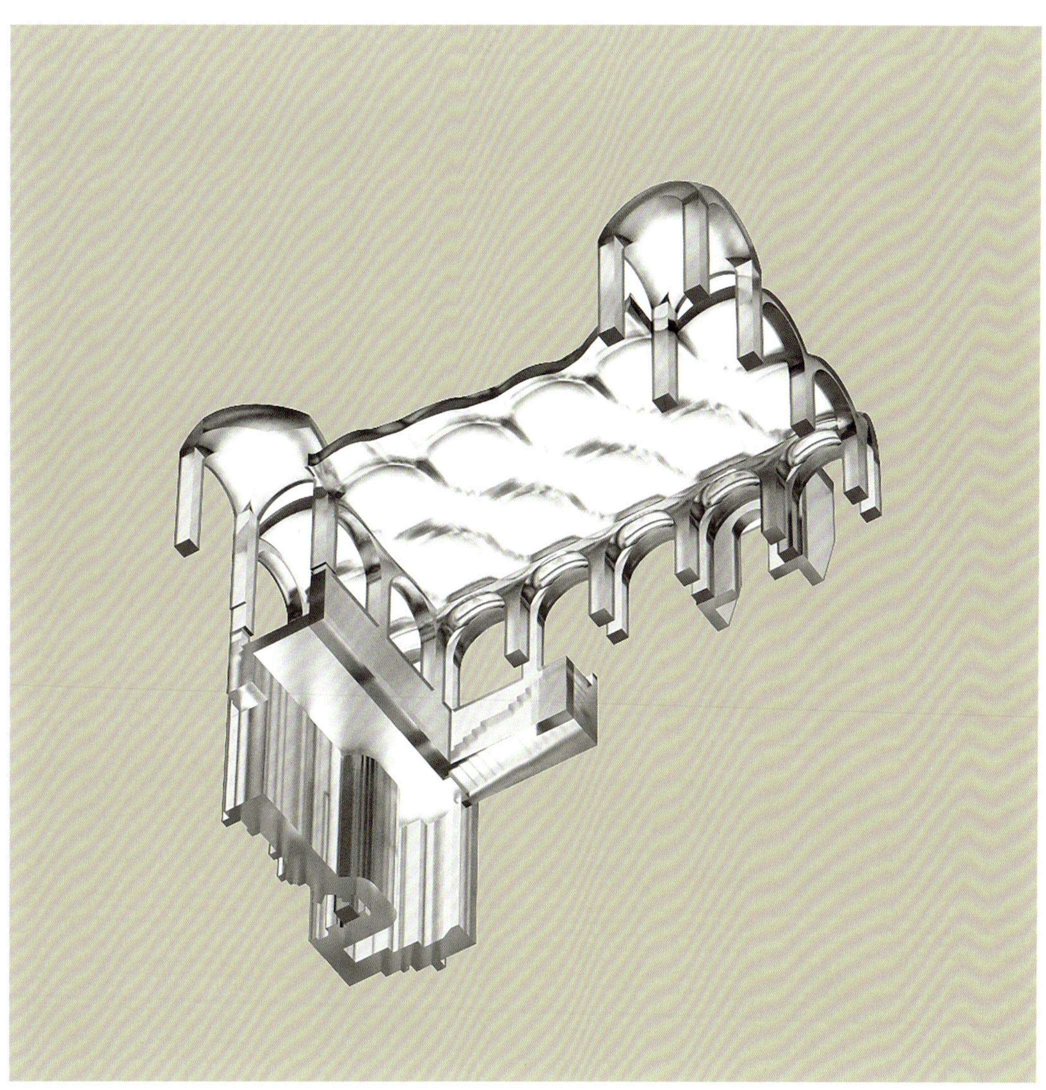

Preceding pages: This image illustrates a low aerial view of the resort's central core. This image shows the integration of the multi-domed restaurant pavilion with the sandstone outcroppings toward its right. Also visible is the carved VIP dining facility, located within the rocky outcroppings but with a cantilevered edge for a massive framed glass window. *This page:* These images were done after the project was complete as a way to try out some new rendering techniques. They weren't part of the design process, but may be part of the design process of future projects—showing a translucent rendering of the restaurant pavilion on the left and an etched image of the ceremonial entrance, minus the stairs, on the right.

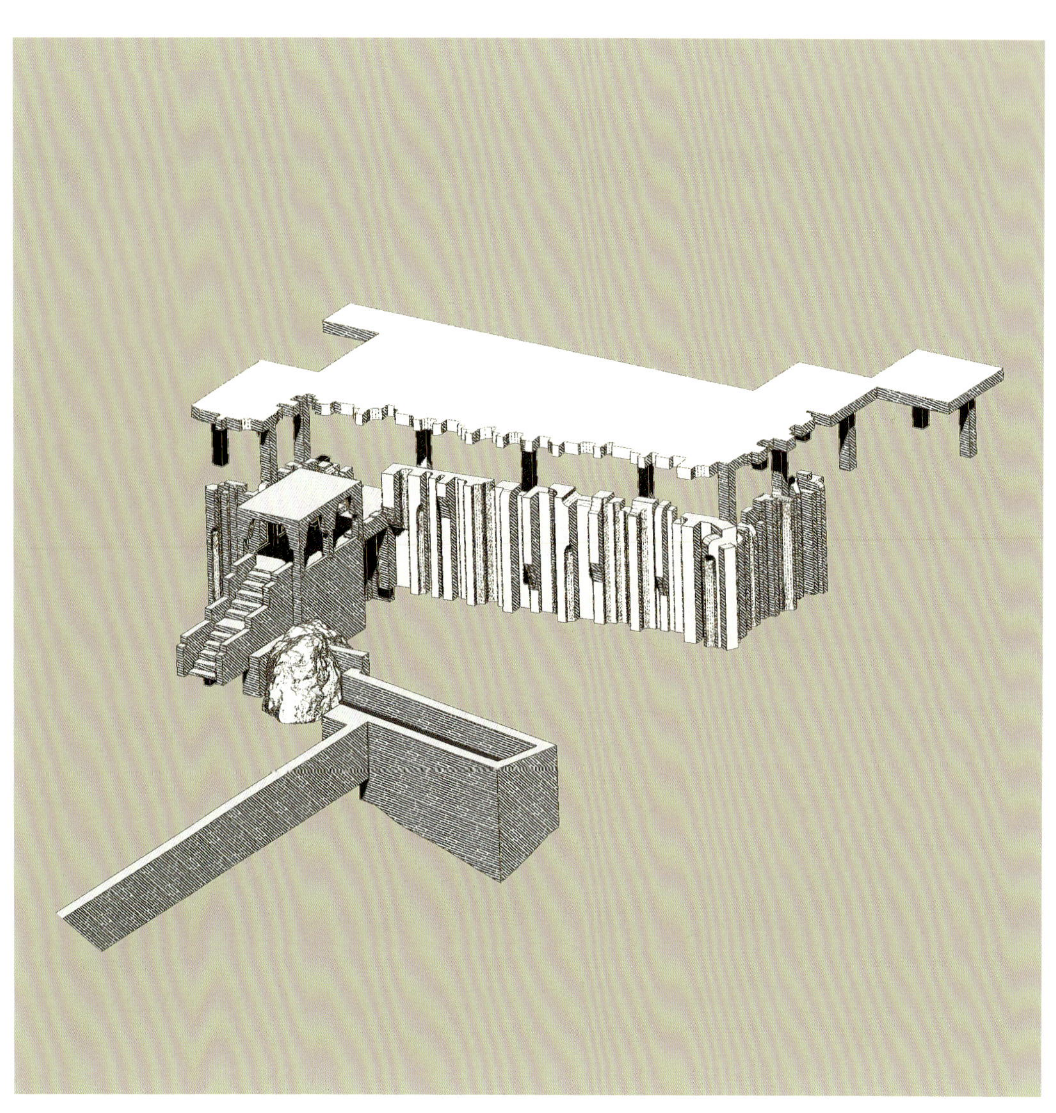

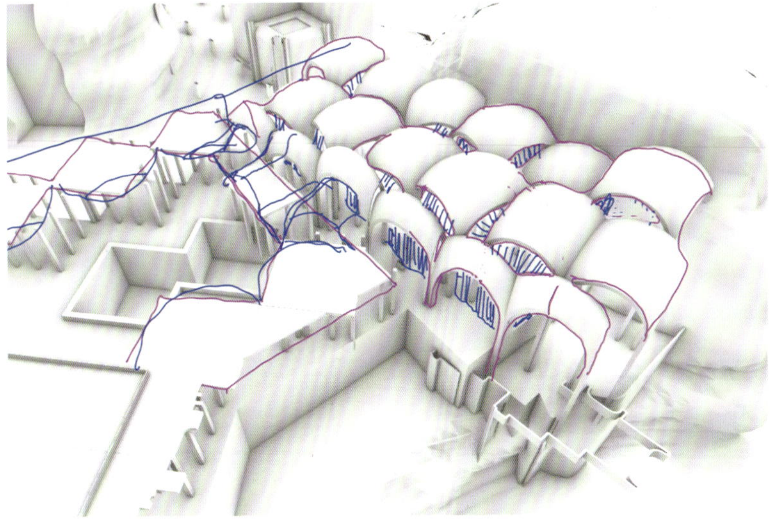

AN INTRICACY OF VAULTING

Underneath the conjoined domes of the restaurant pavilion we wanted to design a fractal/AI vaulting structure—an arabesque version of Henri Labrouste's Bibliothèque Nationale in Paris, which itself seemed to have affinities with some of the multi-domed mosques found in the Middle East. These early sketches show the general ambitions of the interior that were further explored.

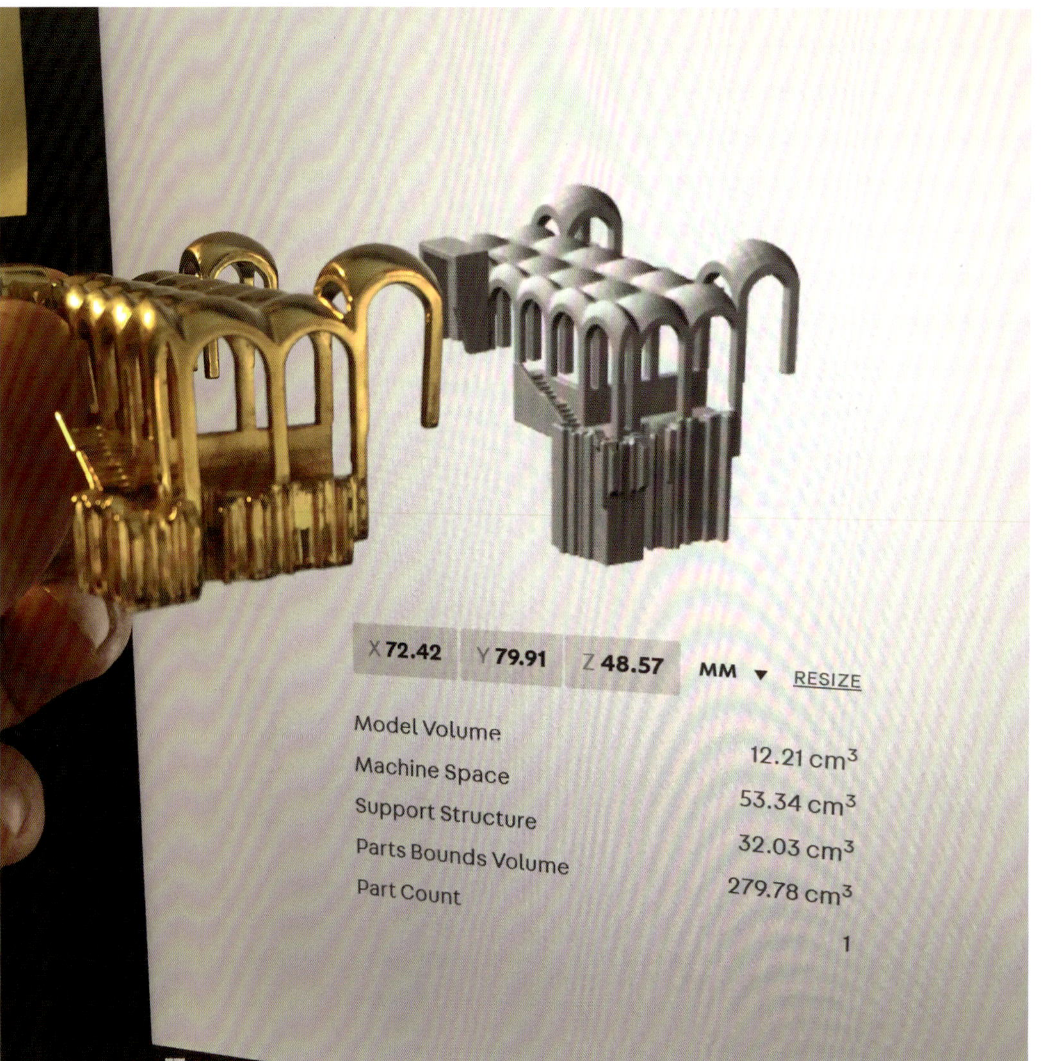

323

STUDY 3D PRINT IN BRASS

When presented with the task of producing a final presentation model, we ultimately decided on solid 3D-printed brass buildings set into a robotically carved high-density foam base. This is because of the intricacy and formal complexity of many of the building forms we were using. The above image shows the restaurant pavilion model in its final brass form, ready to be combined with its site—thus the dangling column which would soon have a base in the carved foam version of the adjacent rocky outcroppings. The digital 3D printing file is shown in the background.

VAULTS FROM FRACTALS

One of the more complex tasks we undertook was to design the underside of the conjoined vaulted domes of the restaurant pavilion. The forms, curving in two directions with multiple intersections, was tricky and caused us to go down a rabbit hole into the process of designing fractal/ AI language dome structures—some earlier project tests of which are illustrated above. While 3D fractal forms based on Mandelbrot set are capable of generating forms that approximate curvature in two dimensions—they don't like to.

Eventually, we developed a higher degree of control as is seen in the above image, which was originally created for a previous project where we introduced a common denominator—coffering, so that the pattern was stable against the intricacy of the vaulted surfaces. This was the final direction, although due to its complexity, it wasn't fully worked out. We were reserving it for a future day after the project was won—which it wasn't, leaving this poor coffered AI intersection of domes homeless. We await your call.

THE LUNAR CANOPY

Our interest in pursing the complexity of Saudi dome structures extended to the exterior design of the resort, notably in the "lunar canopy," which hovers high above the garden oasis. This structure not only provides guests with shading during the day, but also doubles as a water heater for nearby resort functions when the sun is high in the sky. At night, the canopy flips function and acts as a giant radiator to disperse heat stored from daytime air-conditioning units into the cool night sky. This means our air conditioning network can function without requiring fans—a benefit because they produce significant noise, which we thought was in conflict with the serenity of the site. This "lunar canopy" is not only one of the first such structures in the world, but the largest.

This lunar canopy has two functions. During the day, water is slowly channeled through the vast interior area of the lattice to be heated to high temperatures by the sun and is used directly by the adjacent kitchen and housekeeping services. At night, this function is reversed, as the daytime desert air is hot it makes a poor absorber of the stored heat removed by air conditioning. In our system, this heat is removed from rooms and public areas and stored in water tanks during the day. After sunset, the system flips and slowly pumps this unwanted heat, stored in water, through the lunar canopy where it is sustainably radiated into the night sky—noiselessly. This also has the added effect of slightly heating the outdoor oasis garden during the cold desert nights, making the space more usable for nighttime performances and activities.

THE LUNAR CANOPY: PATTERN AND STRUCTURE

These renderings highlight the design of the lunar canopy and show the complex patterning that is formed into vault shapes by being bent in two directions. The arch forms of the taller vaults rest on the arch forms on the lower vaults, thereby transferring their weight without the need for additional columns. Our goal with this strategy was to minimize the columns required to touch the ground, leaving the garden level less obstructed and giving the lunar canopy the appearance of floating high above.

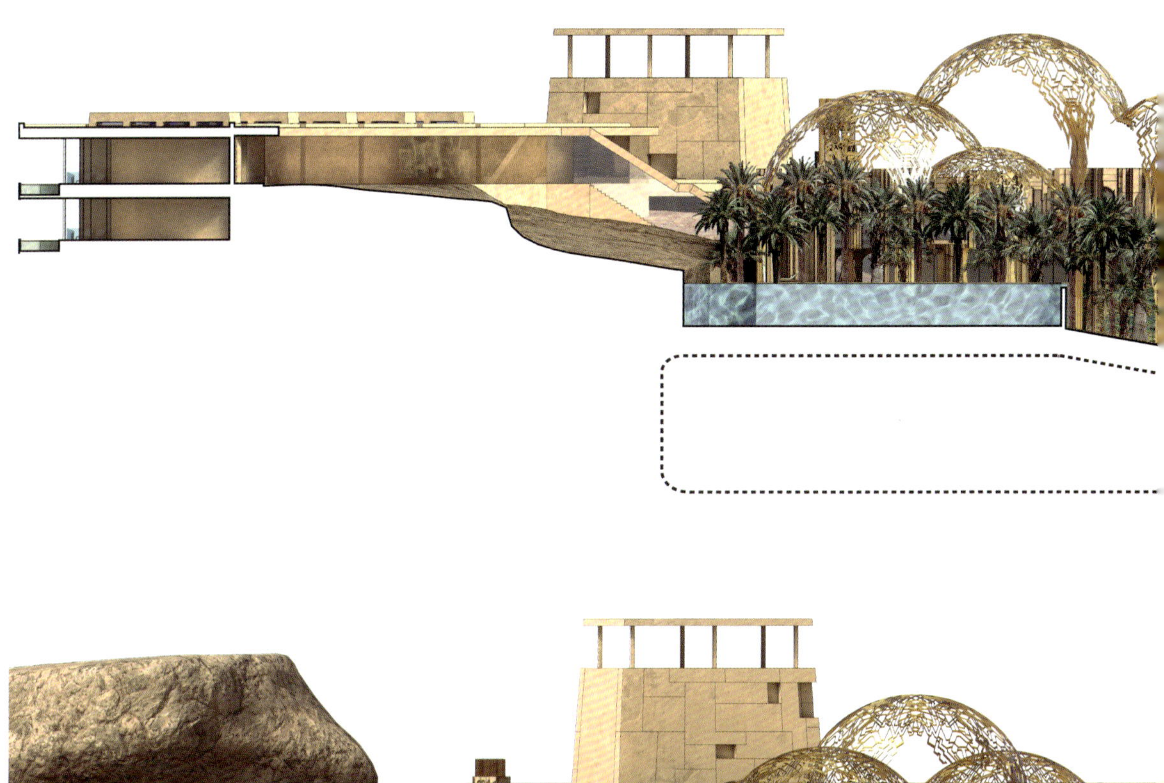

FINAL SITE SECTIONS

The above images are the final site sections presented for the project. They illustrate the highly sloping nature of the basin in one direction, a feature that was important for enabling distant views from each level, but also to aid in the circulation of recycled water. The lunar canopy is visible in both sections, protecting the native species oasis below with additional shade and irrigation, when needed, and turning mist to water the plantings at night.

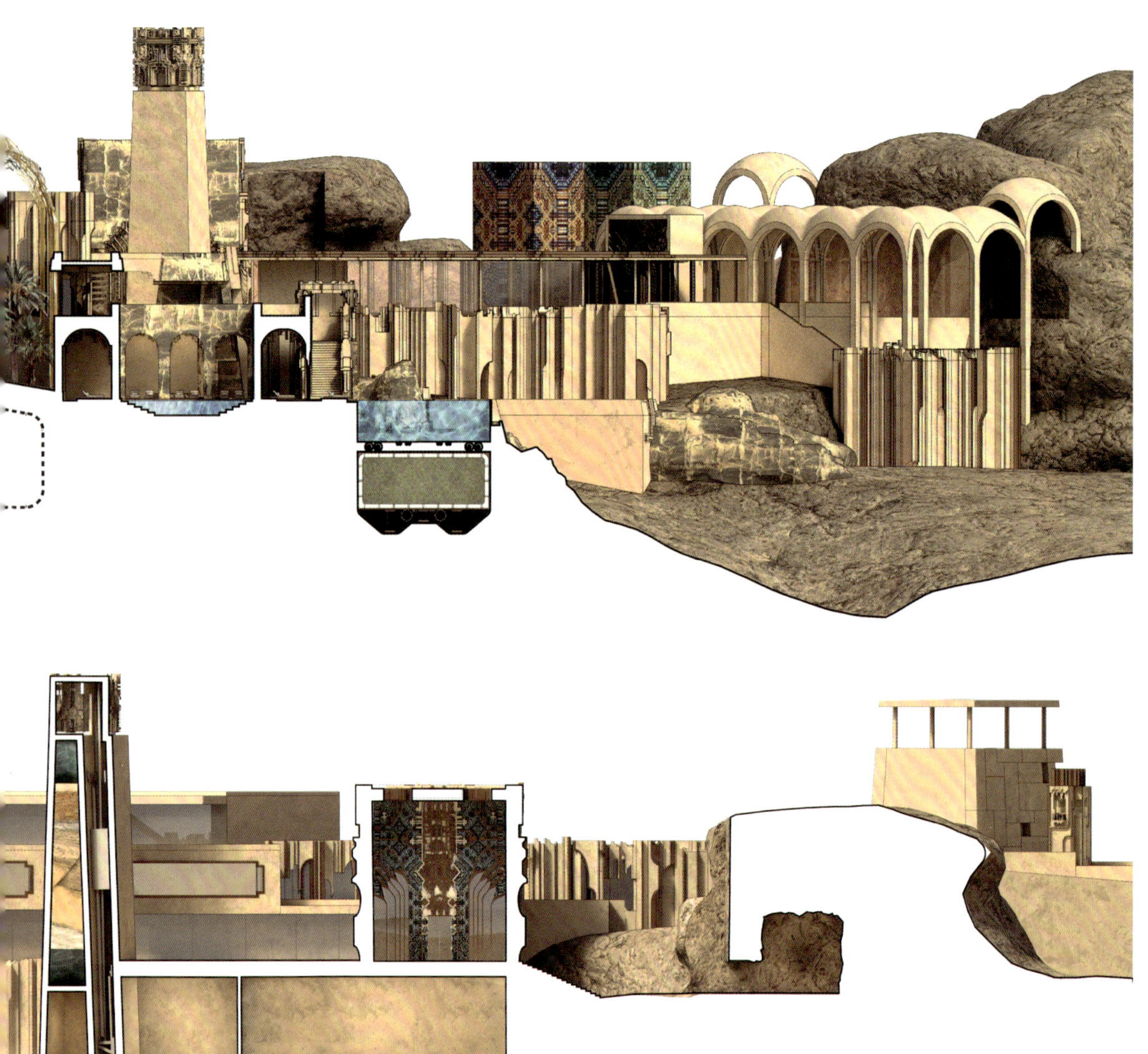

The perpendicular section illustrates the relationship between the two higher guest floors above and the service floor below. The service floor has access to the guest areas via dedicated elevators and to the pool through direct horizontal access. This allows almost all cleaning and cooking services to be centralized and thereby makes it more efficient in terms of spatial requirements and energy use. *Following pages:* Aerial rendering of the resort's central core in its near-final form showing the collection of buildings connected by circulation paths and knots.

XII

BUILDING IN GEOLOGY

Rustication for isolated buildings
Fractal/AI rustication
Developing formal control of techniques
Buildings nestled into ravines
Geological and architecture interiors

Opposite page : This is a multi-story historic residence in Rijal Alma'a, a recently declared UNESCO World Heritage Site located in the 'Asir Region of southern Saudi Arabia. We used this tapering residential typology as a basis for some of our nestled guest suite mini-towers.

RUSTICATED MINI-TOWER ITERATIONS 1-18

In an attempt to re-create the tapering residential forms of Rijal Alma'a, we tested multiple formal languages that combined the rusticated cyclopean masonry made from local sandstone that would be excavated during construction, with higher-resolution CNC carved patterns roughly inscribed into their surfaces. Through numerous iterations we eventually landed on a form almost identical to those of our precedent, but with massive single openings where recessed glass would allow for small balconies and vast viewing frames. *Opposite page:* Additional residential suite building studies. Our final proposal further developed the direction seen in the middle of the top row of this array.

POST IPSO FACTO REPRESENTATION

To properly illustrate the design process of this project required a five hundred page book, but upon creating such an extensive book, we realized we had quite a few of the same representational types. To provide some relief from all the serious content, Chad Miller from my office took our guest suite mini-towers and placed them on a lawn like a bunch of little cows. This image tells you nothing about the project, but it's funny, so here it is.

339

MINI-TOWER POCHÉ

The rusticated stone used in the guest suite mini-towers is thick to produce a barrier against heat gain. As such the floor plan has thick poché, and the occupiable spaces are significantly smaller than the outside envelope indicates. This image shows the interior occupiable space in an x-ray image of the whole tower.

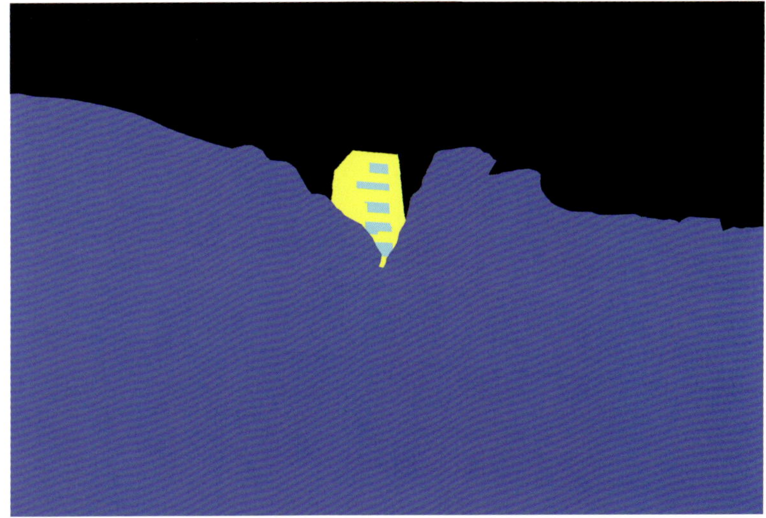

Our ambition for the guest-suite mini towers was that they would be deeply nestled into the surrounding sandstone ravines. The upper image shows the existing sandstone in blue and our sandstone structure in yellow—to indicate the subtle presence we were trying to achieve for these particular buildings. The lower image is a preliminary rendering using digital textures to estimate the camouflaging effects of our material selection—with the aforementioned "elephant skin" rock texture.

The tradition of carving volumes directly out of stone is a uniquely Nabatean strategy, one we applied to circulation rather than carved rooms themselves, as Jean Nouvel would later do in his beautiful proposal for a related resort.

Following pages: These are the final exteriors of two nestled suite buildings, primarily accessed through carved stone circulation corridors.

XIII

HIDDEN ARCHITECTURE MADE FOR SEEING
346–379

Remote desert viewing and shading structures
Abstracted cultural visitation facility
Interior outdoor spaces
Hidden desert mini-pavilions

Preceding pages : **This image shows the** final interior rendering of a typical guest suite room. Note that the existing sandstone structures invade the unit where they are sand blasted and ground to reveal their veining and texturing as an aesthetic feature. Rather than install art into the rooms, we sought to allow the site itself to provide moments of interest in what are rather minimalist rooms intended to allow guests to focus on the extraordinary views.

Opposite page : Merely kilometers from our site sits the majestic Jabal Alfil, or "Elephant Rock," a natural arch of solid sandstone that appears like an elephant and its trunk. The propensity of such vertical structures in the surrounding desert prompted our interest in producing a resort defined by specifically located towers.

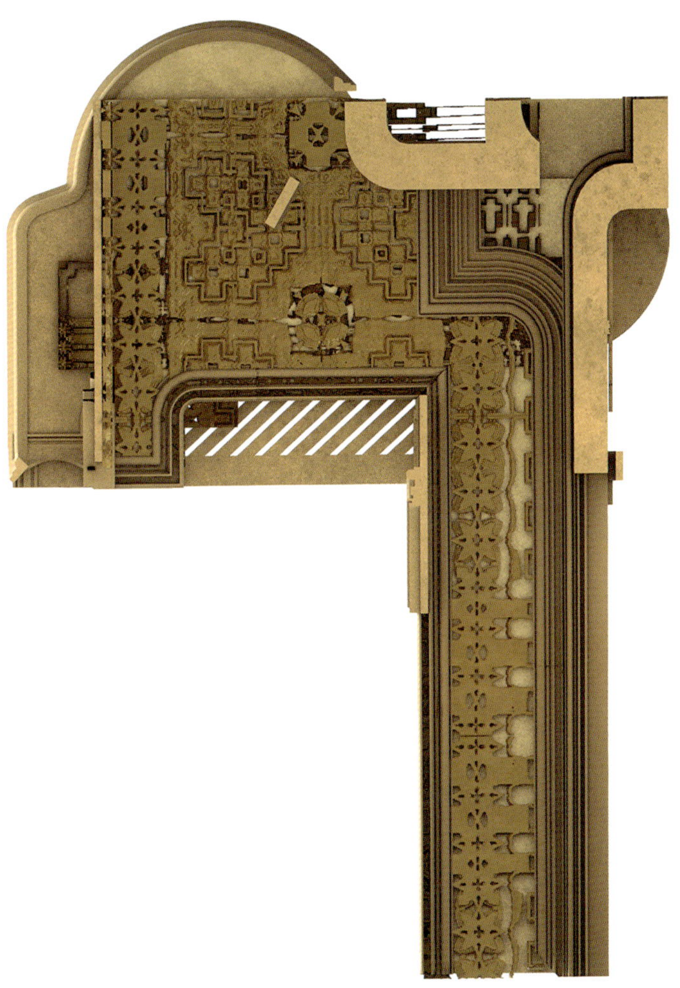

SHADING PAVILION REFLECTED CEILING PLAN 09

As part of our extended involvement with the project beyond the initial competition, we also proposed a series of observation pavilions in specific desert locations. The purpose of these pavilions is to provide shaded and controlled access to views of key areas, as well as tourist infrastructure including access to drinking water, without which visitors could very easily, well, die.

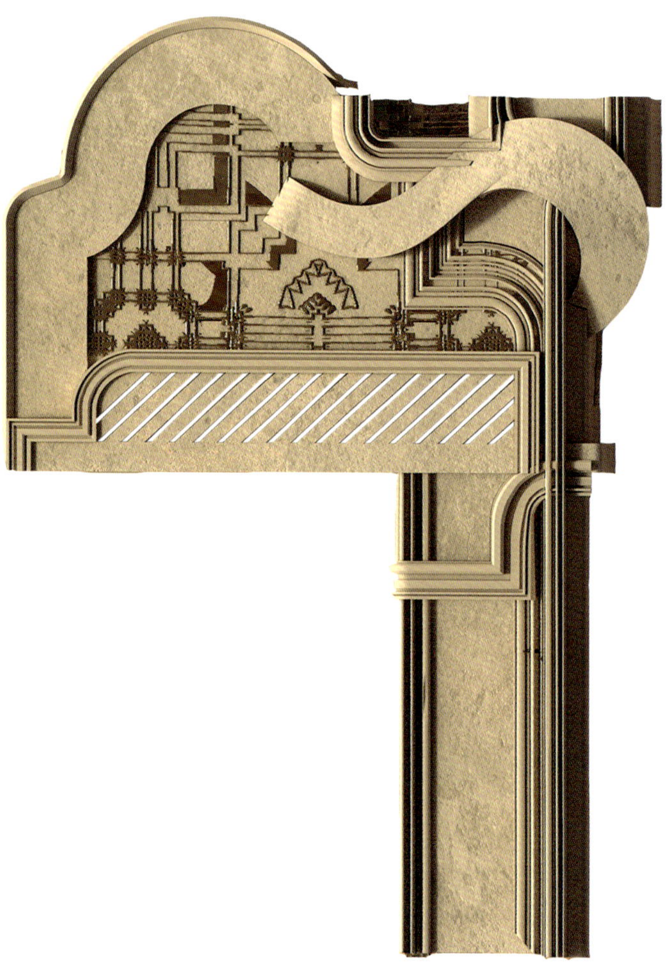

SHADING PAVILION REFLECTED CEILING PLAN 11

The elongated entrance is a covered portico that provides shade to guests emerging from desert vehicles. Both of these images are reflected ceiling plans of planar roof structures, with no walls, that are supported by thin discrete bronze pilotis. Because of this, the reflected ceiling plan is where any architectural design needs to occur. The design uses stone patterns and arabesque carved shapes.

350

REMOTE DESERT OBSERVATION PAVILION #11

351

REMOTE DESERT OBSERVATION PAVILION #16

Some larger observation structures were proposed to accommodate expected increases in numbers of tourists. Our thinking was that in order to maintain the pristine qualities of the desert, including its sand and sandstone structures, it would be undesirable to have tourists driving or being chauffeured in their SUVs all over the extents of the desert and thereby leaving tracks. Accordingly, key points defined by these observation platform structures would encourage tourists to stay on the beaten path and leave the desert pristine.

REMOTE DESERT OBSERVATION PAVILION #19

We often illustrate our design atop large sections of earth, or as "chunk" renderings, a representational type developed by Ferda Kolatan, a friend of mine who is an architect and educator at the University of Pennsylvania. This type of image gives the advantage of an axonometric view. But instead of removing perspective and presence, as the axonometric was intended to do, such chunk renderings use a heavy context and materiality that convey gravitas and human experience in a view that's physically impossible for a human to experience in real life, as the lines of such drawings do not recede perspectively.

REMOTE DESERT OBSERVATION PAVILION #19: REFLECTED CEILING PLAN

The above image is the reflected ceiling plan of the pavilion featured on the adjacent page. This design direction uses a massively thick roof structure that acts as a thermal insulator to keep the underside cool in the desert heat. Within the stone's thickness are very small slits for light and air movement. Such intricately cut apertures are often cut with diamond-studded wires that carve massive depths of stone with razor-like precision.

THE TOURISM SERVICES CENTER

Remote from the desert resort and not visible from, but adjacent to the ruins of Mada'in Salih, we proposed a large centralist tourist "base" that would house information, small dining facilities, access to water, medical staff and most importantly, highly elevated viewing platforms from which the vast desert could be more clearly seen. This is partially to provide these views, but also to discourage climbing on the adjacent sandstone structures which are easily damaged by the presence and weight of human visitors. *Opposite page:* The image shows the tourism hub nestled deep into rocky outcroppings so as to not detract from the views in and around the Mada'in Salih ruins.

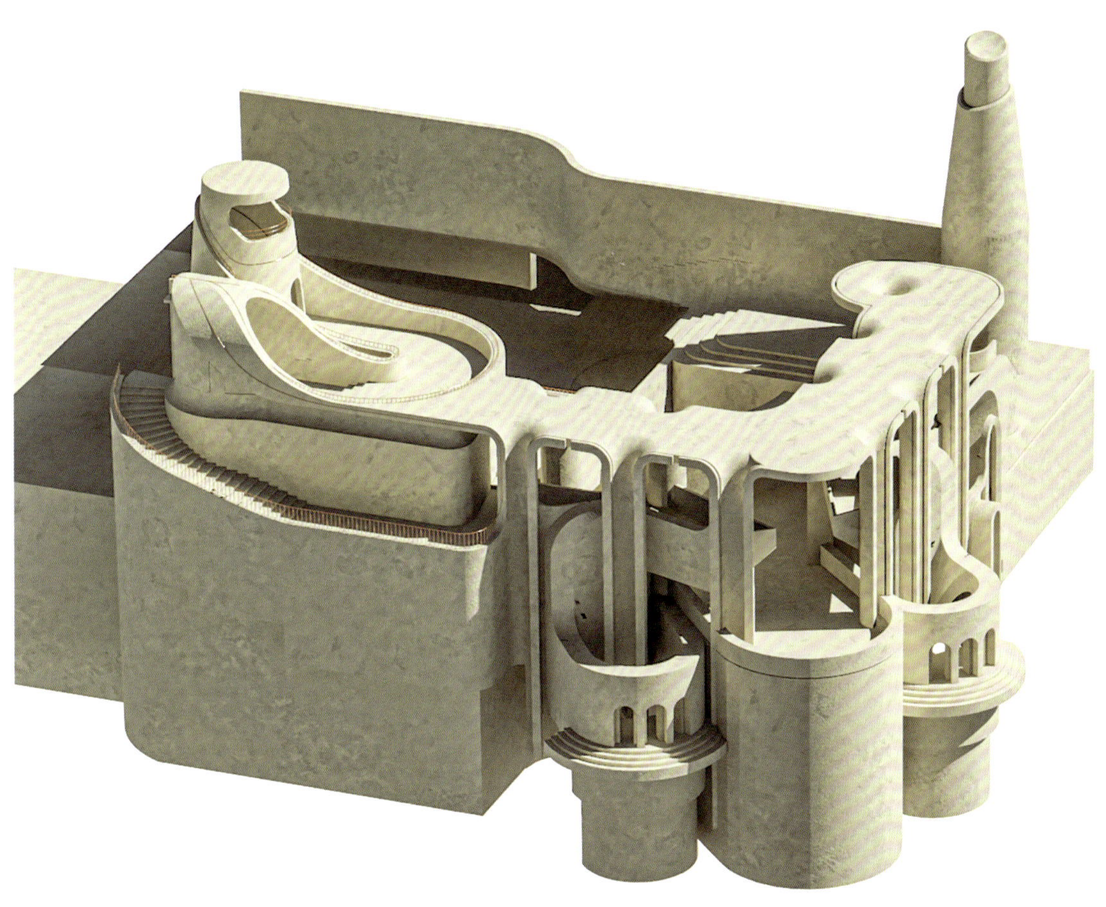

356

THE TOURISM SERVICES CENTER FROM ABOVE

The tourism hub itself is designed with an architectural language very different from that of our desert resort proposal. In attempting to give primary importance to the views provided, our design uses smooth, unarticulated surfaces that provide resistance to wind or sand, but still provide different spatial experiences through the integration of different levels, framing devices, and circulation paths. Materially, the structure is made entirely of poured concrete to produce a highly robust form capable of withstanding the challenges of existing in a harsh and exposed desert environment.

A WIND RESISTANT FORMAL LANGUAGE

The tourism hub is designed to walk up, in, and around—a circulation object that reveals new views and programs, rather than a simple volume which simply contains them. Visitors walk in and out of covered and open spaces, where new views and spaces are experienced as part of a journey rather than a destination. As the sandstone outcroppings are off limits to tourists, we wanted to provide the experience of climbing and exploring in this more controlled and less destructive manner.

This page show a vignette of the tourism hub. The material selected for use is a solid, thick concrete that takes a long time to heat up in the desert sun, and releases heat into the cooler nighttime air after daily use. The concrete is also intended to resist wear in the harsh and unforgiving desert environment. *Opposite page:* These images show ground level views from within the tourism hub with views of the desert beyond. *Following pages:* These images illustrate important desert vistas framed by shading devices.

DESIGN FAST FORWARD: FRACTAL DOME STUDIES 1-2

At times the office tends to work rather schizophrenically. In this case, it was designing the smooth, minimalist and wind-resistant forms of the tourism infrastructure and nearly simultaneously studying possible directions for 3D fractal-generated vault and dome structures at high resolution. Theses languages would eventually come into contact in the primary restaurant facility that is defined by a roof of smooth, conjoined domes, with a highly articulated, coffered and vaulted underside. These are study images for the vaults.

365

DESIGN FAST FORWARD: FRACTAL DOME STUDIES 3-4

The above images show different techniques for generating dome-like structures out of fractal coffering—by stepping the coffers back sequentially to produce a tapering volume, or by using continuous structural elements to produce the curvature of the dome itself. These studies are distantly related to the work of Guarino Guarini, one of my favorite architects, who used the former strategy in his San Cappella della Sacra Sindone and the latter strategy at his dome of San Lorenzo. Look 'em up.

THE STACKED CYLINDER TOWER: HAND SKETCHES

Above are hand sketches of some of the desert observation towers that are part of the larger tourism infrastructure design proposal. We opted to continue to use the less detailed architectural language because the observation pavilions and towers needed to be low-maintenance—and solid concrete surfaces seemed an ideal way to achieve this. The smooth surfaces of the concrete structures are slippery to the wind and particularly storms that carry sand—meaning that their surfaces will not be "etched" with wear in the same way a flat surface with corners would. While our desert resort is protected from such wind by the sandstone outcroppings, the observation towers and pavilions are more exposed.

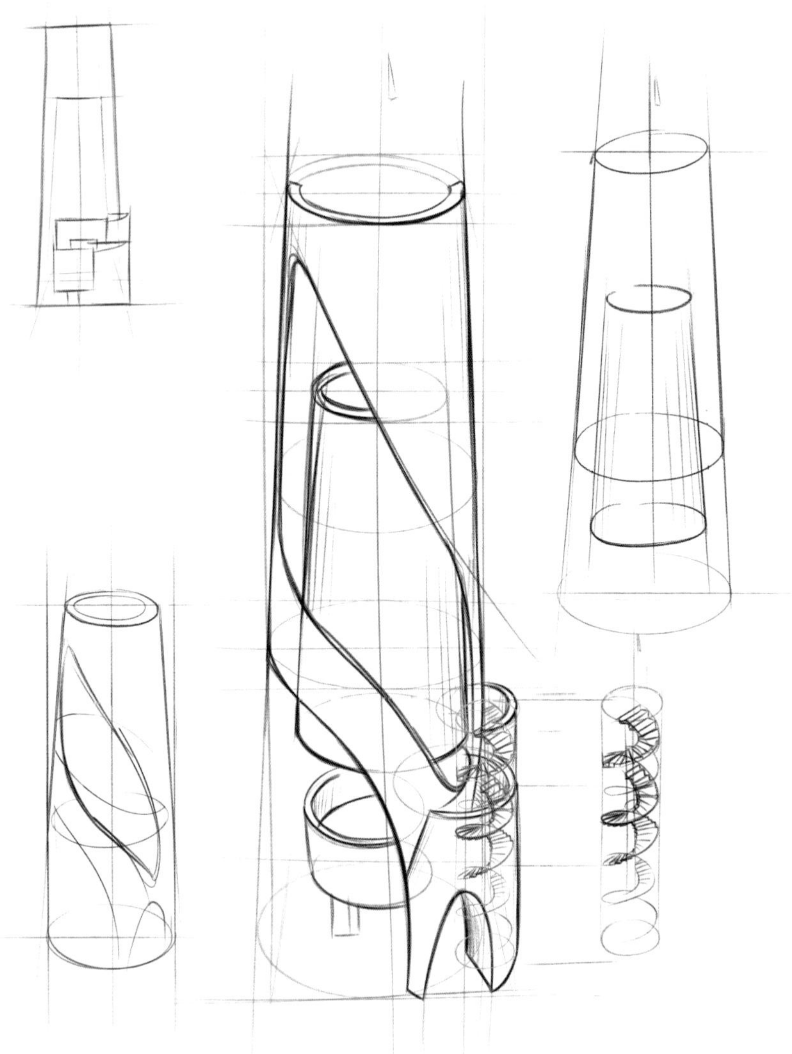

367

THE CARVED CONIC TOWER: HAND SKETCHES

These desert observation tower sketches illustrate our desire to provide different levels and view heights which focused on different view directions. The tower is not only an object that you go up and look out from, but also one that you journey within. You are presented with different desert vistas and visual experiences as you ascend to the top. Much of the elevator equipment is hidden in the thick poché space where multiple shells intersect.

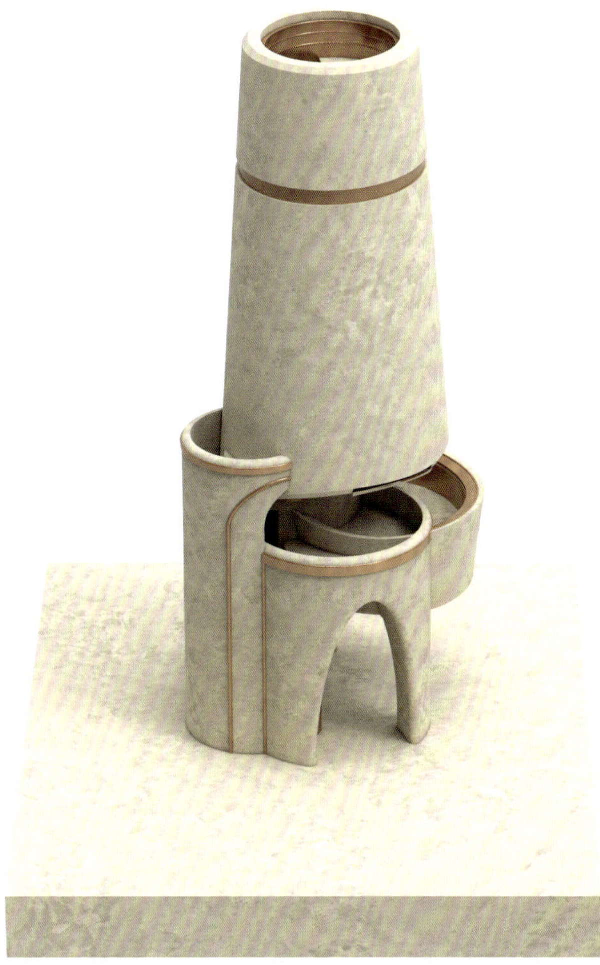

THE STACKED CYLINDER TOWER

These images show a rendered digital model of one of the multi-level desert observation towers. Here you can see the softened forms that are intended to provide less resistance to the wind. Although this design was not taken to full completion, you can see the multiple levels of access and their arrangement toward different directions. The top tapered cylinder is not only an additional elevated observation platform, but also provides shading for the lower platforms.

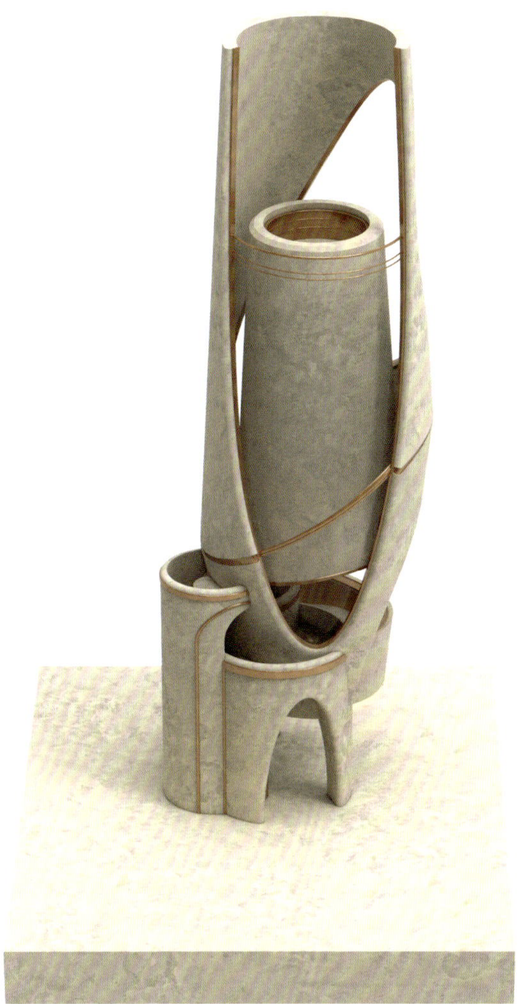

THE CARVED CONIC TOWER

Seen here is the rendered digital model of a desert observation tower that has a shell to protect visitors from the dominant wind direction. Certain tower locations have very predictable wind erosion patterns on the surrounding rocks. As is visible above, this observation tower has an outer "shell" that protects from wind and focuses views at different points on the vertical journey. The structure is inlaid with bronze detailing, as it is one of the most robust materials one can use in architecture—illustrating the goal of these towers to have lives spanning millennia as their Nabatean neighbors continue to do.

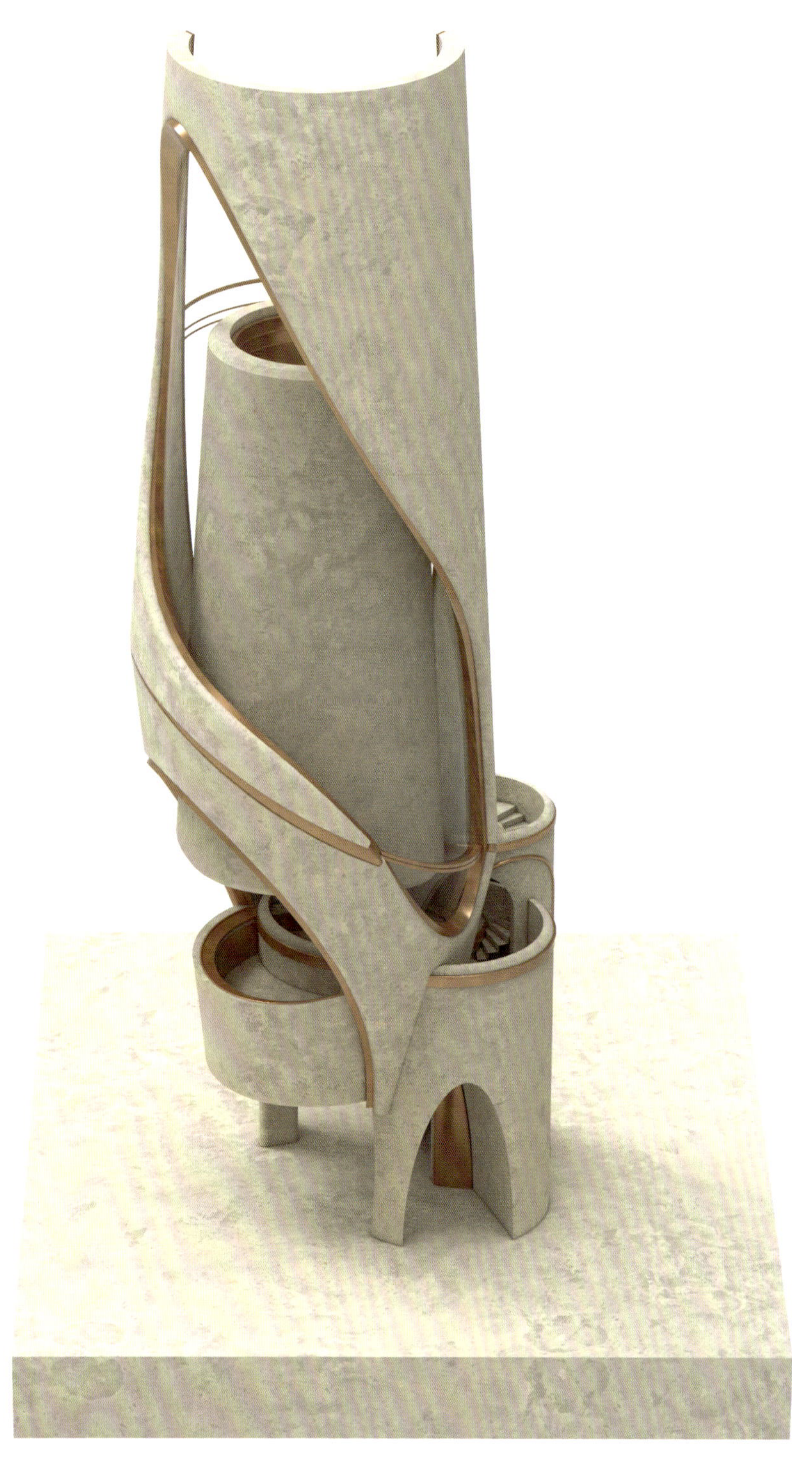

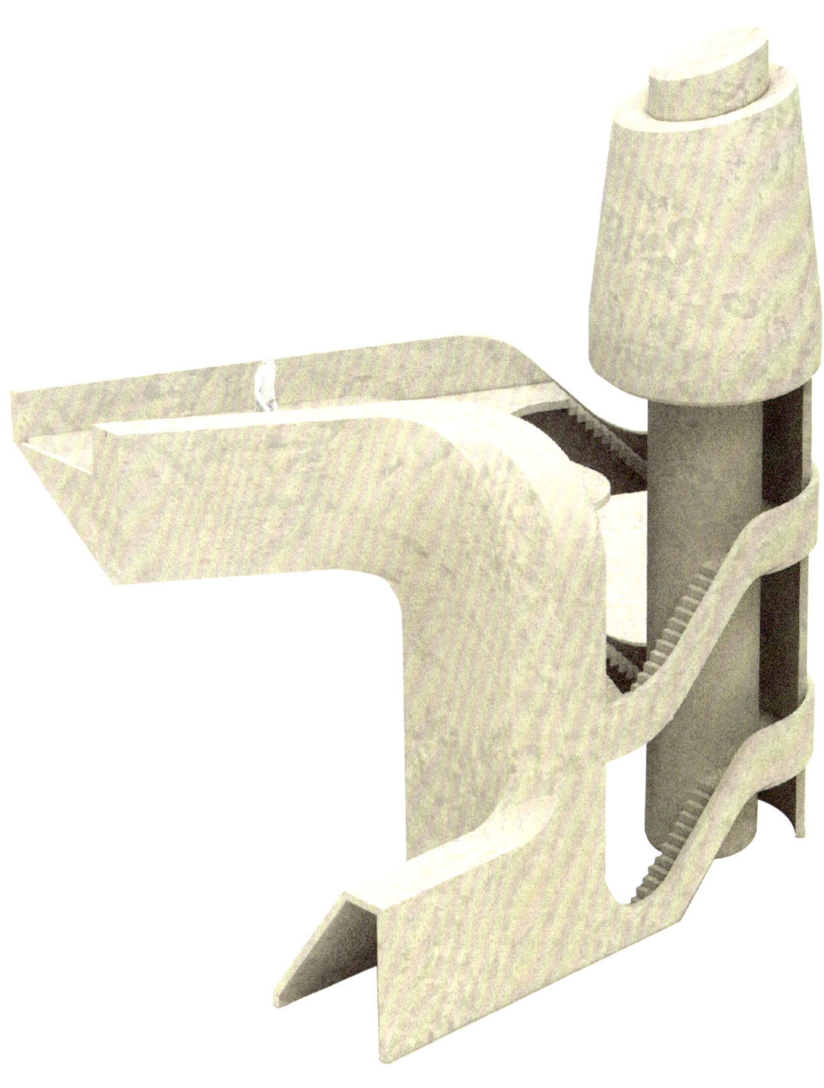

THE CANTILEVERED TOWER

For tower structures that need to accommodate more tourists than the cylindrical options, we also proposed a series of towers that led to observation cantilevers oriented toward particular views. While the entire structure is poured concrete, there is a sparing use of glass for the railing at the end of the cantilever, so that photos can capture more of the view beyond. Although the bridge connector is not shown in this image, the elevator is located in the tall cylindrical tower around which the stair is wrapped.

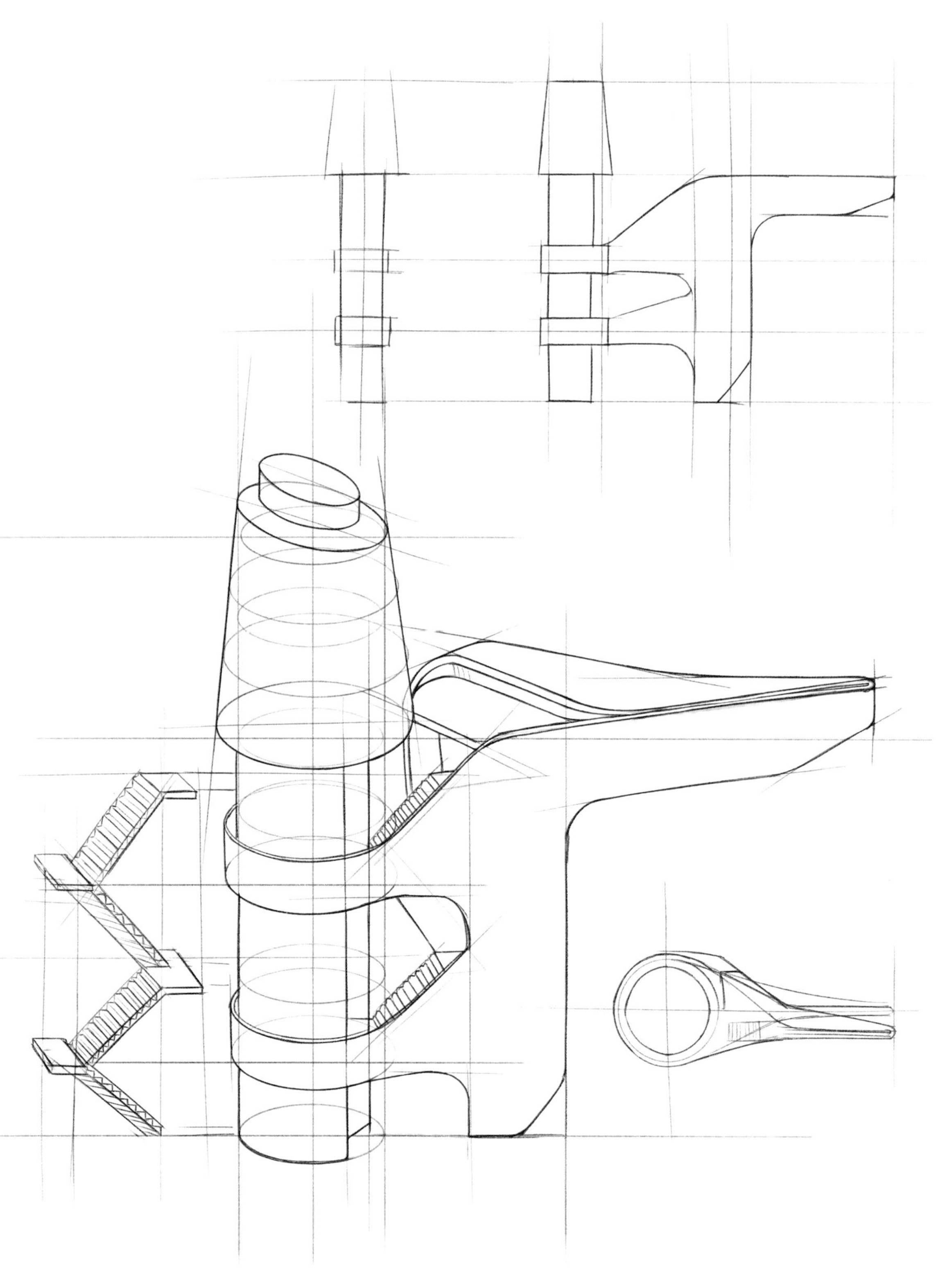

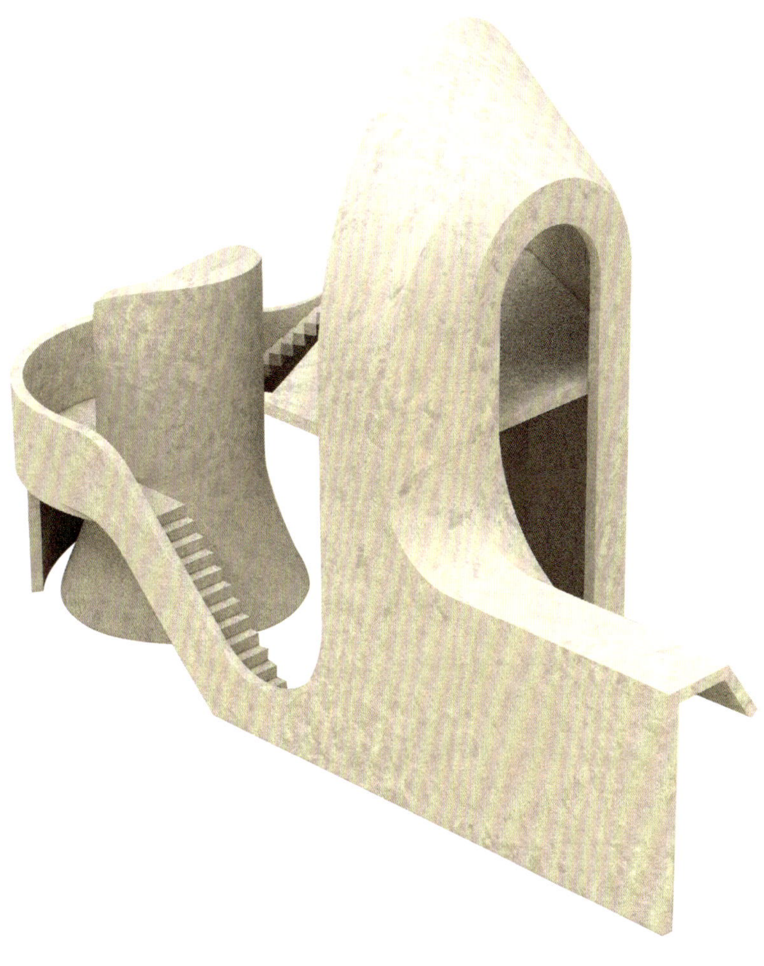

THE AMPHITHEATER PLATFORM

For the tourist infrastructure, we proposed numerous pavilion types. Some were for views best seen from up high, some for refreshment such as water and shade, and some to provide more intimate views of rock formations lower to the ground. *Opposite page:* In these images, you can see the "exhaled" form of the opening that allows access and leads to the amphitheater seating. Beyond the amphitheater is an additional door that leads to the truncated observation tower, which can also be made part of the theatrical set for different performances. We thought it would be great location for a staging of Rapunzel.

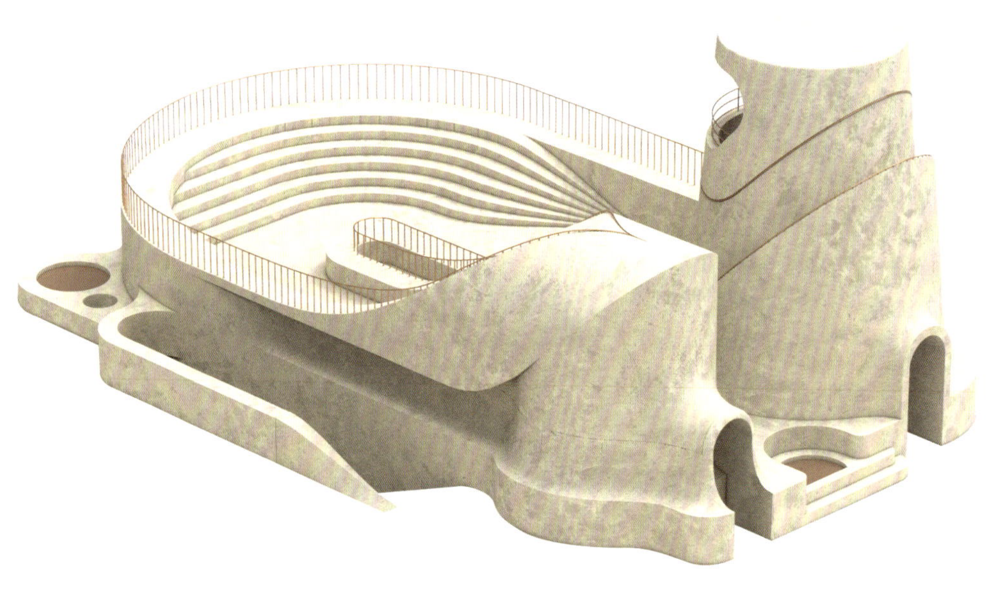

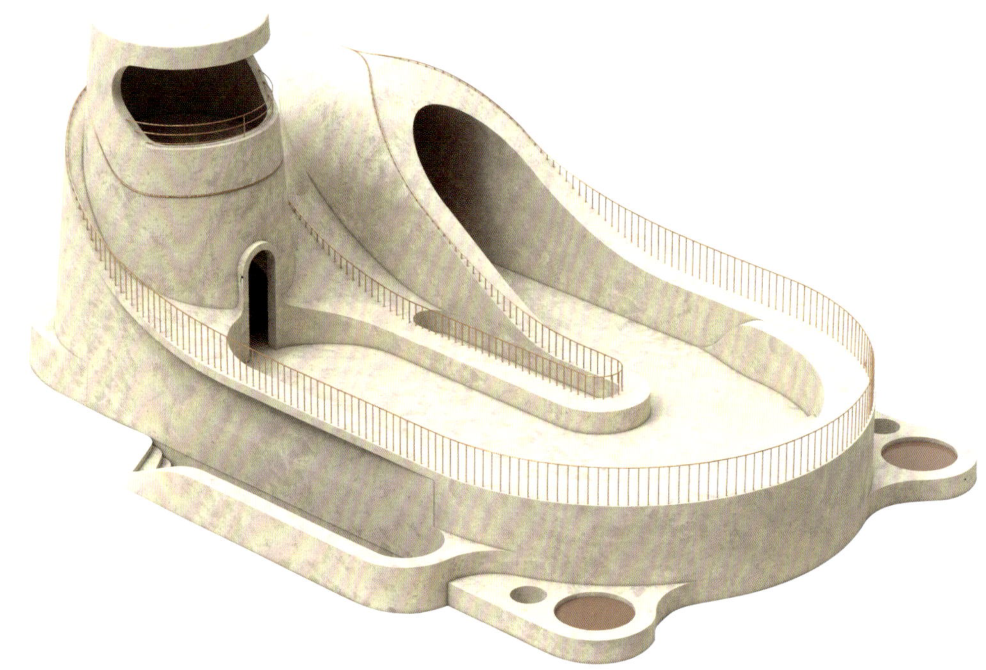

THE LITHOPS AIZOACEAE PAVILION

These two pages illustrate viewing pavilions that we tried out, but ultimately didn't use because they were less functional and a bit too weird—perhaps ugly. This one above is based on a species of succulent called a "stone plant"—which is odd as we don't generally design toward specific symbolic or metaphorical effects. Perhaps this is why it came out so bad—almost immediately rejected for being not only non-functional, but creepy. While we provide wide design latitude for experiments, sometimes they backfire.

377

THE REJECTED BIRDCAGE FOR TOURISTS

The above pavilion is an attempt to integrate a metal framework that spanned in an arch form between two distinct pavilion masses. The metal cage is a framework for fabric that provides shade inside the mesh, but also casts larger shadows on the surrounding ground areas. Good intent was there, but the design came off looking more like a birdcage for tourists. Another backfire and instant rejection.

378

THE HUMBLE OUTHOUSE

This tourism pavilion is only for a small isolated restroom—essentially an outhouse. As it is open to the desert, it has to be protected from high winds and blowing sand. It also needs to provide privacy, thus the extended wall that blocks wind and views. These structures are to be placed more deeply in ravines to both assure privacy, but also remove them from view. Despite this they were given the same design attention and goals toward longevity as their more prestigious siblings.

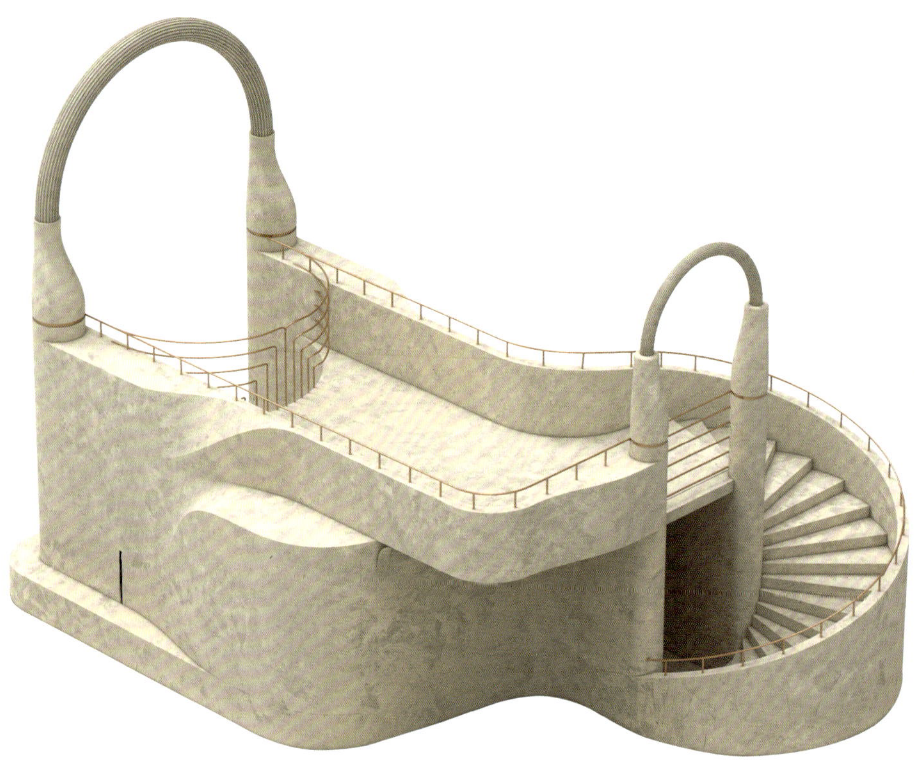

THE STAIRWAY TO HEAVEN, OR NOT

Pictured above is an elevated viewing platform with an air-conditioned room and restroom facilities on the ground floor. The two are connected by a grand spiral stair. The arches in the design accommodate the stretching of a tensile fabric between them for shading—not shown in this image. The larger arch is also a framing device for the key views toward which the entire pavilion would be oriented.

AESTHETIC CHOREOGRAPHY
380–403

Opposite page : **This is a photo depicting the interior** of Al-Masjid an-Nabawi, or "Prophet's Mosque" in Medina, Saudi Arabia

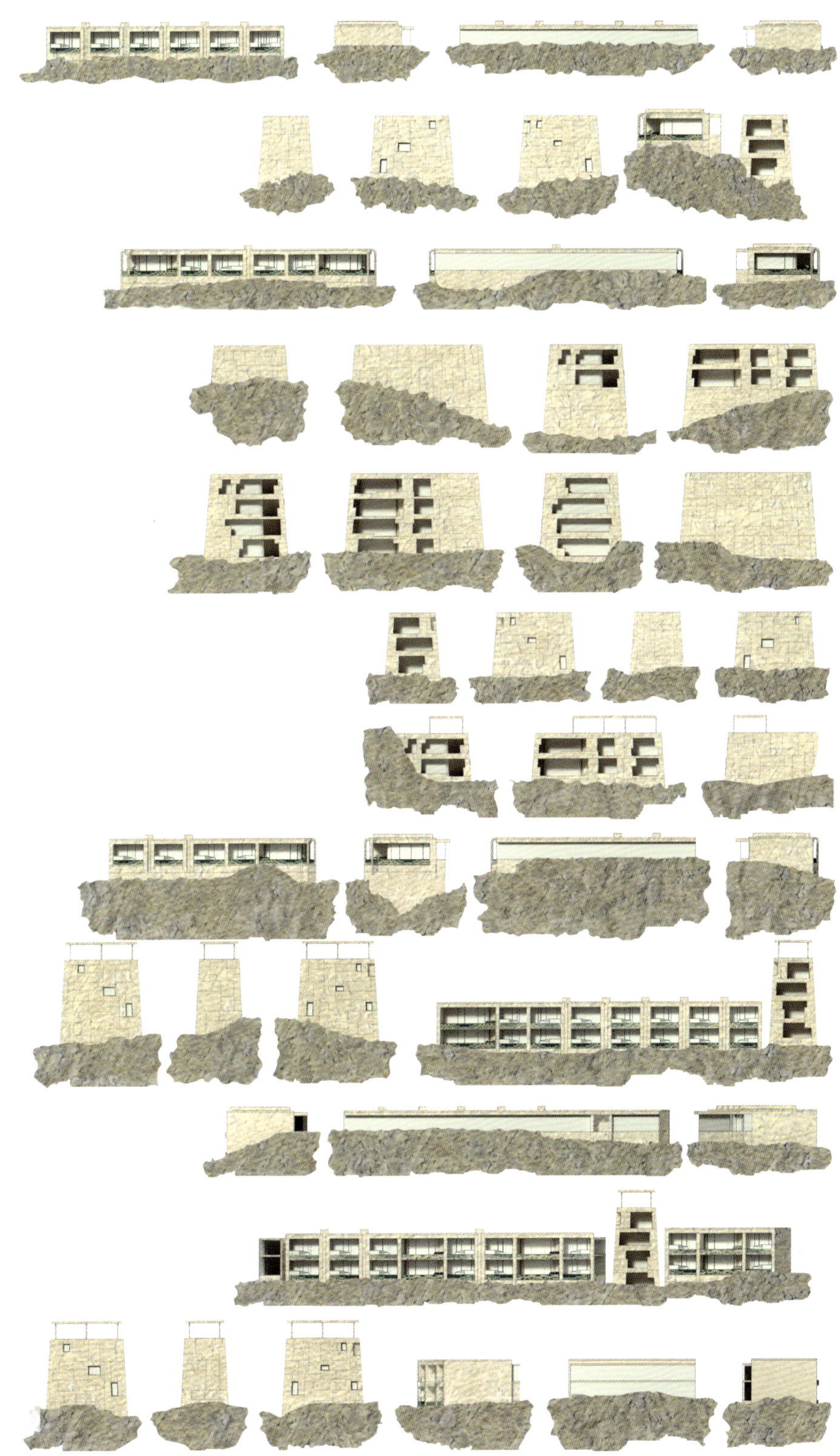

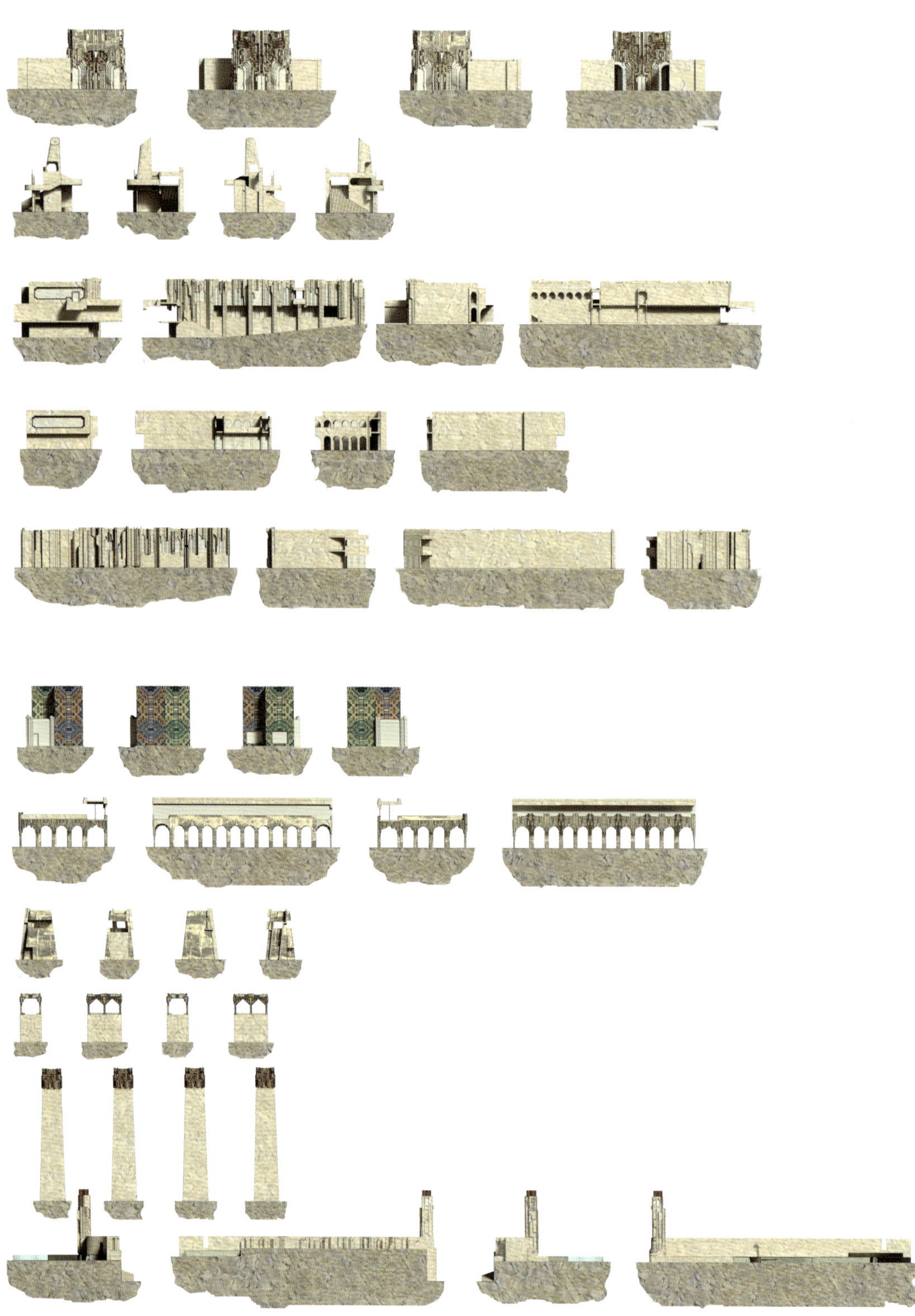

VIEW AND MATERIAL SKETCHES: POOL CIRCULATION

Preceding pages: All building elevations are layed out here, "unrolled" for material calculations as part of the cost estimating process. *This page:* As most of the primary design for the proposal was complete, we moved onto the development of more specific materials and details that would be made visible in carefully selected views. This often involved the study of numerous camera angles that would allow us to not only develop, but show key materials and systems in the final presentation. This image series shows explorations of the shaded walkways between buildings and if they should be left as unarticulated rustic stone or have ceilings with custom tile patterns.

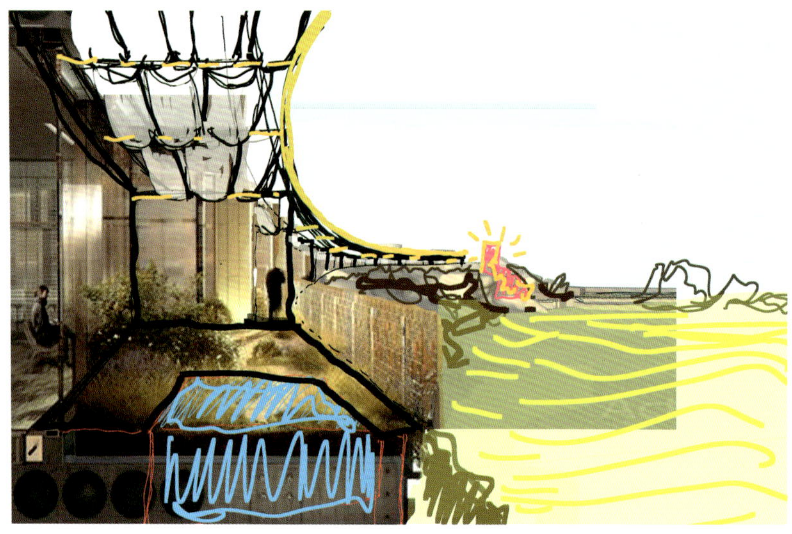

VIEW AND MATERIAL SKETCHES: GUEST TERRACES

Our design proposes that each hotel room have its own balcony and plunge pool. The desert environment is so bright and unforgiving that we also studied the use of retractable fabric shades that could allow guests to control the level of light on their balcony areas. After calculating wind loads and imagining the wear that sandy desert winds would cause, we abandoned this idea in favor of more robust stone roof structures for most balconies.

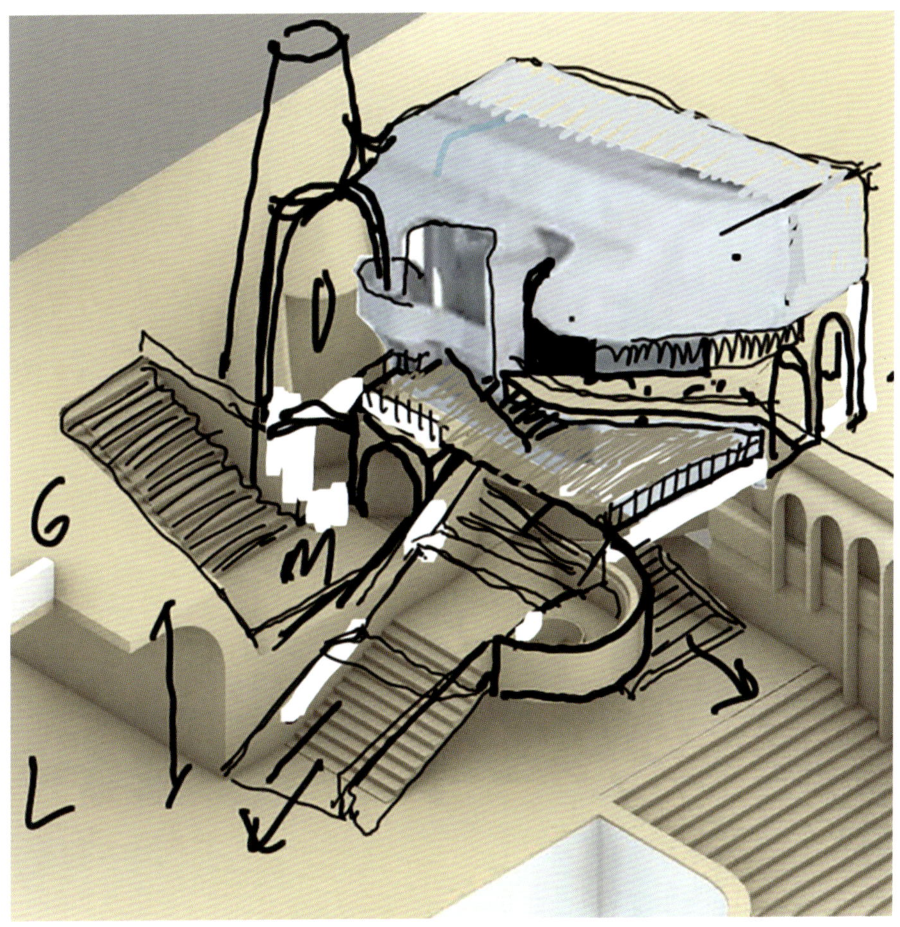

CIRCULATION KNOT, INTERRUPTED

Even toward the end of the design process, we found ourselves working out the kinks of particular areas we weren't quite satisfied with. The above sketch shows my ugly sketches that suggest modifications to the circulation knot that connects the pool and spa. In this sketch I was trying to more directly link the circulation experience with the nearby cafe, so that one of the larger terrace landings for the circulation path would double as a place for outdoor seating. This was abandoned as it was trying to do too many things at the same time and went against our ethos of allowing the parts of the project to remain more distinct, each having their own aesthetic qualities.

387

CIRCULATION KNOT, REFINED

Above is a 3D-rendered model of another iteration of the circulation knot at the north end of the pool area. This direction is close to the design used in the final proposal, as it provides a circuitous journey that focused the eye on some of the most stunning desert vistas. The central occupiable mini-tower would later become larger to provide a pavilion for outdoor private guest massages. This image does not illustrate that the lower left corner would all be embedded in solid sandstone, including the pool, as shown in the final images.

"OPENING DAY" IMAGE: DEVELOPMENT SKETCHES

Developing final views isn't only about producing dazzling imagery in the form of eye candy. In a competition with such limited presentation materials, particular views that convey multiple ideas are more useful than ones that convey only one. It can take us weeks to select views for our projects—they are composed and designed to achieve very particular ends. The above images illustrate the process of moving from hand sketches through collaging, usually in black and white, as we tried to imagine this celebrational "opening day" image for the resort, with the red carpet rolled out, literally.

389

"OPENING DAY" IMAGE: COLOR COLLAGE

Once we've set a particular view, we often loosely collage it with context elements, in this case a mix of our own renderings, hand drawn digital sketches, cropped areas of photographs, and other artworks. As we had a similar stair arrangement to Leon Krier's "Atlantis" proposal, we borrowed his people and stair carpet—it's ok, we're friends. The end result is a collage of representational types and levels of detail that allow us to work with a professional rendering team, in this case our collaborators at Arqui9, or in other cases to further develop the images internally in our own renderings.

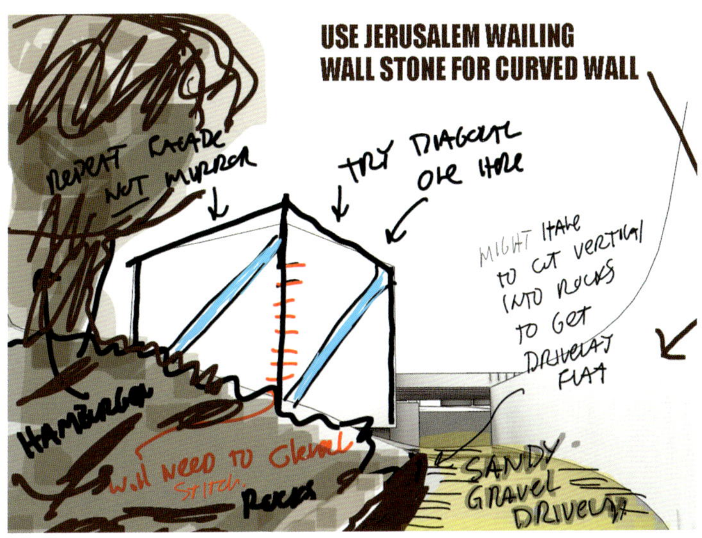

UGLY SKETCHES: RECEPTION APPROACH

These digital hand drawings show possible views of the approach sequence from the desert. The arrival sequence is choreographed to produce certain views of areas in a specific order. How to convey this idea about movement, in a series of still images, proved difficult. We abandoned the above views, but continued with those of the recreational complex circulation, observatory and water filtration tower.

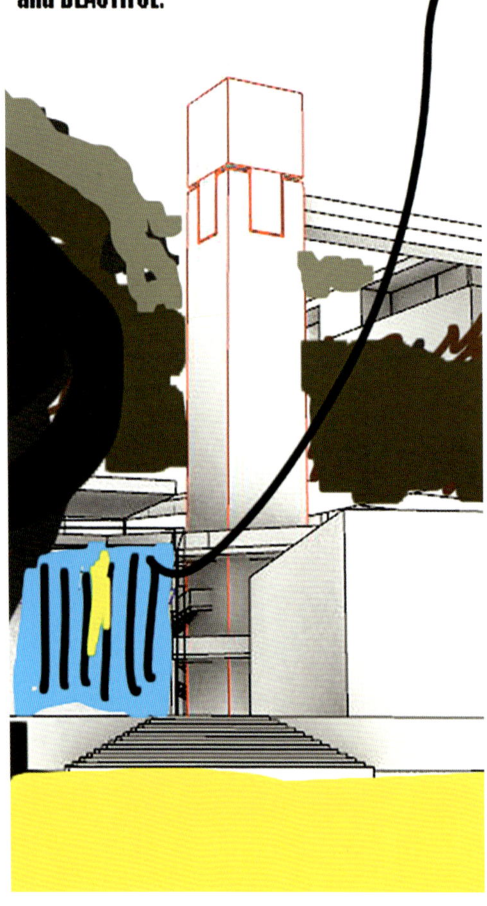

UGLY SKETCHES: RECREATION CENTER APPROACH

The above images show further development of the recreational complex tower, with the preliminary addition of material information. When determining these views, there are a vast array of variables—lighting type, direction, time of day, where the shadows are cast, what elements are emphasized, the focal length of the camera, etc. While many architectural renderings seem to border on downright deceit, we aim for photo-realism that shows the building as it would appear if it existed in reality given the information we have. As you can see in the above images, some of what we presented had to be guesswork as we didn't have dimensional information for things like the foreground rock.

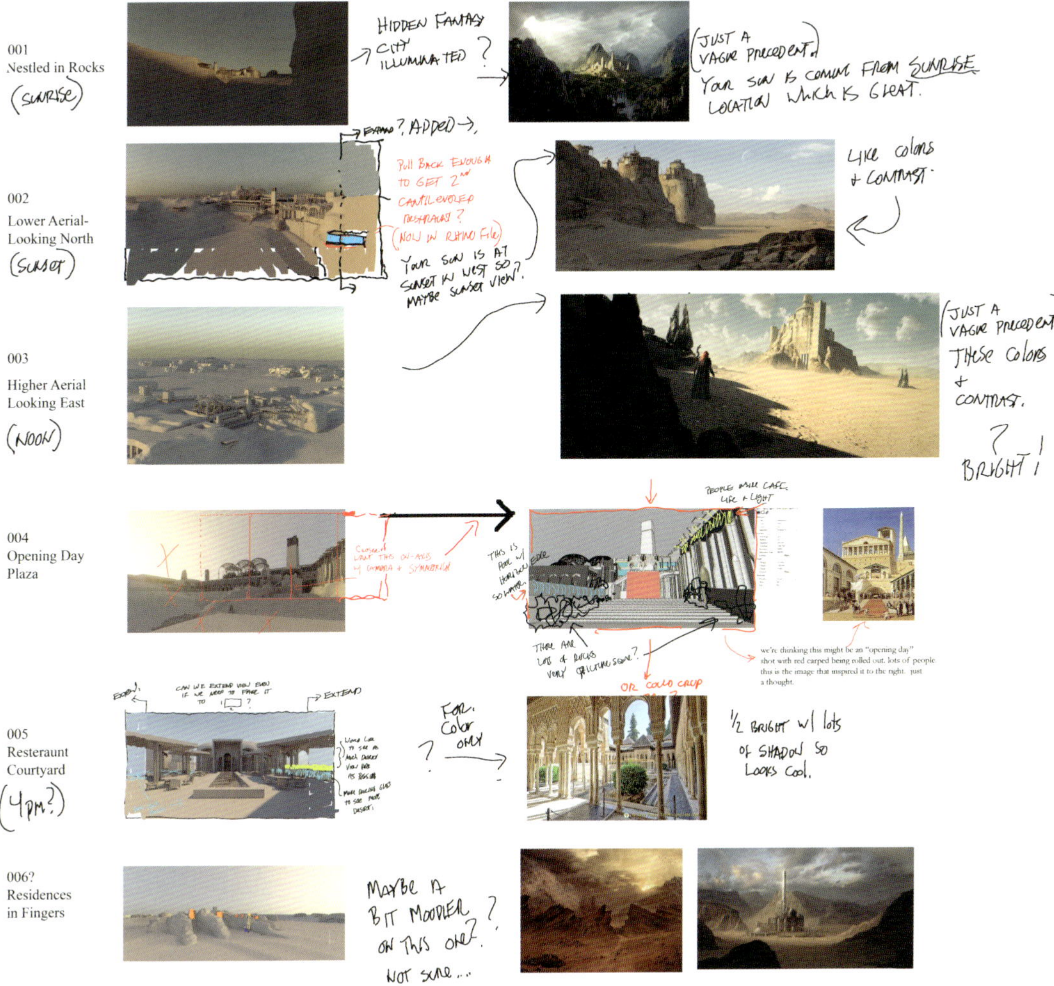

FINAL IMAGE PREPARATION: COLOR AMBITIONS

When selecting views, we often compile images from online as source material to imagine how similar perspectives and color tones might illustrate our design. These sources can be from anywhere and include digital matte paintings, concept art from movies, our own work, projects of other architects, photographs of existing places, and other speculative imagery. The reason for this, is to convey to the rendering team how we'd like to present the project in various lighting and atmospheric conditions.

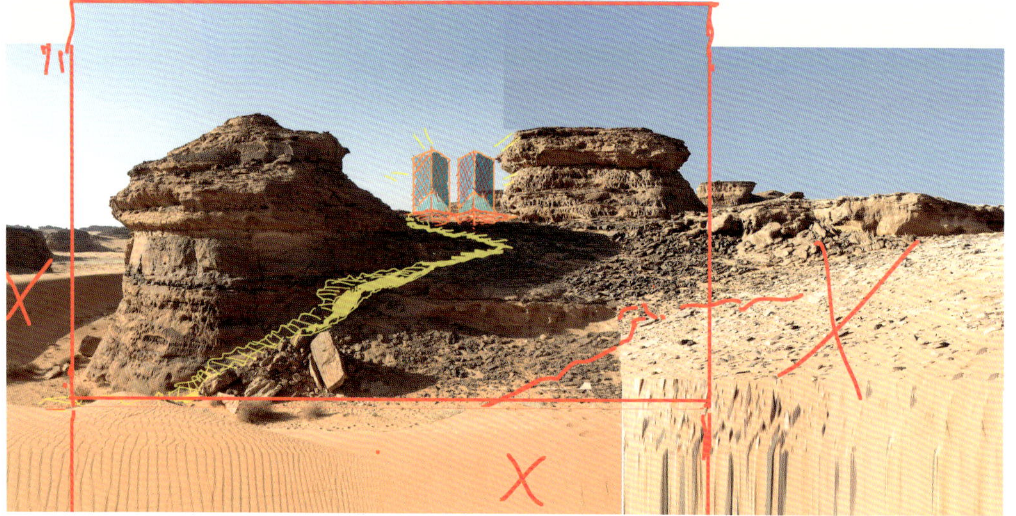

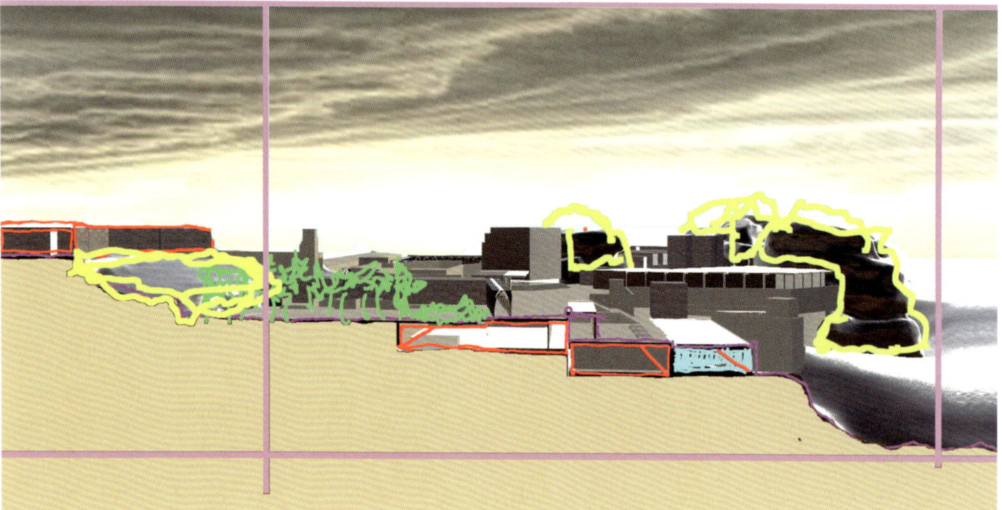

393

FINAL IMAGE PREPARATION: CROPPING AND PROPORTIONS

As the view development process continues, one important decision is where to crop—which is really a decision on how to balance what we're trying to show from the context and the project—both at the same time. If we show too much of the context, we are unable to see the design, but the reverse is also true. In these images you can see the struggle between these poles—the original images are much larger than what we ultimately decided to illustrate, as outlined in the digitally hand drawn boxes.

A BRIEF FORAY INTO ETCHING

I've always been fascinated with etching and wood engraving, particularly in the work of historic figures such as Albrecht Durer and Piranesi. Every few years, I go through a phase where I'm convinced that the right direction is to present an entire project through etchings, as presented in the above image. Techniques that involve silverpoint, etching, and wood engraving are incredibly labor intensive, so we've developed some internal techniques to have our computers do the hard work. Ultimately, I decided that the incredible colors of the context and atmospheric information that is lost in the etching process was too much of a sacrifice for this particular effort. Nonetheless, we did a series of etchings of our buildings that we ultimately didn't use. Others are peppered throughout this book to illustrate different aspects of the project in different ways.

CAMERA AND LIGHTING TESTS: AERIAL VIEWS

For larger competitions and projects, we collaborate with professional rendering teams for some of our final images. For this project we worked with Timon Van Wynsberghe, Matteo Ferrari, Lukasz Mildner, and Kelly Torres from the London-based visualization company, Arqui9. Their office has an incredible gift of being able to capture the architecture being presented, but also the atmospheric qualities of the context through stunning control of lighting. The above images are early tests of possible views at various times of the day.

CAMERA AND LIGHTING TESTS: LOW AERIAL VIEWS

The above images show additional lighting and view tests done in collaboration with Arqui9. Both images illustrate the effects of bright and dramatic sunlight. The upper image emphasizes the shaded areas that are produced—an important aspect of a project in the remote desert. The lower image is a view into the sandstone ravines that hide the smaller guest suite mini-towers, showing the effect of morning light on the scene. Aerial views are incredibly important to this project as they allow us to show not only the arrangement of our architectural elements, programs and connections, but also show the vast, uninterrupted desert horizon.

CAMERA AND LIGHTING TESTS: AERIAL VIEWS

One difficulty present in aerial views that show the horizon, as the above image does, is to figure out how to develop an image that shows off miles of empty desert with very specific rock formations—without 3D modeling each individual form. Fortunately, the human eye has difficulty seeing such vast distances because of naturally occurring particular matter in the air, which is further amplified in the desert. This, called "turbidity," produces the effect of a hazier appearance the farther away an object is—which is why distant mountains or similar objects appear washed-out or faded to the human eye. This effect is incorporated into the final renderings which produces a far more accurate depiction of the desert views.

CAMERA AND LIGHTING TESTS: DESERT APPROACH

The above image is a study in how the human figure relates to the resort complex through its approach on foot. While this was a beautiful image of a sole figure walking along the top of a dune toward the resort beyond, it was decided that it was simply unrealistic. Unless that guest had been wandering around in the one hundred-plus degree heat, they would likely not find themselves in this position of returning to the complex on foot. Each image inherently produces a narrative and for us it is important that narrative aligns with the projects. In this case it did not.

399

CAMERA AND LIGHTING TESTS: NESTLED INTO SITE

This is a distant view of the resort that illustrates its siting in the raised basin. This provides the "nestled in rocks" approach we wanted, which allows the majority of the resort to be protected from desert winds and sand—yet is elevated enough to provide views from nearly all programmed areas. Ultimately, this view was rejected. While it shows the siting rather well, it was decided that it did not do justice to the architectural composition. This was also a ground-level view that nobody would ever see the project from as it was not along the established desert vehicle circulation paths.

CAMERA AND LIGHTING TESTS: BRIGHT DAYLIGHT

The above images illustrate the interior of the resort's central core in different lighting conditions. The top image shows the horizon pool level, restaurant court, and main tower beyond, but it didn't include enough of the desert context and wasn't a particularly important location that guests would see the resort from. The lower image, however, formed the basis for one of our final renderings, which we titled "opening day"—an important view from the bottom of the grand stair up toward the reception areas. For the final view, we significantly altered the lighting so that the scene was in a more realistic bright sunlight, as it would be for the majority of the day.

CAMERA AND LIGHTING TESTS: THE OASIS AND LUNAR CANOPY

One of the key features of the resort proposal is the inclusion of a water-purifying oasis of plants, which process water through root networks, and the "lunar canopy," which exists above it. These two images are attempts to capture the aesthetic effect of this massive metallic vaulted canopy on both the resort "skyline" and the appearance from within the oasis garden. Neither of these views were used in the final presentation namely because they didn't illustrate the vault's pattern clearly enough, which was based on an AI deconstruction and reconstruction of Nabatean and Dadanite scripts.

A VIEW FROM THE POOL

This rendering is an early, in-house collage to test what was visible to guests when they were actually in the horizon pool looking back toward the complex. It illustrates an earlier courtyard garden and its associated trees to the right. This rendering helped us realize that we actually did not want so much vegetation visible to guests when they were in the resort's central core, as we wanted to focus their views on the natural desert beauty, rather than an artificially created botanical one. The oasis garden was therefore relocated further away where it was part of the resort composition, but not a dominating feature.

COLORS, MATERIALS AND TEXTURES

Opposite page : **This is a photograph of a** bright green door in Rijal Alma'a, a village located in 'Asir Region. The careful use of intense colors against a normally monotonous desert context was a feature of Saudi Arabian architecture we prominently used in our design.

MATERIALS AS SHADERS

Architecture has, in recent centuries, become a discipline dominated by lines. Lines are used to draw plans, sections, and elevations—leaving material selection to often be made much later in the process. In recent decades, however, architects have been given access to higher levels of control regarding material effects through digital representation—the ability to more accurately see the data of sensible experience that materials convey. An even more recent development in architecture's digital technologies is the ability to move beyond the mere appearance of materials to approximation of their textural values through the development of software programs such as Mudbox and Z-Brush, in addition to more commonly available technologies involving bump maps on software shaders.

SHADERS AS MATERIALS

The above images are some of the texture shaders we used in the project—a palette very much in the historic sense of the term "palette" as used by a painter. We think of the buildings as curated collections of materials and textures, rather than the assembly of products, which is, unfortunately, what architecture often becomes. The textures and shaders pictured form the aesthetic ambitions of the project and are usually established before knowing the exact materials that will produce them. This often forces innovation, in that we try to produce the material effects through new interconnections of technologies, materials and fabrication methods.

MONOLITHIC MATERIAL STUDIES: SMOOTH STONE

As an early test of material and textural properties, we will often apply a single material to the entirety of a project. This has the effect of over-saturating the proposal with a particular material property and, therefore, helps us establish the limits of each material's reasonable use. The top image illustrates the application of a non-material—the standard default gray shader used in numerous software programs. In contrast, the image below shows the application of a yellow sandstone similar to that of the ruins of nearby Mada'in Salih.

MONOLITHIC MATERIAL STUDIES: RUSTICATED STONE

Here are some additional texture and material studies. The one above shows a heavily veined version of the regional sandstone. The one below illustrates what we referred to as "stained" sandstone—the accumulation of dirt in porous sandstone surfaces which occurred over thousands, if not millions of years. This suite of material and textural options represents the stone most readily available in the region. Our desire was to use only stone available within a several mile radius of the construction of the project, which limited our palette to these presented options and combinations thereof.

ARTIFICIAL INTELLIGENCE AND MANDELBROT SETS: PATTERN ITERATIONS

While the building exteriors use local stone materials in large quantities, the interiors of our proposed buildings are either simply reflections of their exteriors, or alternatively and in limited moments, intensely colored and patterned.

To generate these patterns, we used our previously developed artificial intelligence and fractal generation systems that fuse historic pattern excerpts from Dadanite, Nabatean, Bedouin, and Saudi cultural references.

ARTIFICIAL INTELLIGENCE AND MANDELBROT SETS: CERAMIC TILE PATTERN

The above image is a result of the aforementioned processes, designed in a teal and blue recursive patterning with metal and ceramic tiles. The fabrication technique proposed is a common one—often used in the production of tile murals and swimming pool bottoms. Tile companies such as Bisazza allow architects to upload jpeg images which are pixelized and translated into tiles as small as a half-inch square. Our AI and fractal design patterns can be easily pixelized into these dimensions, allowing for their exact reproduction at a 1:1 scale. The above image was a test version of the reception building interior generated according to these manufacturer dimensions.

THE RECEPTION INTERIOR: AI TILE PATTERN ITERATIONS 1-4

This series of images illustrates iterations of the fractal/AI tile design pattens deployed in the reception building interior. The idea is that upon completing a lengthy journey across the monotone desert, the guest is immersed in an explosion of color, refraction, and light. While many of the resort buildings are oriented toward particular views, others, such as this one, are internalized. The goal with these interiors is to produce specific and intense aesthetic effects, emerging from ancient and historic cultural forms from the region, that provide a mysterious, contrapposto relief from the raw desert surroundings.

THE RECEPTION INTERIOR: AI TILE PATTERN ITERATIONS 5-8

These eight studies illustrate different source materials and parameters within the fractal/AI recombinant processes. Some results produce linear, angular interiors that have a closer relationship with Bedouin weaving patterns, while others exhibit qualities of arabesque tracery or intricate jewelry inlays. Each of these studies took days to produce. Of the ten that we created, the final one used is closest to the lower left image on this page.

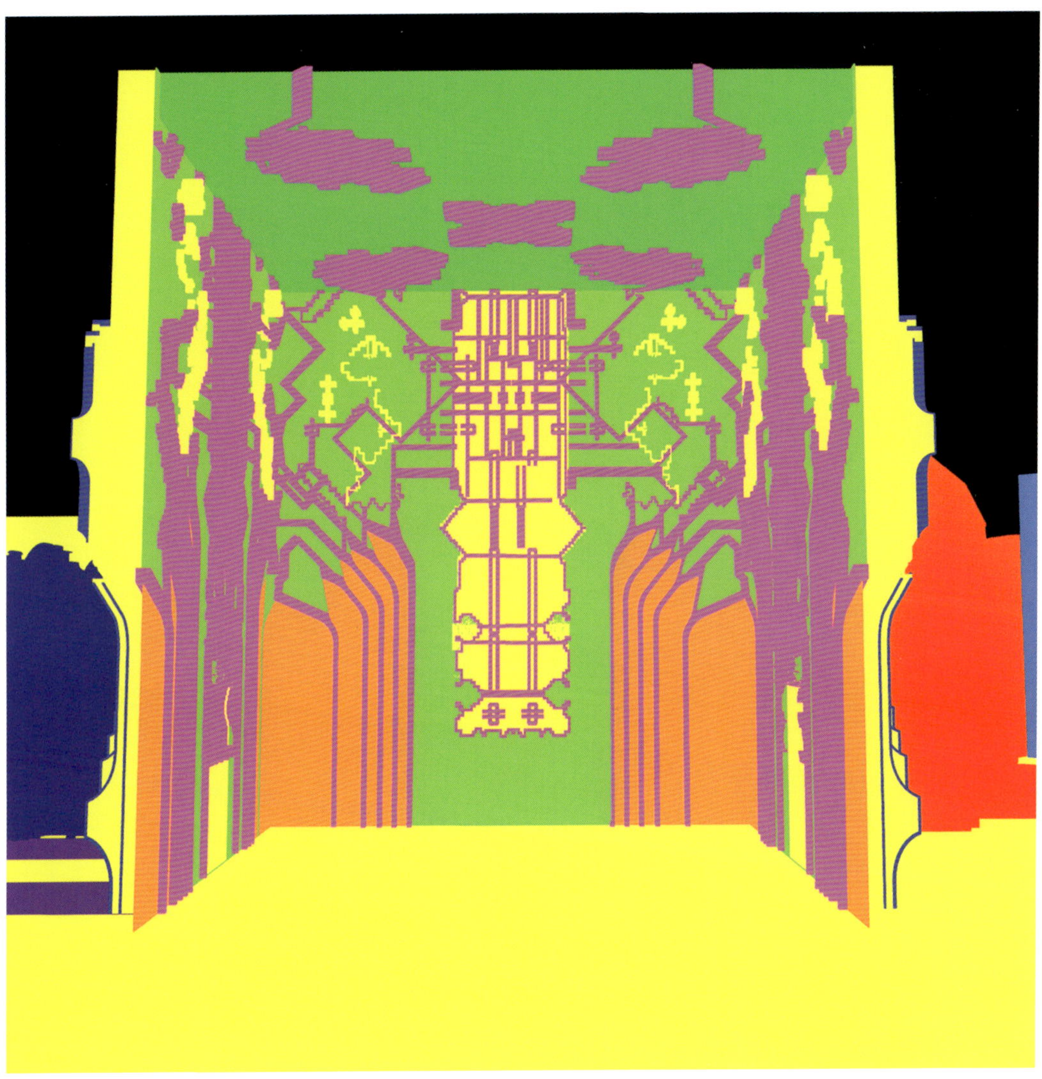

THE CLOWN PASS

As our patterns became incredibly complex, it was difficult to deal with them in terms of design changes. Because of this, we made extensive use of what in the digital world are called "clown passes," which establish block colors for certain layers of design elements. Compositions through isolated blocks such as this allowed us to design images and mask changes with specific parameters much faster than considering the entire pattern and form all at once.

RECEPTION INTERIOR FINALISTS: BIOLOGICAL PATTERN

One of the design iterations of the reception interior placed a heavier emphasis on the formal inlay languages found in Bedouin jewelry, which were also unusual in that they produced asymmetrical compositions within a symmetrical space. We eventually decided that this direction was too patchy and slightly biological looking, like the mitosis of amoebas, which while interesting didn't produce the same cultural reference we were interested in.

THE FINAL RECEPTION INTERIOR

The final iteration we developed for the reception interior was based on the stepped forms of Nabatean architecture combined with orthogonal arabesque metalworking patterns. Together, they produced an architectural pattern with a high degree of scale variation. The various forms that emerged were colored with intensely saturated tiles in greens, teals, blues and golds—colors that are rare within the desert and accordingly provided the most intensely luxurious environment we could imagine given the desert journey the guests had recently completed. To the left of the image, two guests have recently left their desert vehicle and are walking through the watery entrance courtyard to check in with the front desk. To the right of the image is the neighboring rock formation and lower incense tree garden proposed as part of our larger landscape ambitions.

418

MONOTONE AI TILE STUDY

Less intensely colored versions of our fractal/AI tile generation techniques were used in less important resort areas, while also becoming less saturated in tone the farther away they were from the resort's central core. The above image is an example of a pattern that was used as a ceiling condition for a shaded arcade in a primary circulation corridor to one wing of guest suites.

419

DIGITAL CERAMIC TILING

A variation of the previous pattern was used as the underside of a similar circulation arcade closer to the resort's central core, therefore it received more saturation and color variations than the left image. The degree of color complexity and saturation therefore became an orienting device, as more saturated areas were closer to the reception building and the farther away one traveled from the center, the colors became more faded and less chromatically intense and diverse.

TILING PATTERN: GUEST SUITE ARCADES

Above is the interior view of the previous arcade, showing a human-level view of the immersive colored vaulting. This particular example uses a mix of the raw, exposed stone, shown in beige, which is inlaid with the printed pixelated tiles. The mixed use of stone and tile indicates this arcade's position as rather distant from the resort's central core. Hanging light fixtures, not pictured here, would be designed to occur at the rondel intersections of the vault crossings.

421

TILING PATTERN: LOWER GARDEN ARCADES

Some of the arcade colors are darker in order to provide relief from the relentlessly bright desert sun—such as this version that uses gold fractal/AI-generated patterns that reflect sunlight to appear particularly vivid against the black background of the Bedouin goat hair tents. This direction was not pursued as it was decided that the black surfaces applied to stone would absorb too much heat over the course of the day. We did, however, use this interior patterning in some of the interior residential corridors.

THE ETCHED STONE ARCADE: EXTERIOR STUDY

As a counterproposal to our strategy of tiling more simplified arcade structures, we simultaneously developed an arcade language entirely constructed out of stone, where the fractal/AI patterns are translated into carvings as opposed to colors. This allows the shadows produced by the bright environment to function as kinetic pattern-generating devices over the course of the day. The axonometric image pictured above illustrates a hybrid arcade/trabeated system defined by vertical fins, which produce their own shade and reduce the solar radiation absorbed by more typical arcade structures.

423

THE ETCHED STONE ARCADE: INTERIOR STUDY

The above image shows a view from the pool area arcade. The carved ceiling forms are derived from recombinant AI fusions of Nabatean and Lihyanite forms of writing and ancient petroglyphs found as etchings at Jabal Ikmah, known as Al Ula's "open air library," mere kilometers away from the resort site. A variation of this design direction was used in the final project where the edge of the script patterns were offset and edged in gold leaf. Ultimately, this carved-stone arcade strategy was used exclusively on the areas immediately surrounding the lower pool level. This produced a single unified aesthetic for the wet world below the regular activities of the resort.

24

425

THE TILED OBSERVATION CORRIDOR—VERSION 05

One strange problem with our tiled fractal languages is that they sometimes resemble the interior of a computer—like circuit boards. This is an odd and accidental result of a design language literally constructed from historic architectural and cultural DNA from throughout the region's history. *Following pages:* This is the final image of the lower pool arcade with a carved-stone articulated ceiling edged in gold leaf—developed through the aforementioned fractal/AI fusions of Nabatean and Lihyanite forms of writing and petroglyphs found at Jabal Ikmah.

THE PRESENTATION MODEL
428–437

Final CNC milled model base in high-density foam
3D-printed brass for public buildings
Model photographs of final presentation
Masterplan drawing of final model arrangement

Opposite page : **This is an** aerial view of two stone carved temple fronts at Mada'in Salih.

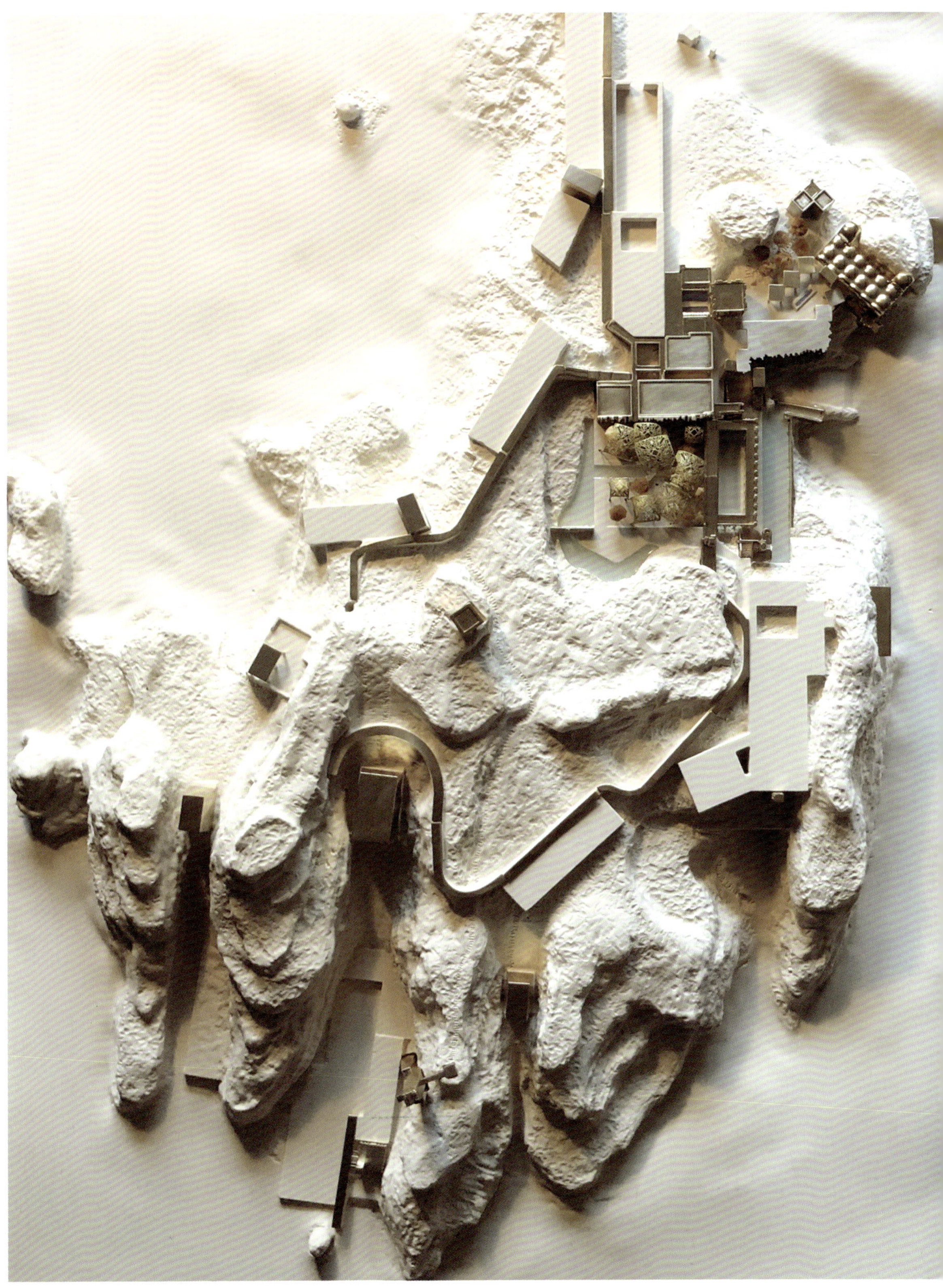

THE PRESENTATION MODEL: AERIAL VIEW OF CORE

Preceding pages: This shows the final presentation model of the project made from robotically carved high-density foam and solid brass, 3D-printed buildings. *This page:* While our study model was made out of clay it was, as with all such clay models, mildly greasy and smelled funny—hardly presentation model material. Instead, we produced a rather elaborate final presentation model for the sole purpose of presenting in Riyadh. The above image shows a zoomed-in image of the resort's central core, which is 3D-printed in solid brass.

THE PRESENTATION MODEL: LOW AERIAL VIEW OF CORE

Our final presentation model was assembled in-house, with parts sub-contracted out to various suppliers. With the base CNC carved from one supplier, the 3D-printed brass buildings supplied by a second, and the foam trees and "lunar canopy" provided by a third—there was not much room for dimensional error. We found ourselves carving foam, sanding and grinding brass for several days in order to get everything to be as perfectly coordinated as possible. For areas such as the pools, we hand cast clear resins into the model itself and added slight coloration to appear as pool water.

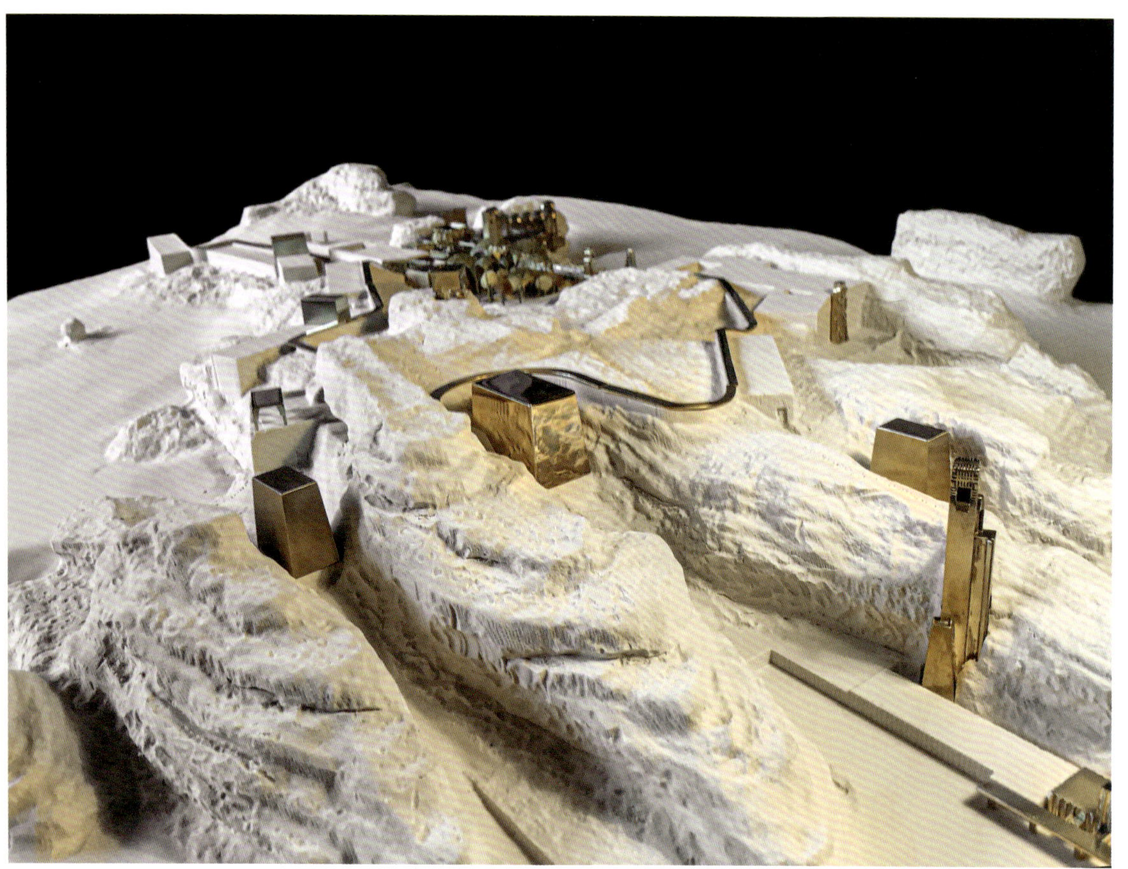

435

THE PRESENTATION MODEL: AERIAL VIEW FROM NORTHWEST

While done at the end of the project, the presentation model was valuable in illustrating aspects of the project that we were unaware of, despite having worked on the design for months. We found new and surprising vistas as well as much more accurate information on the performance of shade and shadow—given that we could use actual spotlights and receive feedback in real-time. Our original clay study model wasn't able to produce the same level of information as it didn't have the same degree of detail as this presentation model. We discovered this in areas such as the 3D-patterned lunar canopy, which cast stunningly intricate shadows on the trees and ground below.

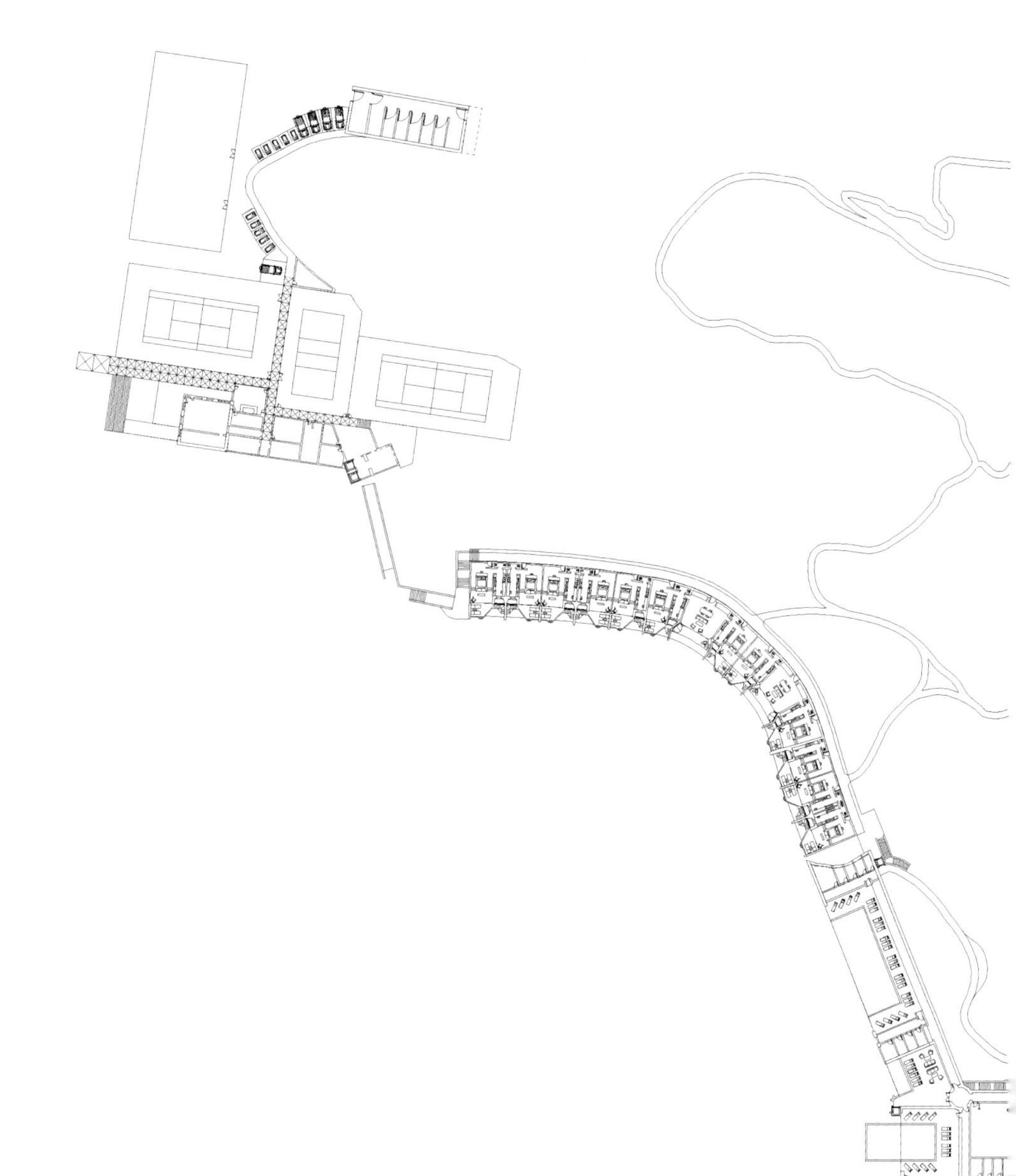

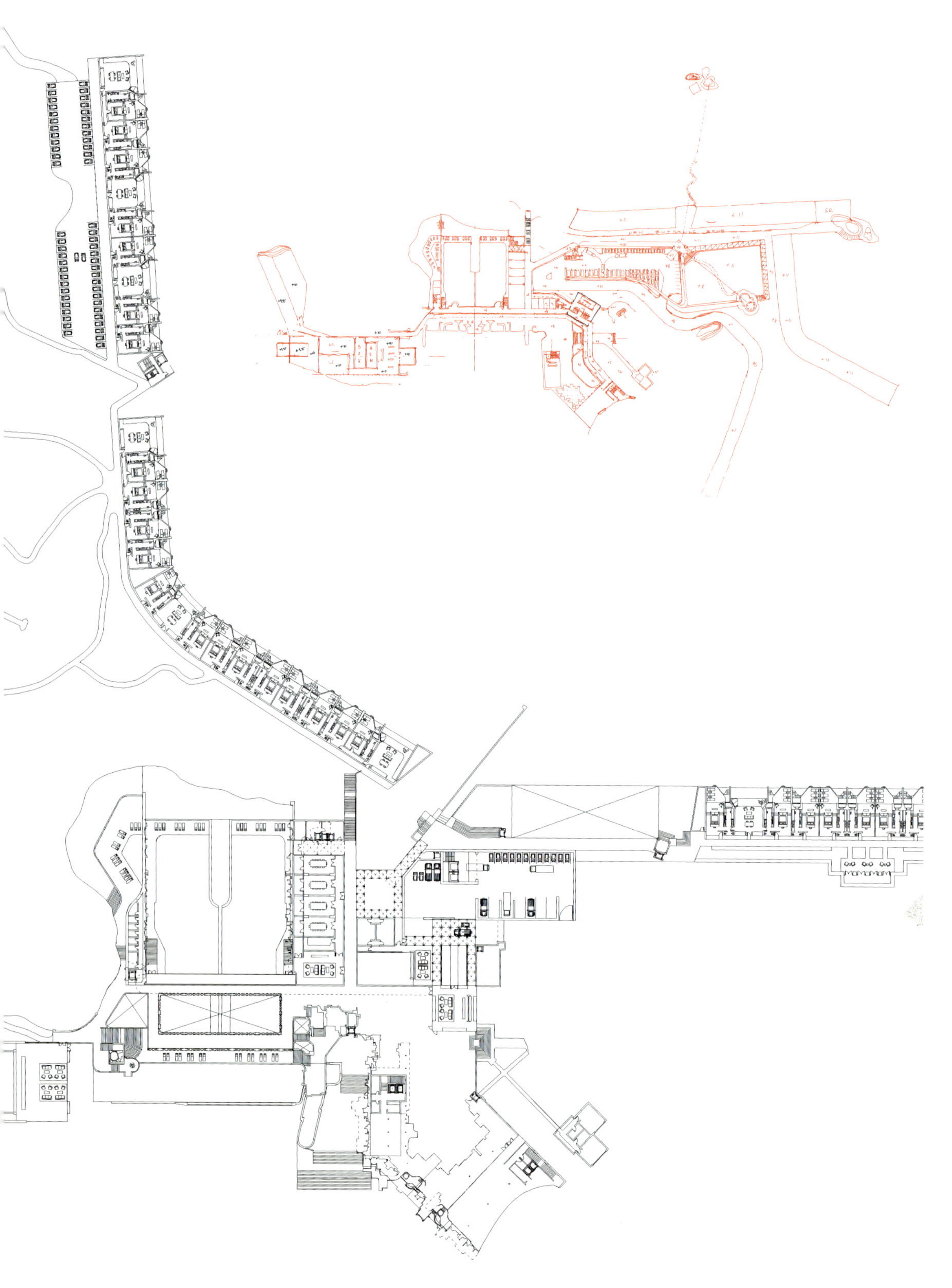

ISOLATED LUXURY VILLAS
438–453

Opposite page : **This photo was taken in** the village of al-Baha, a four hundred year-old abandoned stone settlement in Saudi Arabia built atop a marble hill, recently declared a UNESCO World Heritage Site.

REMOTE VILLAS: HAND SKETCHES

One of the proposals for the resort project was the inclusion of a number of remote luxury villas, ranging from four to ten bedrooms. These isolated residential compounds are intended to house larger families and events in more remote and private locations than the resort proper can accommodate. In our proposal, villas were all nestled into or up against large protective rock formations. This assured that each unit had the benefit of views out to the vast desert horizon, as well as proximity to stable geological foundations, which allowed for better structural support, wind protection, and the opportunity for natural changes in level.

REMOTE VILLAS: EARLY 3D STUDIES

The villas are all divided into two sections—a "living section" and a "private section." Both areas are connected by a glass hallway which acts as a "hinge" between the two. Early studies of these building types are pictured above, where each section could be mirrored or rotated to align with the immediate site conditions—the only element requiring custom alteration being the glass connector itself. This early 3D model illustrates the two sections divided by a sandstone outcropping through which the snaking hallway that connects the two buildings and program areas is woven into.

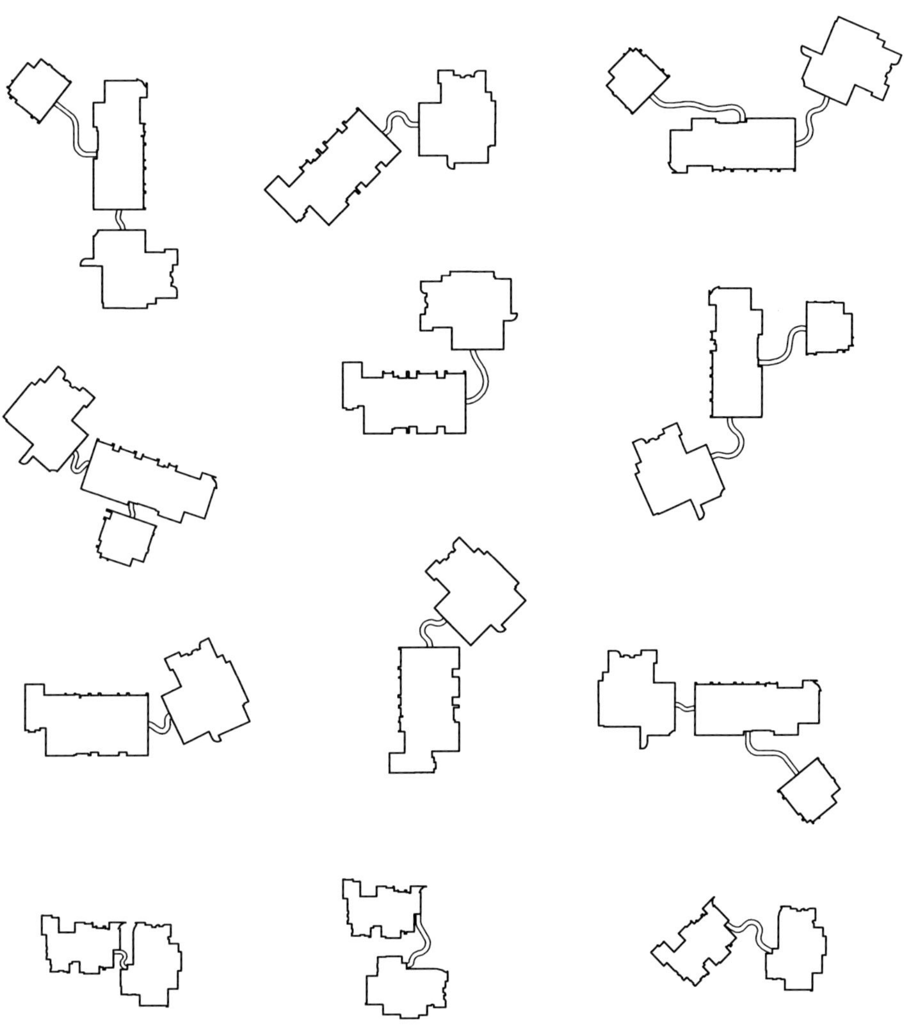

REMOTE VILLAS: THE MODULAR SYSTEM

In order to design a large number of villas without designing each of them individually, we developed an architectural module system that uses the same elements to produce highly customizable homes out of similar components. This allows each villa to be integrated closely with the rock formations that are unique to their carefully selected sites. This series of diagrams shows the unlimited palette of possible "living section" and "private section" relationships, as sections were mirrored and folded to accommodate a nearly infinite number of site types. Some villas are comprised of two of the modular system buildings with large compounds made possible through the use of additional modules connected with flexible corridors.

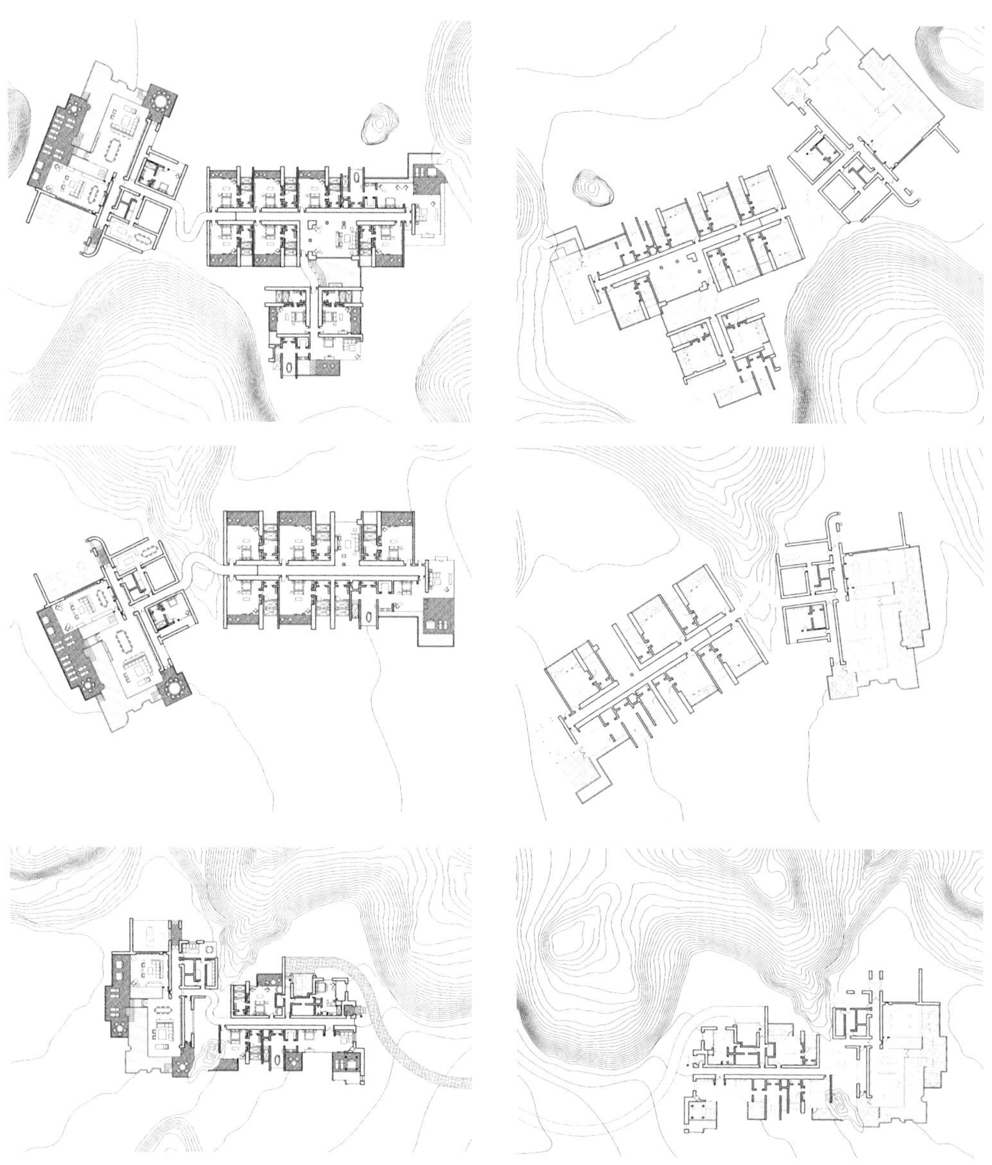

REMOTE VILLAS: TOPOGRAPHICAL CONFIGURATIONS

The above images are preliminary floor plans showing how the villa modules wrap into and around the sandstone outcroppings to which they are adjacent. This flexible system allows a villa to wrap around a stone peninsula, fold into a crevice, or be situated within a more private rocky basin—all of which are illustrated above. Drawings such as the middle ones show a four-bedroom villa that is built on two sides of a sandstone peninsula with the flexible connector puncturing the stone to connect the two modules. This strategy allows for the production of villas that were often built directly into the rocks, using the geological formations in lieu of walls and, in some locations, floors and ceilings.

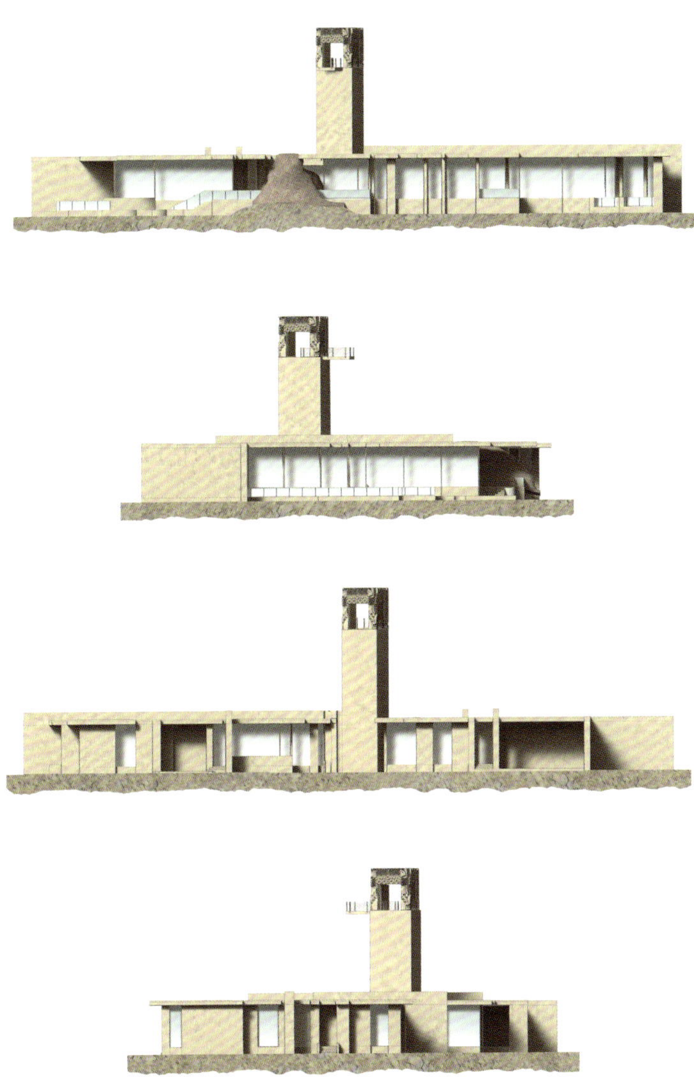

REMOTE VILLAS: RESIDENTIAL TOWERS

The villas all have the option of including a small observation tower linked to the glass corridor hinge, which allows guests and owners to have a visible and picturesque wayfinding marker from far away, including a small lounge elevated high above the desert floor with spectacular views. As with the resort proper, the towers can also be gravity-fed water filtration systems intended to assist in the water recycling process.

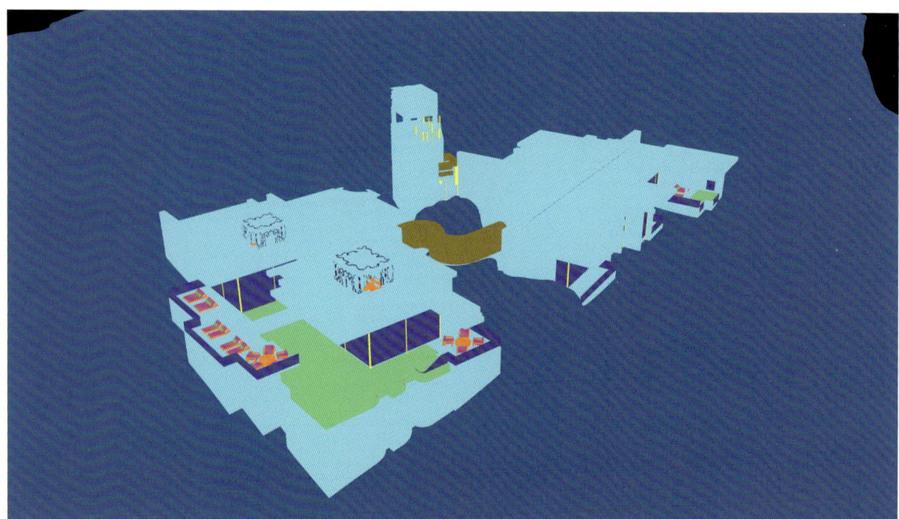

REMOTE VILLAS: CONTEXT AND VIEW STUDIES

When designing the villas, we wanted to leave as little of a visual footprint on their context as possible. To accommodate this, we used stone materials that matched their immediate surroundings. The above study images highlight the sympathies between the color and smoothness of the villa surfaces against the rocky and sandy context in which they are placed.

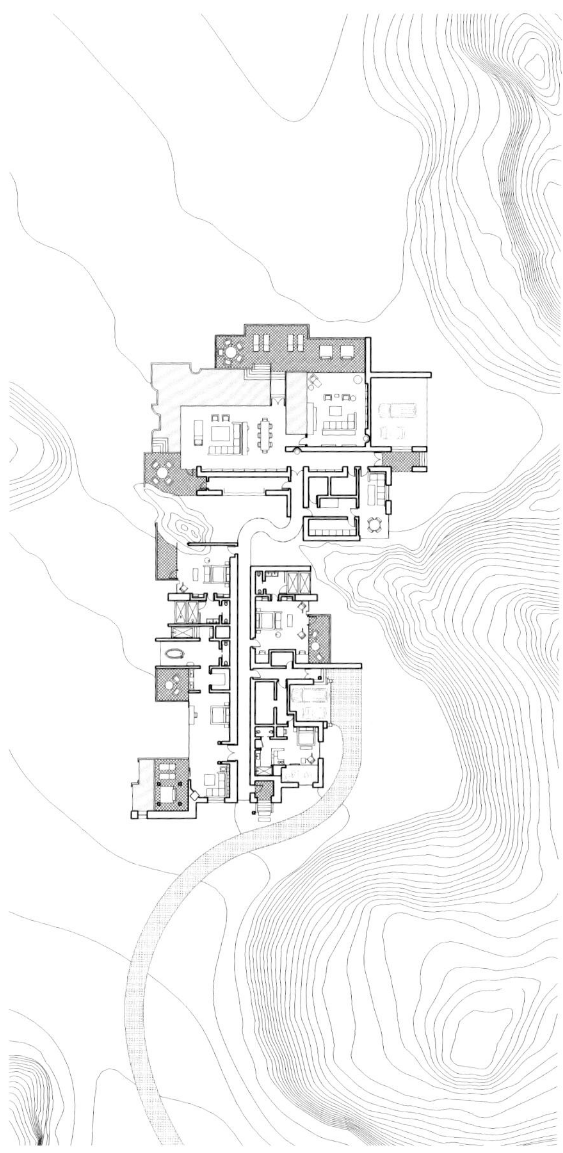

REMOTE VILLAS: A FOUR BEDROOM UNIT

A standard four-bedroom villa shown with a flexible connector that allows the living and private modules to be orthogonally related to one another. *Opposite page:* This image shows a zoomed-in view of floor plan that better illustrates the furnishings, layouts of rooms, and internal workings of the villa plans. As with many Muslim residential arrangements, there are separate living rooms for men and women.

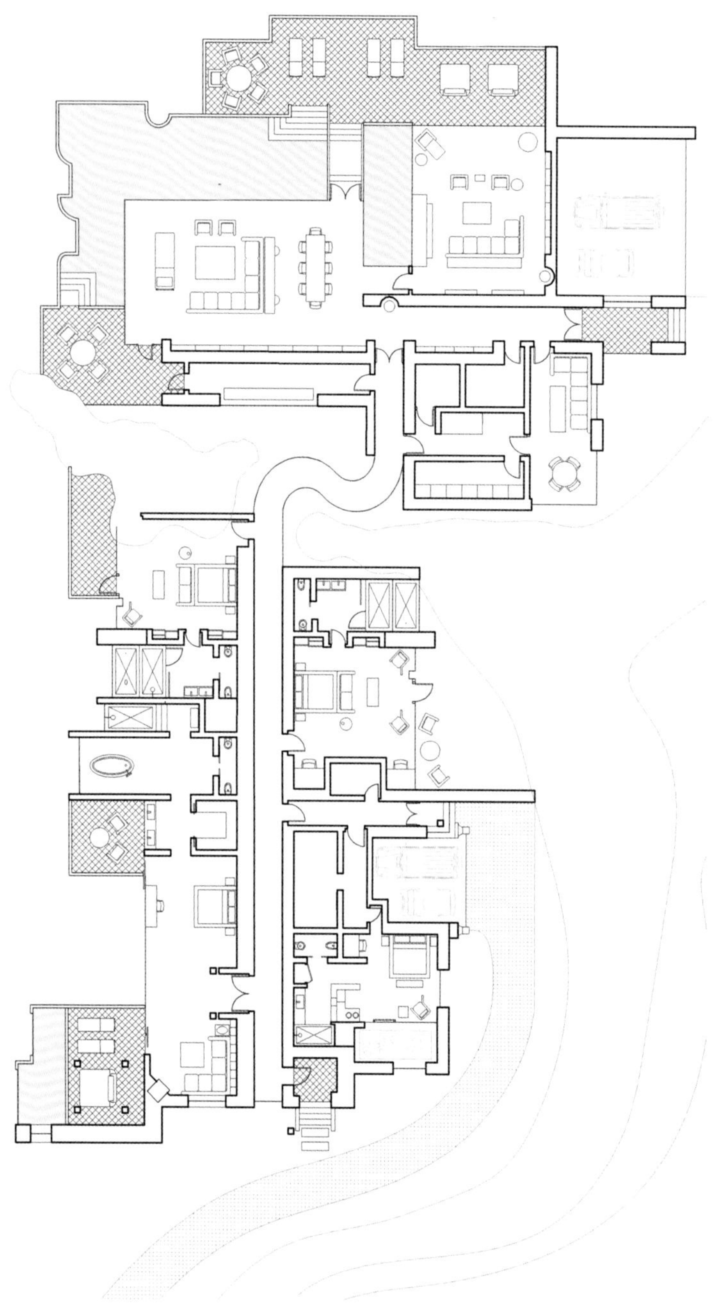

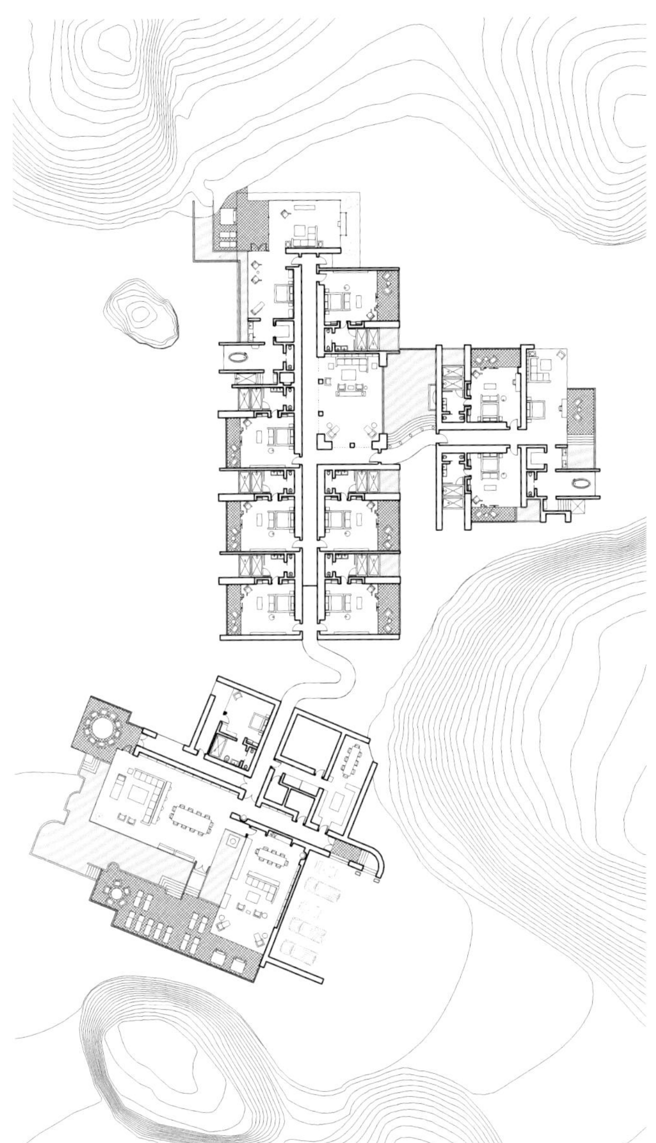

These images show a more highly customized ten-room villa with an exaggerated curved connector that allows the living and private portions to be more distinctly isolated from one another. *Opposite page:* The enlarged floor plan shown here better illustrates the relationship of furnishings to rooms and internal workings of these larger villa plans, including the introduction of a more private family room and an adjacent plunge pool for smaller gatherings in the private building module.

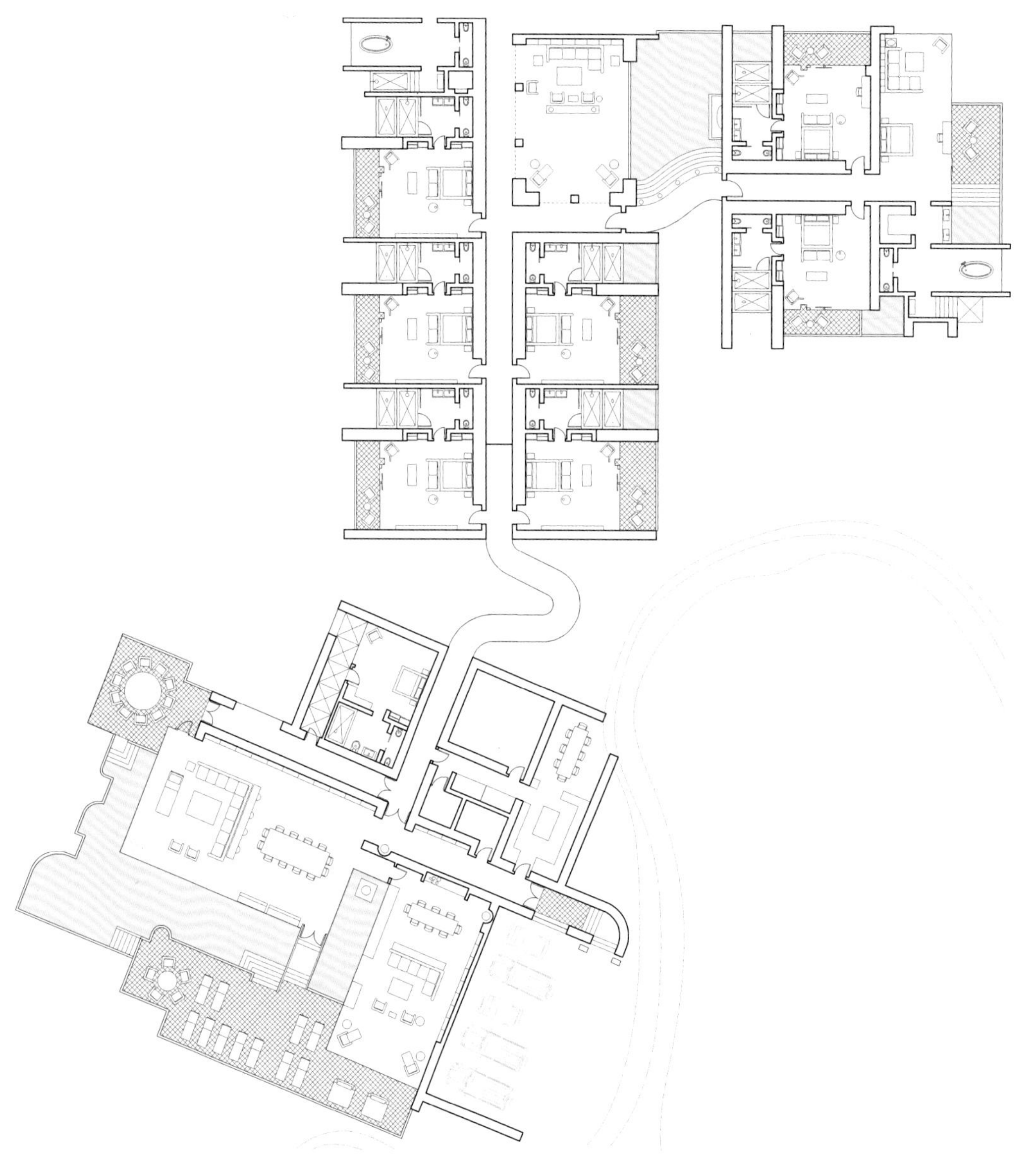

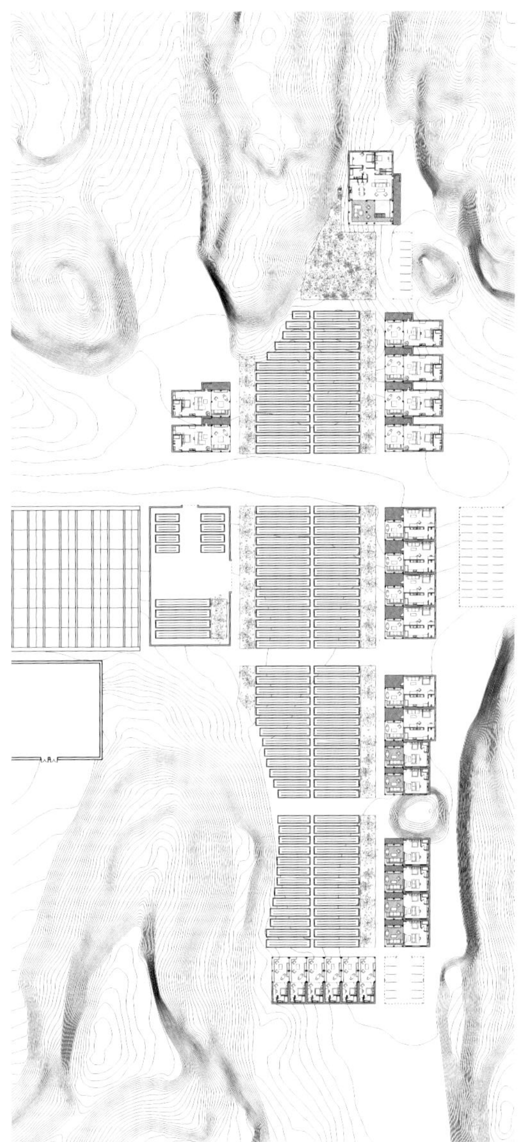

STAFF ACCOMMODATIONS: THE NATIVE SPECIES NURSERY

Preceding pages: This is the final rendering of a standard four-bedroom villa against the sandstone outcroppings of its site. *This page:* Given its remoteness, the desert resort would need to accommodate a large number of its staff members on-site. Therefore, we developed a satellite campus, hidden from view of the resort, that housed the native plant nursery and was surrounded by the residential quarters of the required staff. This arrangement provides protection of the plants from wild camels, and also provides the staff residences with access to and views of vegetation and greenery. The above plan shows this with horizontal rows of plantings surrounded by joined residential units of varying sizes.

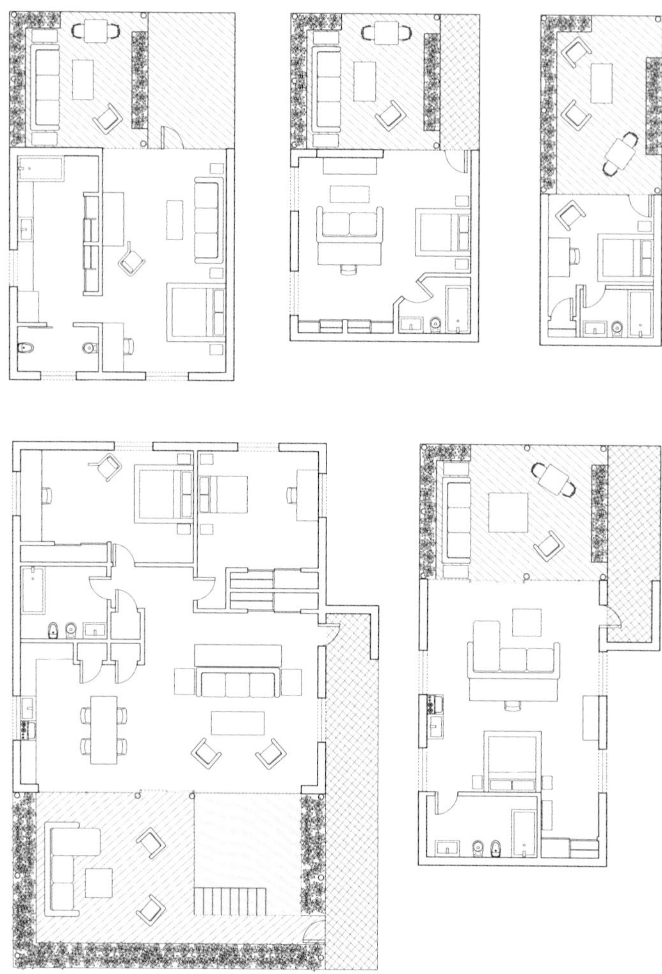

STAFF ACCOMMODATIONS: UNIT TYPES

The staff residences contains multiple housing types for different levels of responsibility and seniority, but also to accommodate families. The primary plan types are shown above, ranging from small studio apartments to larger two-bedroom complexes. All residential units for staff contains shaded outdoor spaces made more private by the additional planting of native species around the patio perimeters.

FINAL BOARDING
454–463

Seven A1 final presentation boards
Resort tower at sunset

Opposite page : One of the activities available to guests was falconry, which is a more common recreational pursuit in Saudi Arabia than I was aware of. The falcon in this photograph is blinded, which I thought appropriate to introduce a section on our final boards because after the presentation we felt similarly blind to the impending outcome.

1/7 PLACEMAKING: SITE LAYOUT, VISION AND RESORT EXPERIENCE

mfga Stantec Transsolar KlimaEngineering FOCUS LIGHTING MIC Front VIA DOMANI

PROJECT VISION:

NEW NABATEA

~

A feeling of otherworldliness cannot be produced using the common tools of our own everyday world. In order to move beyond this limitation and into the realm of the mysterious and awe-inspiring, our office proposed a question- what if the Nabateans were still with us today? What might their architecture have evolved into given an additional 1800 years to mature and incorporate all of the technology era, that merges design techniques from this ancient civilization with those that followed -including those of today. The result was, we believe a fantastic fusion of not only landscape and architecture, as called for in the project brief, but also of history, all enabled through the use of new and advanced technologies. One thing is clear of the Nabateans of Meda'in Saleh- their culture was not only one of wealth and power, but one that vibrantly exchanged ideas with neighboring cultures. This is seen in the architecture that remains at Meda'in Saleh today, as, in even singular buildings such as masterpiece tomb of Qasr al Farid there is not only the exquisite precision of Nabatean stonecutting, and innovations such as the Nabatean column capital found nowhere else in the world- but there can also be found clever reinterpretations of entablatures, triglyphs and metopes from Greek antiquity, curved stone cornices from ancient Egypt, and the stepped "merlon" motifs from early Mesopotamia. Nabatean design culture was one of beautiful fusion, so to imagine a New Nabatea in the 21st century we must imagine that, above all, they would have continued to combine into their architecture aspects of design from more recent regional and Saudi design traditions. We have therefore imagined a new and mysterious resort city, complexly integrating into Nabatean design techniques newer influences ranging from the details of Bedouin jewelry and the patterns of early Islamic architecture to the contemporary graphic design trends of Saudi culture today. In order to accomplish this fusion of cultures, patterns, materials, technologies and the forms in our architecture we turned to the new technologies of artificial intelligence to assist us in our fusing several millennia of history and design innovations into an architecture that is as rooted in the deep past as it is in the cutting edge of today's technologies and design culture. Welcome to New Nabatea.

mfga tower top facade

guest access to resort site

THE SKY NECKLACE

~

While societies after the Nabateans left less in the way of monumental architecture, that does not mean they did not have fantastically innovative cultures of design. One of the most fascinating trajectories of such design we identified was that of Bedouin jewelry from the region, that tracks, over time, changes in pattern, form, and material technologies, resulting in some of the most stunning and unusual body adornments in the history of the world. Our organizing form for the relationship between our circulation paths and buildings was inspired such an object—a heavy, highly adorned, and segmented 'hilal' shoulder necklace. The site of our project is on an elevated escarpment that allows for the majority of the resort to sit above the desert floor yet be protected by being integrated into the rocky peaks. The combination of the formal circulation strategy with the location of the site developed into the concept of a "sky necklace," which vividly describes the overall form and geological siting of the project- connected, elevated, beautiful, and with stunning views out in all directions.

bedouin hilal shoulder necklace with filagree, pre-1950

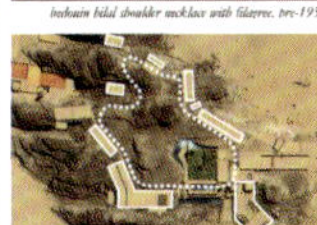

resort from above

FINAL PRESENTATION BOARDS

Final board #1: First impressions and initial approach

2/7 DESIGN QUALITY: RECEPTION, DINING AND LEISURE FACILITIES

resort from south

grand stair and outdoor event space

observation tower

reception entry

reception sectional perspective

restaurant courtyard

250 chilled pool

pool arcade and terrace

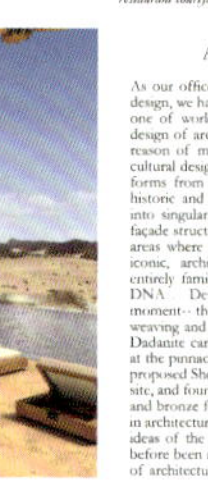

OTHER WORLDLINESS: ARTIFICIAL INTELLIGENCE

As our office is on the cutting-edge of the use of technology in design, we have, for our Sheraan Desert Resort proposal, developed one of world's first uses of artificial intelligence to assist in the design of architectural forms. This, however, was not done for the reason of mere novelty, but instead to help us to take the many cultural design references we gathered in growing digital library of forms from Dadanite, Lihyanite Nabatean, Islamic, Bedouin and historic and contemporize Saudi design cultures—and fuse them into singular, intricate, and deeply three-dimensional architectural façade structures. Over the extent of the project there are multiple areas where such design strategies are used to produce signature, iconic, architectural moments unlike anything, anywhere- yet entirely familiar given their generation from historic architectural DNA. Defining the resorts main point of arrival is one such moment-- the reception "cube," fused from the forms of Bedouin weaving and jewelry, Nabatean patterns and gestures from historic Dadanite carved writing. Such surprises can also be found placed at the pinnacles of elevated observation towers, encasing the newly proposed Sheraan Observatory at the highest elevation point on the site, and found in more subtle ways in rustication patterns, tile work, and bronze forged elements throughout the project. This is a first in architecture and a first with a noble cause—to combine the design ideas of the past with those of the future in a way that has never before been attempted, yet shows great promise for the production of architecture of beauty, meaning and deep historical connections.

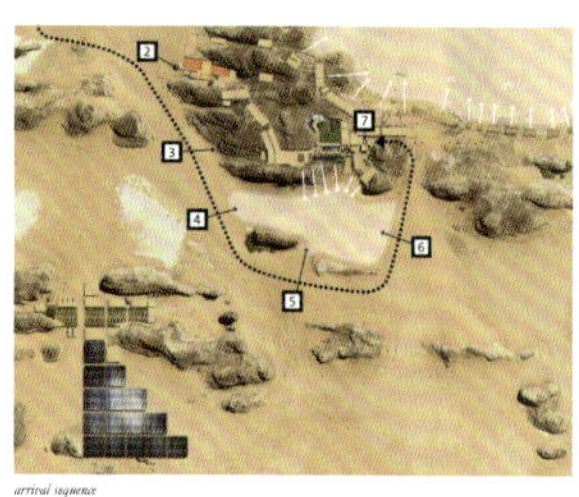

arrival sequence

457

FINAL PRESENTATION BOARDS

Final board #2: Choreography of guest experiences

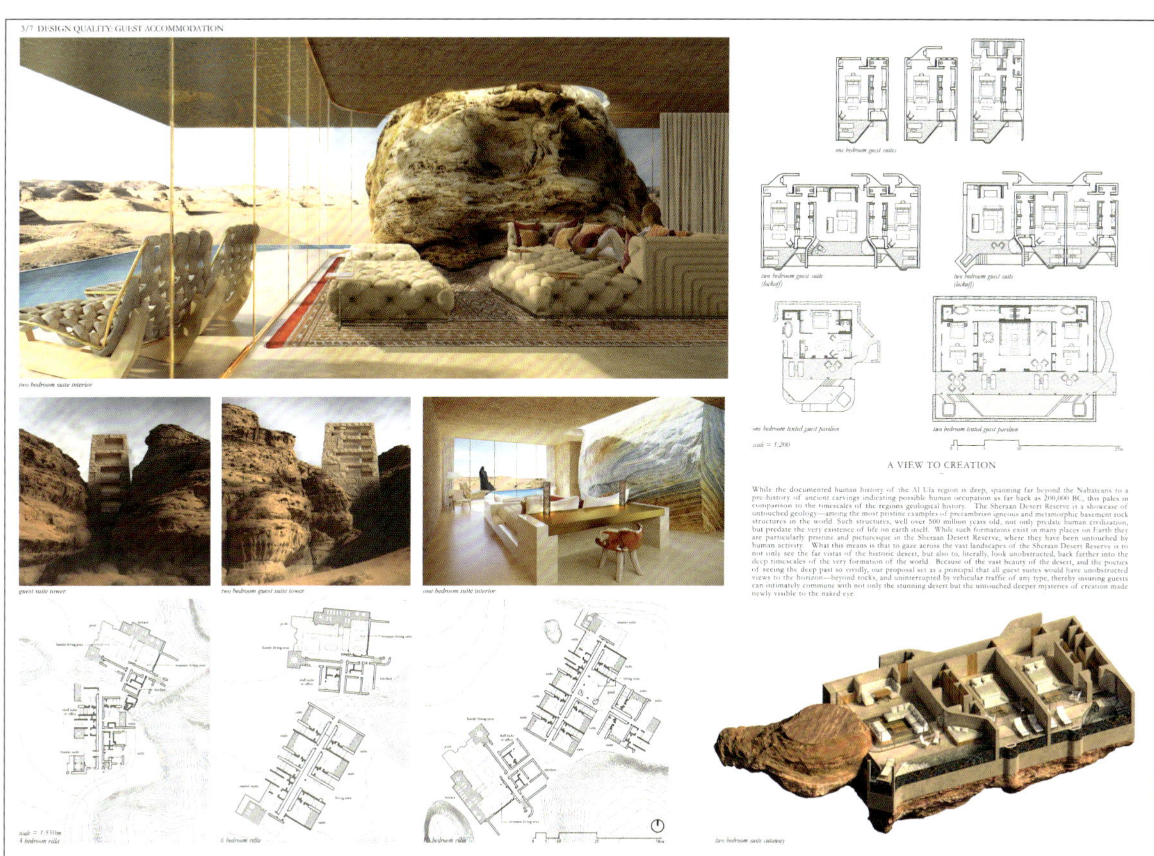

Final board #3: Guest suites: plans and interiors

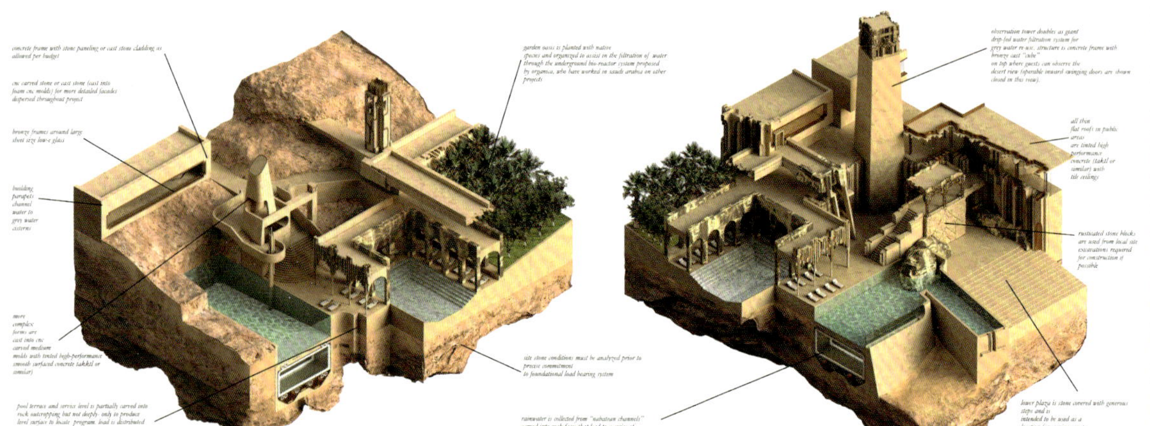

PROJECT FEASIBILITY

To produce an iconic and world-class resort requires world-class expertise. As such we have gathered a team of world leaders in all aspects impacting the design, construction, maintenance, function and sustainability of the resort. We have left nothing to chance—every design and proposal found in our design has been vetted by an extensive team for not only feasibility the immediate term but also in terms of long term maintenance, function and appearance. We believe as a larger team that there are very few opportunities in the world for a project a meaningful as the Sheraan Desert Resort—and as such we have formed a collective of the worlds leading minds to assure that it deliverable at a level of quality that the region deserves as a showcase of not only history and nature—but technology and skill.

GUIDELINES FOR REGIONAL CONSTRUCTION PRACTICES

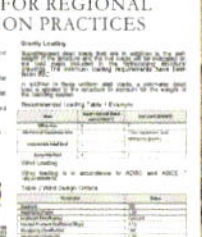

resort axonometric from northwest

pool terrace and service level

Final board #4: The resort center and ecological footprint

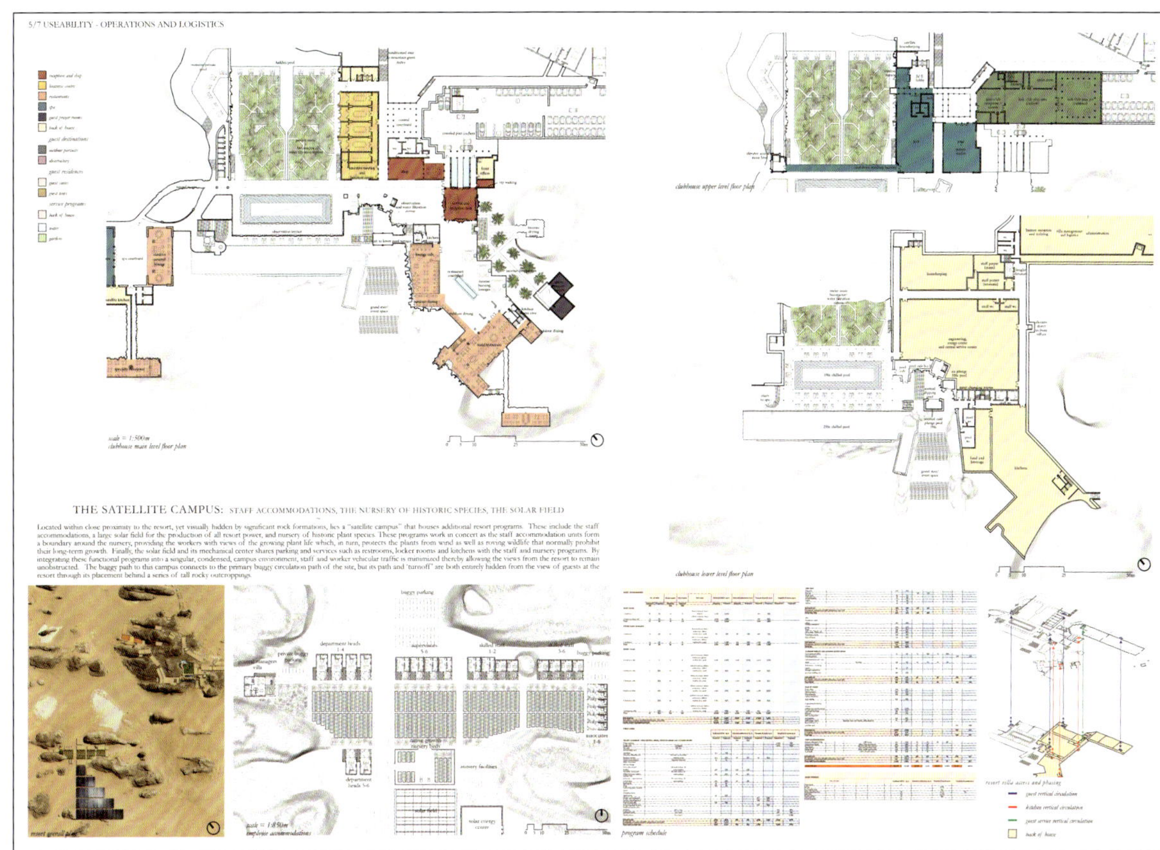

Final board #5: Planning, service, and access

6/7 PERFORMANCE: SUSTAINABILITY AND ENERGY

PIONEERING SUSTAINABILITY

~

The Sheraan Desert Resort will be a showcase of sustainable technology working in concert to produce a building that is net-zero on an annual basis. This will be done through the choreography of common sense, tried and true technologies and smart addition of the most advanced and emerging technologies of tomorrow. The project utilizes an ecology of these strategies including but not limited to the intelligent use of thermal insulation through masonry construction, low emissivity glass, radiant cooling, natural ventilation where appropriate, calculated sun shading, night irrigation, rainwater collection using "Nabatean channels" carved into the rock that lead to multiple grey water cisterns, a new "bio-reactor" system located underneath our garden oasis which uses the vegetation above to assist in the filtration of water, wind-catching towers, giant gravity-fed water filtration towers, a singular solar field hidden from the view of guests to generate all resort power, and the world's largest "lunar canopy" which is a giant patterned hollow bronze-toned lattice placed high above the garden oasis/bio-reactor below. This lunar-canopy has two functions; during the day water is slowly channeled through the vast surface area of the metal lattice to be heated to high temperatures by the sun and used by the adjacent kitchen and housekeeping services, as well as nearby guest rooms. At night this function is reversed- as the desert air is hot it makes a poor absorber of the stored heat removed during daytime air conditioning. Instead this heat is removed from rooms and public areas and stored in water tanks which, after sunset, then slowly pump this unwanted heat through the lunar canopy where it is sustainably radiated into the night sky. Outdoor guest spaces take advantage of an intelligent range of strategies as well-- including breezy shaded areas, water features with plantings, radiant cooling, the use of dry-mist evaporative cooling systems, deep shading overhangs, operable windows and wind-channeling towers that all assure that all of the Sheraan Desert Resorts spaces offer guests the uncompromised levels of comfort to which they are accustomed.

sustainability aerial

~THE WATER RECYCLING OASIS ~
DESERT PLANTS AS BIO-REACTOR

~

While water filtration is a part of everyday 21st century life, it is rarely beautiful to behold. Through working with the company Organica, we are proposing that our garden oasis sit above a "bio-reactor" cistern which uses the plant roots and bio-films to purify water for resort re-use. This provides the resort with, literally, a 21st century oasis that provides the same functions as those of yesteryear but with the most advanced strategies of ecological engineering.

~THE WORLDS LARGEST LUNAR COLLECTOR ~
THE FUTURE OF DESERT SUSTAINABILITY

~

Both beautiful and functional the 'lunar canopy' hovering high above the garden oasis not only provides guests with shading during the day but also doubles as a water heater for nearby resort functions. At night the canopy becomes a giant radiator to disperse heat stored from daytime air-conditioning into the night sky. This would be not only among the first such structures in the world-but the largest as well—providing the Sheraan Desert Resort with an additional unique asset.

~ THE SAUDI TOWER AS WATER FILTER~
FROM HISTORY TO THE FUTURE OF GREEN LIVING

~

Saudi architectural history is filled with towers, wind-catchers, turrets and other vertical elements and forms. We have included multiple vertical structures in our proposal to not only reflect this heritage but use them for a wide range of uses both old and new- including guest observation platforms, wayfinding points, wind catching functions, and as large gravity-fed water filters that recycle the grey water generated by the resort for efficient and sustainable re-use.

~ THE NURSERY OF HISTORIC PLANT SPECIES~
REVIVING ANCIENT ECOLOGY

~

The Sheraan Nature Reserve has made it a priority to protect plant life from consumption by camels and re-introduce native species to the region. The Sheraan Desert Resort should be a part of this worthy endeavor. We are proposing that staff accommodations surround and protect a new working 7500 square meter outdoor nursery to grow native and historic species for use at the resort and region at large, which provides the staff with views of greenery and protects the growing plant life.

~THE INCENSE GARDEN ~
SCENTS OF THE PAST

~

Meda'in Saleh existed largely because of its importance to the incense trade. We are proposing to acknowledge this with the cultivation of a small incense garden that surrounds our guest prayer towers, and includes, and protects, the Frankincense and Myrrh trees native to the incense production of antiquity. Carved deep within an adjacent rock is incense drying room and gallery where guests can experience the process of incense production and take home the scents of the past.

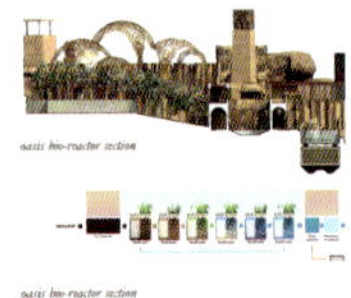

oasis bio-reactor section

oasis bio-reactor section

lunar collectors

observation and water filtration tower elevations

observation and water filtration tower section

planting palette

employee accommodations & native growth nursery

garden cutaway

Final board #6: Systems of sustainability and special features

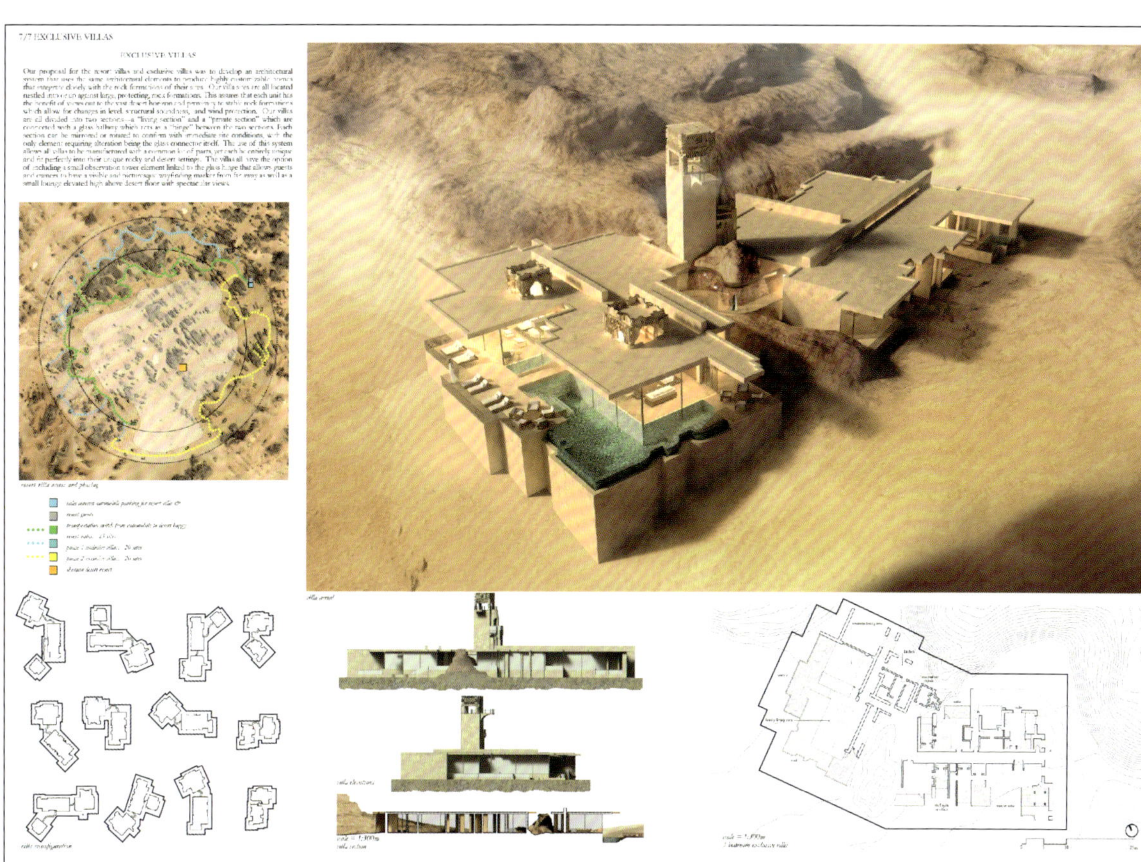

FINAL PRESENTATION BOARDS

Final board #7: The remote villas, *Opposite page:* The central resort tower at sunset

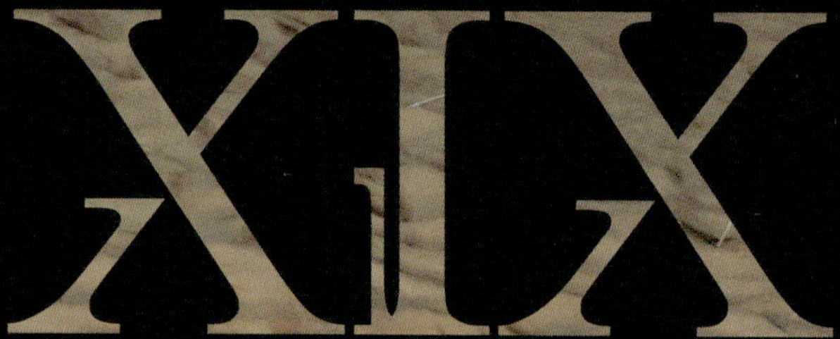

FINAL BOOKLET
464–475

The fifty-three page competition booklet
Resort observatory at night

Opposite page : Arabic coffee pots, also called *dallah,* in a desert campsite.

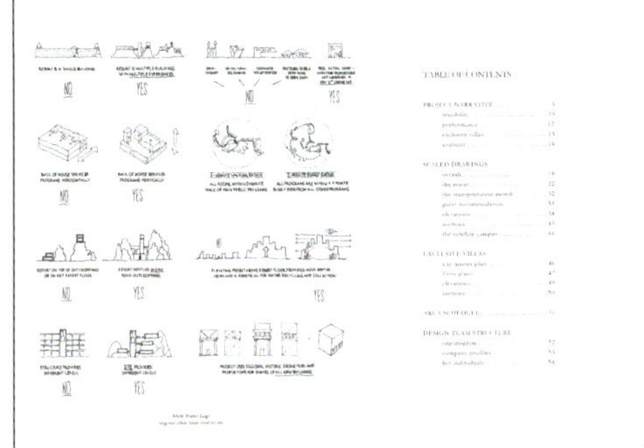

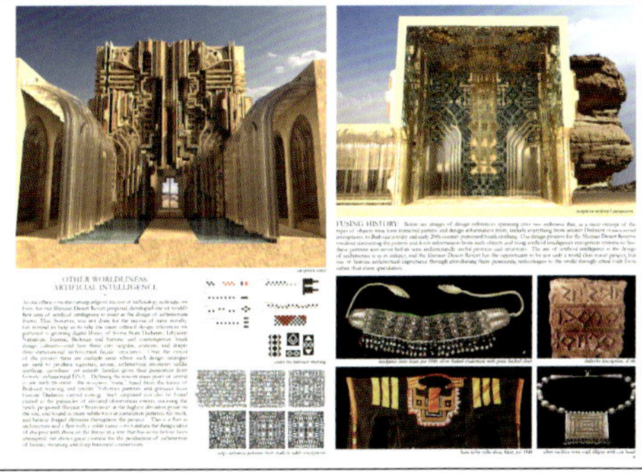

PRINTED BOOKLET FOR RIYADH JURY

Pages 01–06

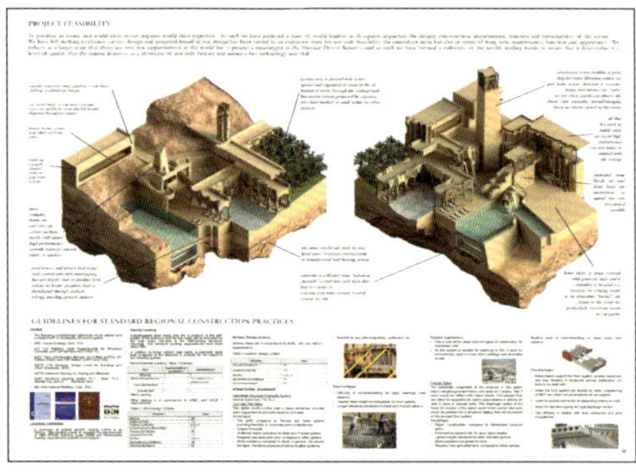

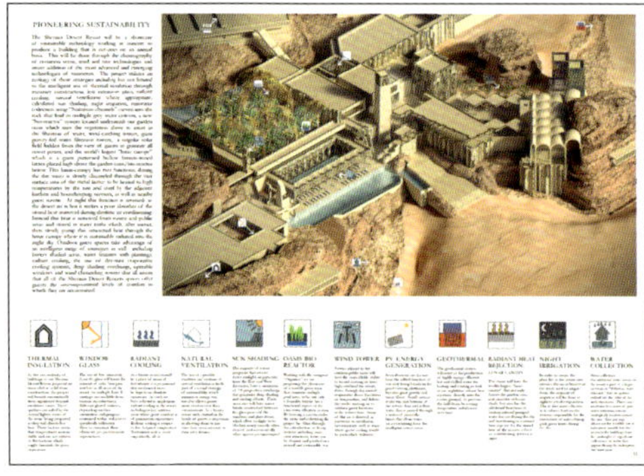

PRINTED BOOKLET FOR RIYADH JURY

Pages 07–12

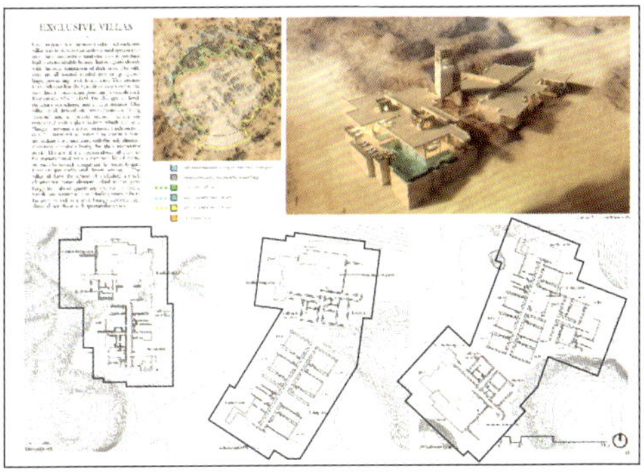

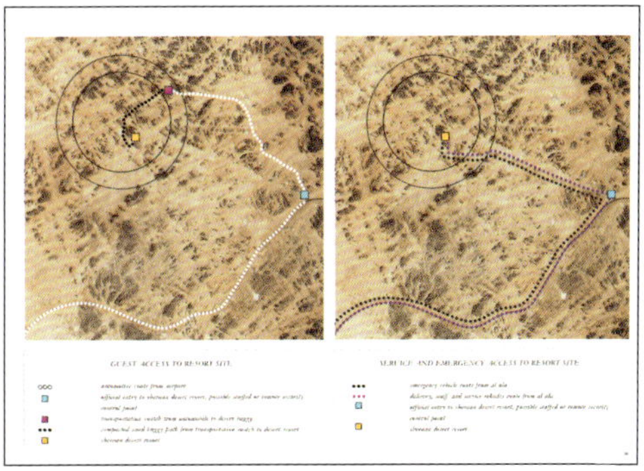

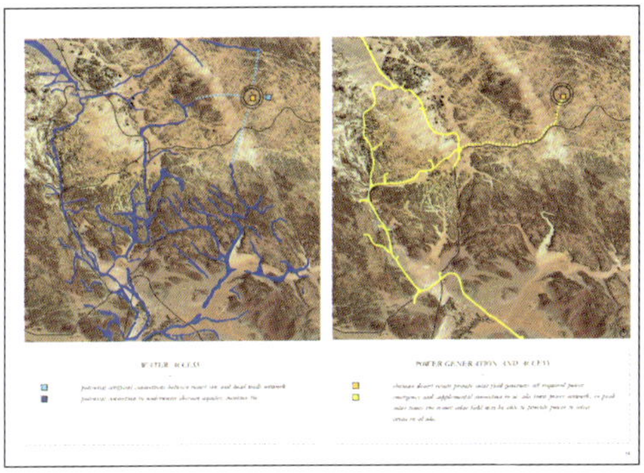

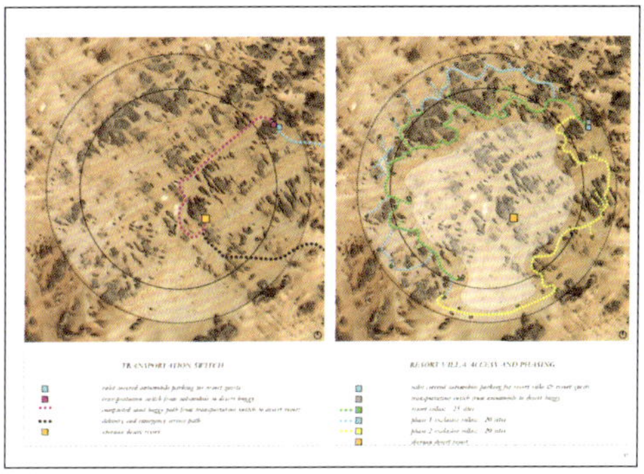

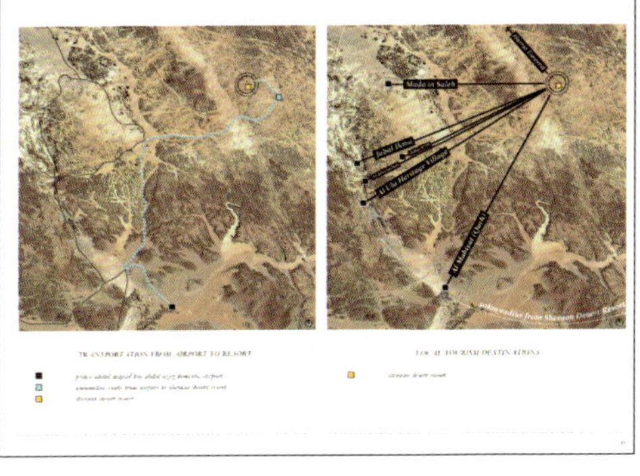

468

PRINTED BOOKLET FOR RIYADH JURY

Pages 13–18

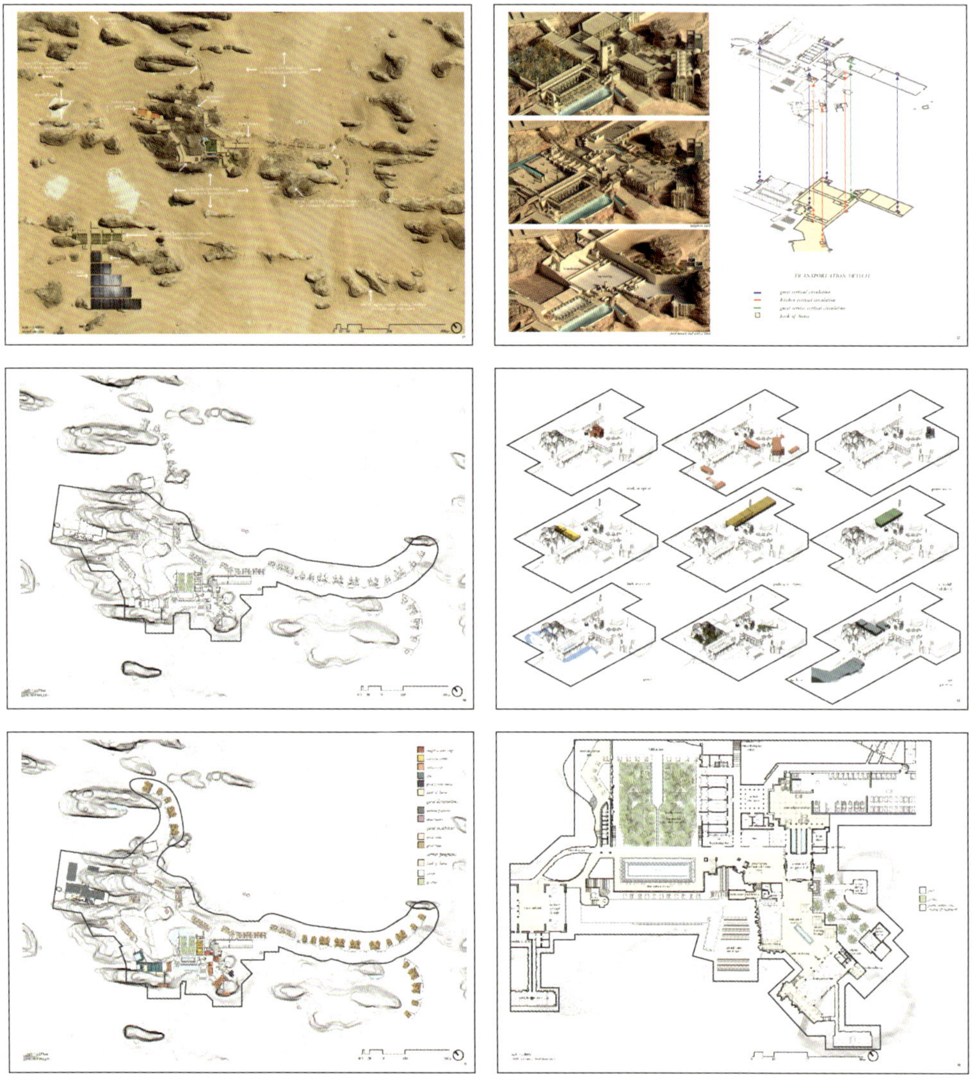

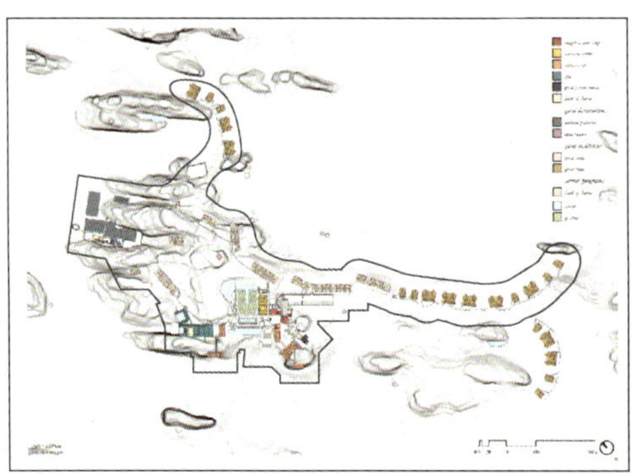

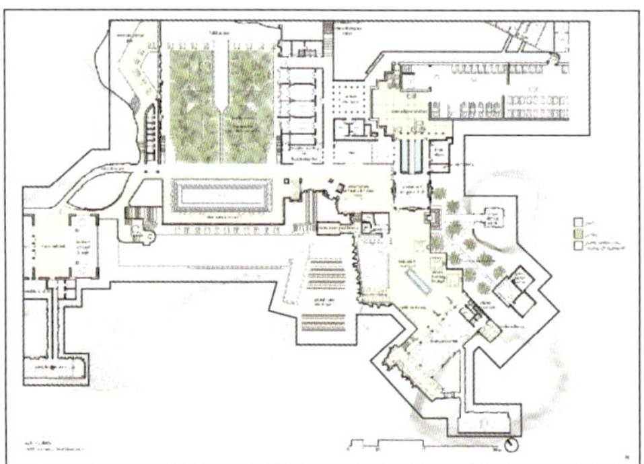

PRINTED BOOKLET FOR RIYADH JURY

Pages 19–24

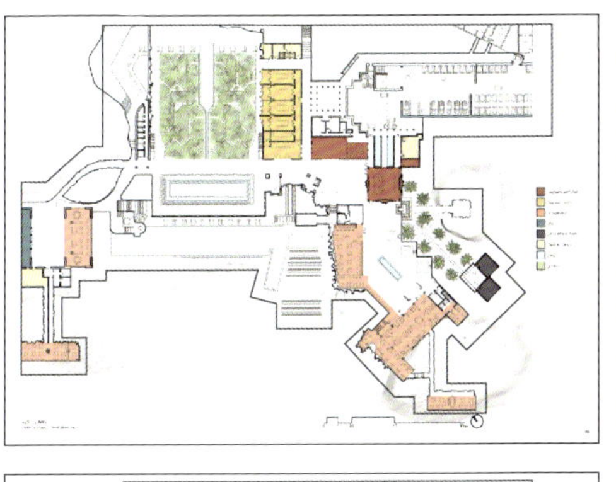
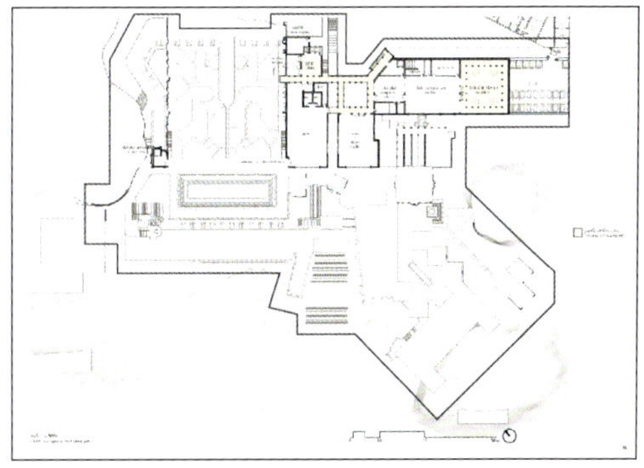
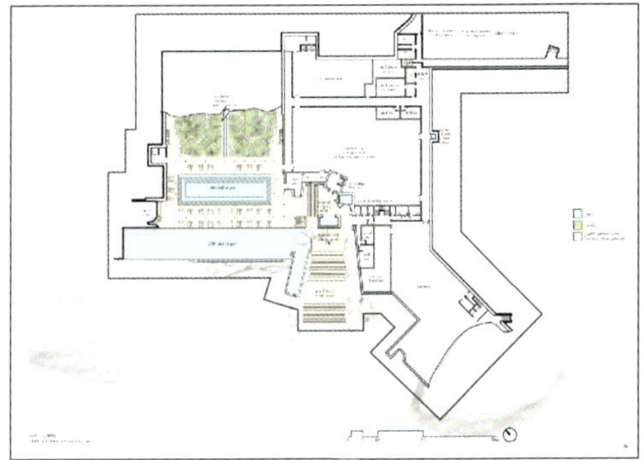
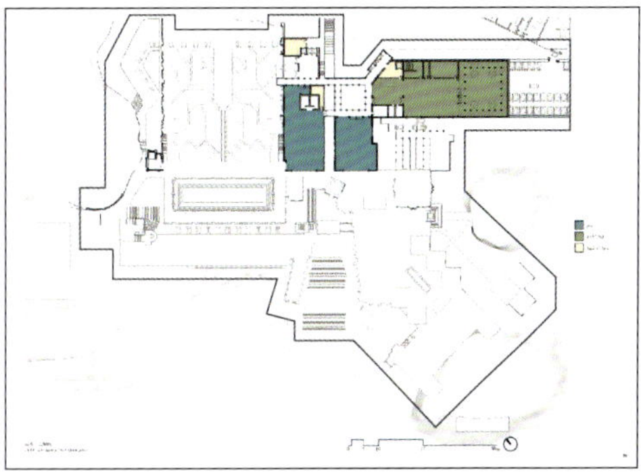
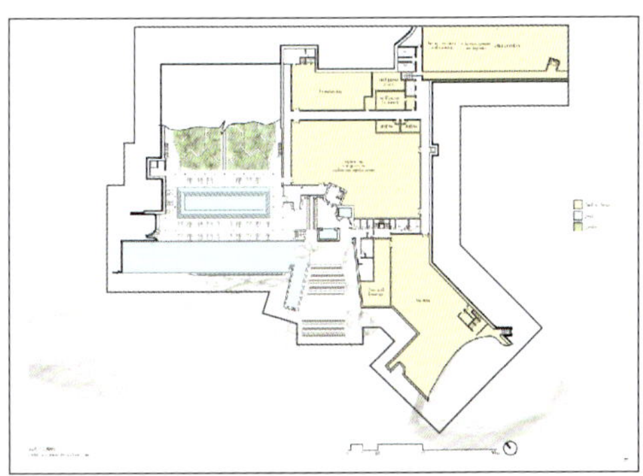
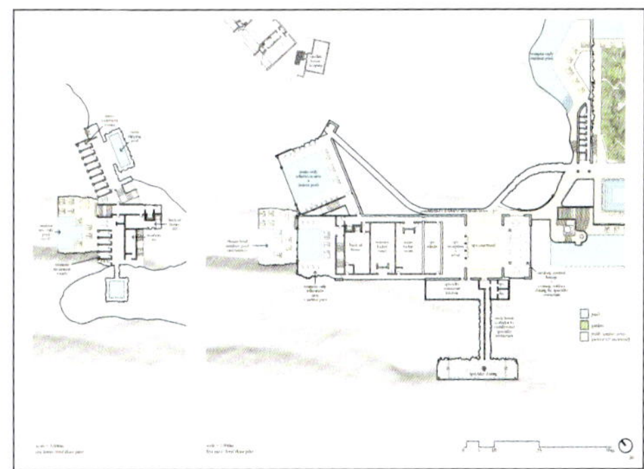

PRINTED BOOKLET FOR RIYADH JURY

Pages 25–30

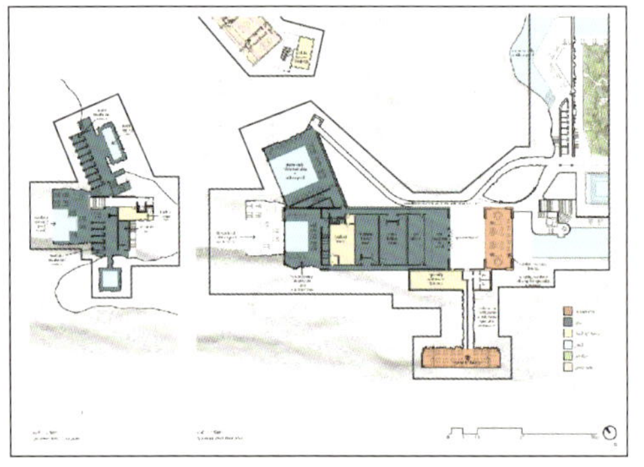

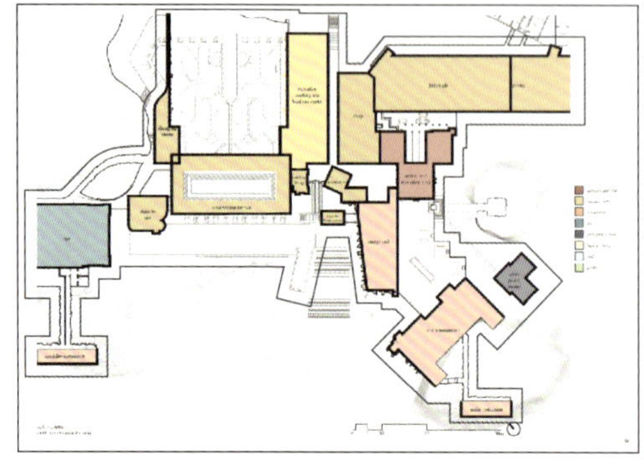

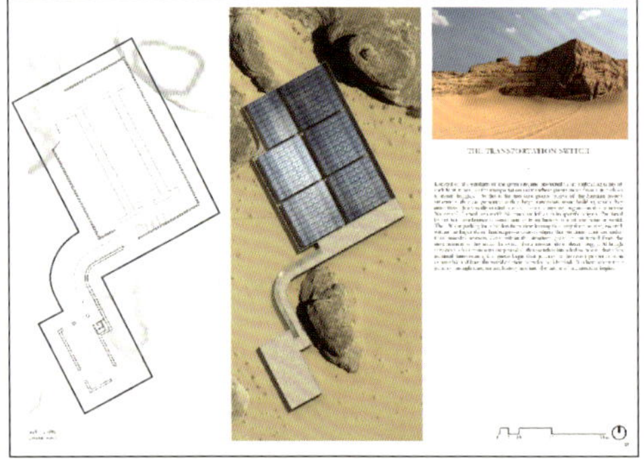

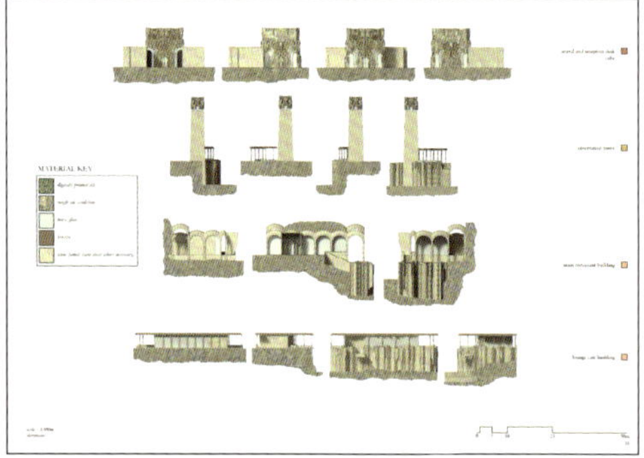

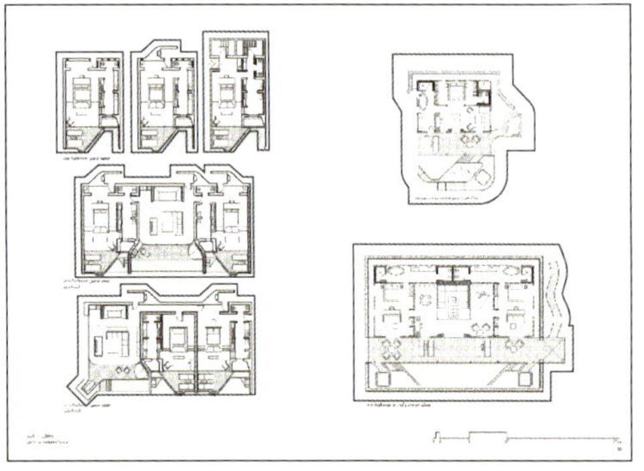

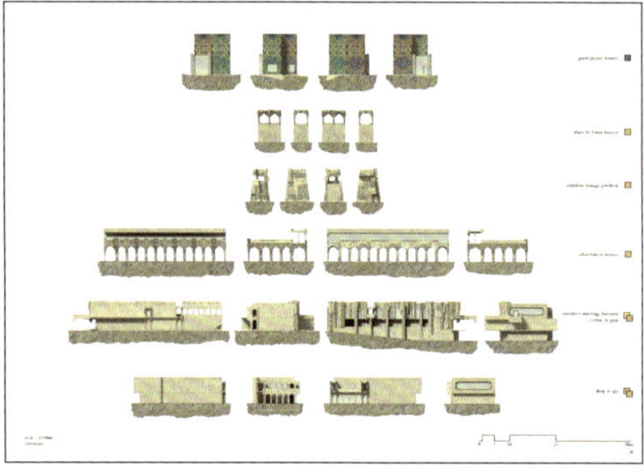

PRINTED BOOKLET FOR RIYADH JURY

Pages 31–36

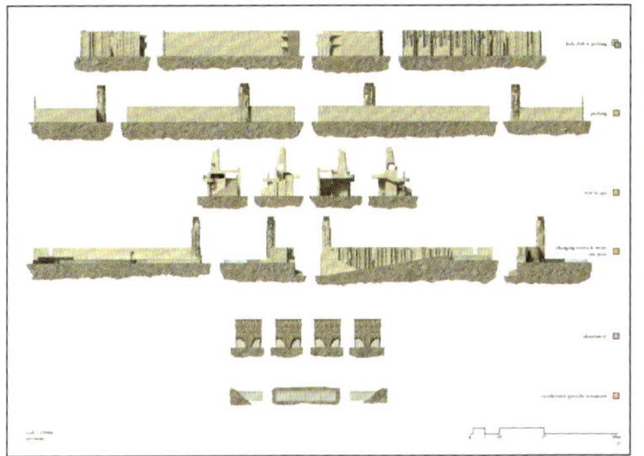

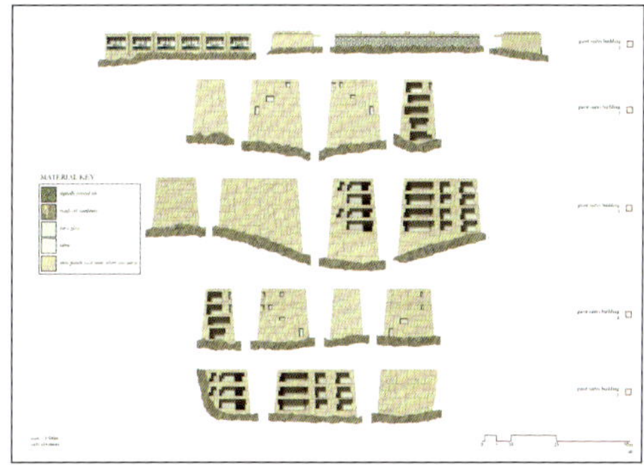

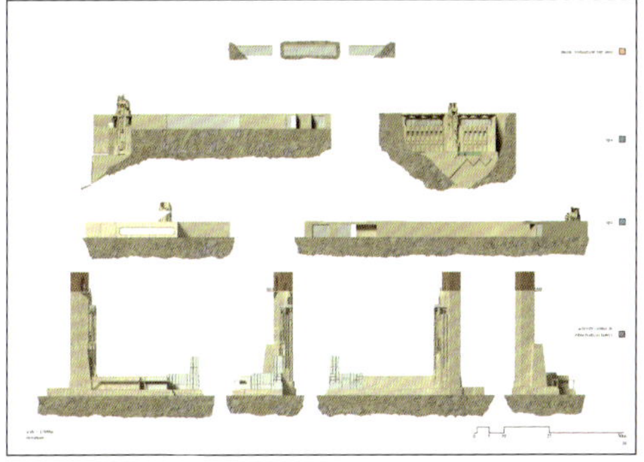

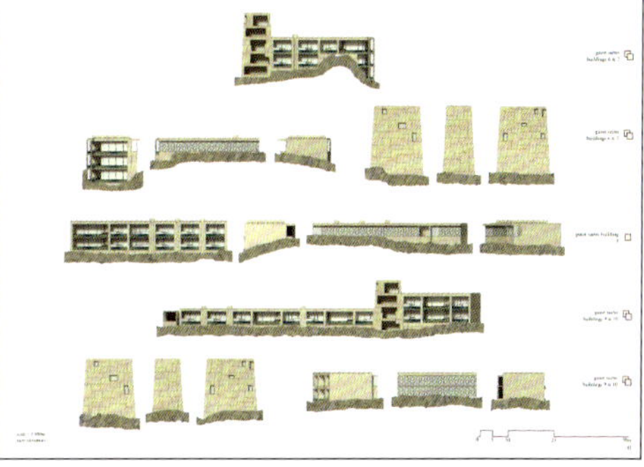

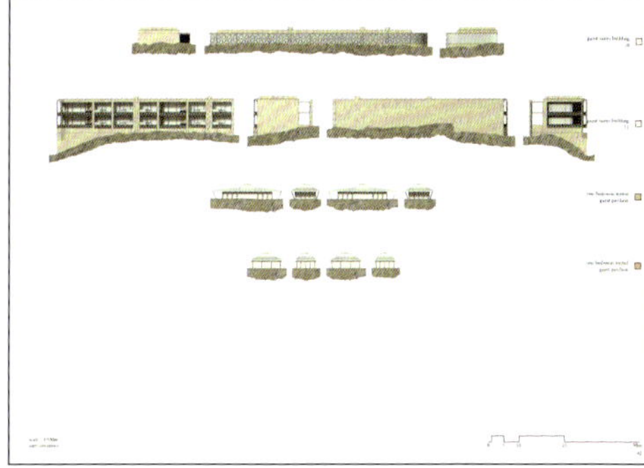

PRINTED BOOKLET FOR RIYADH JURY

Pages 37–42

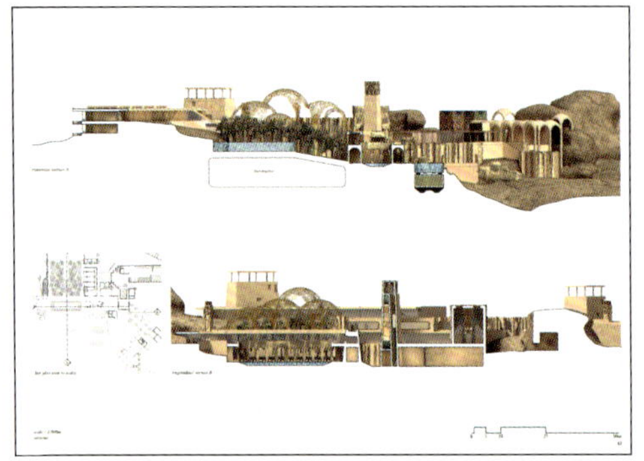

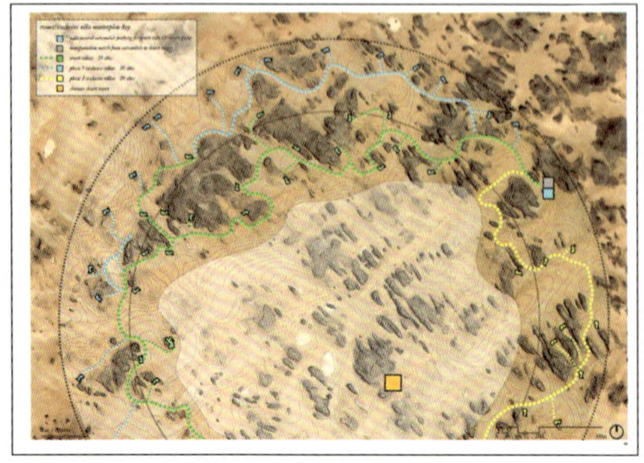

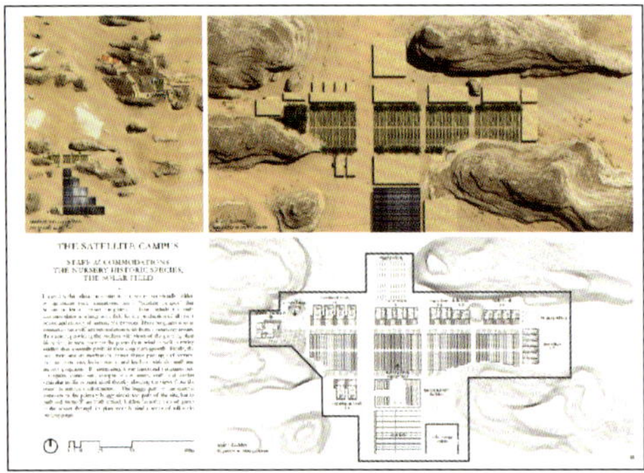

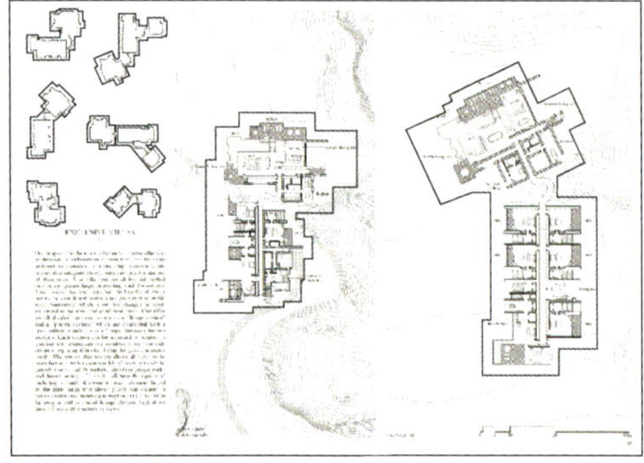

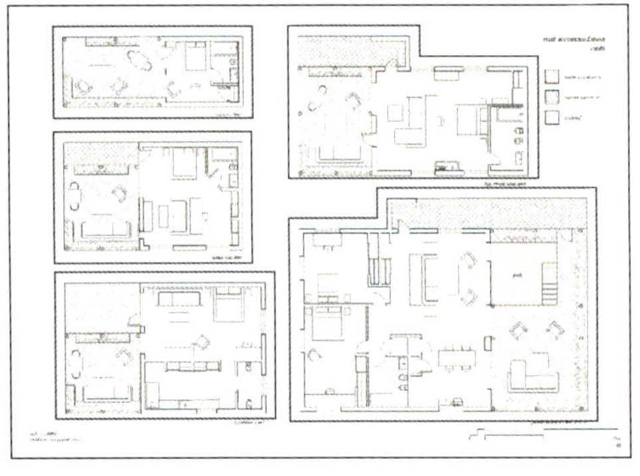

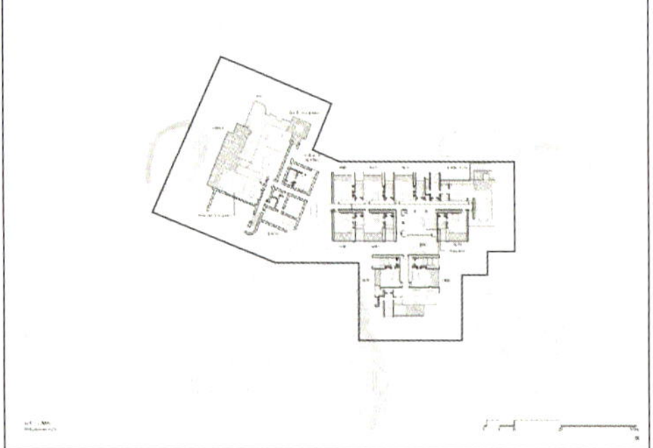

PRINTED BOOKLET FOR RIYADH JURY

Pages 43–48

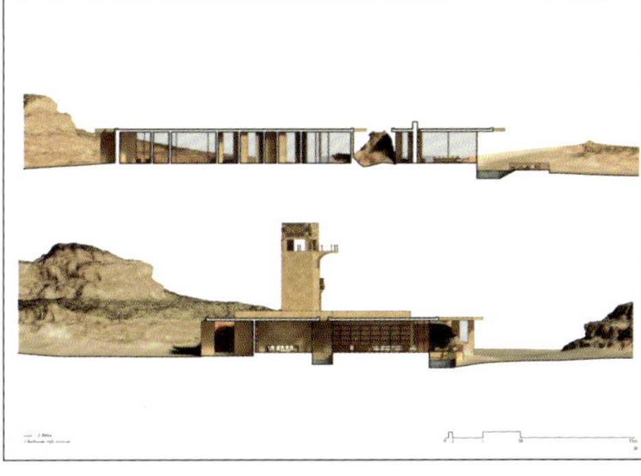

PRINTED BOOKLET FOR RIYADH JURY

Pages 49–53. *Opposite page:* The astronomical observation pavilion

CODA
476–481

The final presentation experiences
Life during a competition

Opposite page : **A computer icon of** Mada'in Salih.

BEHIND THE SCENES

Here are images from design competition life at MFGA. Clockwise from top left: being interviewed by press on-site in Saudi Arabia, at a meeting in Riyadh, still at a meeting in Riyadh, dancing, having coffee in the desert, presentation room in Riyadh.

BEHIND THE SCENES

More images from design competition life at MFGA. Clockwise from top left: wearing a new suit at our Riyadh hotel, typical Saudi men's hanging-out room, all alone at the hotel pool, visiting the site with "Waterfall Rock" in the background.

BEHIND THE SCENES

More images from design competition life at MFGA. Clockwise from top left: behind the wheel of me driving an Al Ula-colored car; MFG photo at the ruins; presentation model packed for travel; peace sign rocks in the desert; first class cabin on Saudi Airlines with no alcohol but an extensive water menu, "dinner" in the Jeddah airport at 3am.

BEHIND THE SCENES

Some final images from design competition life at MFGA. Clockwise from top left: selfie before heading off to present; project team probably watching Bojack Horseman. Bedouin-flavored hotel room in Al Ula; epic Saudi feast in Al Ula, showing my feet; my 1983 Diamond Back Silver Streak dirt bike from age nine, that I rediscovered and rode everywhere in NYC during the competition.

Image Credits:
All images are exclusive copyright of Mark Foster Gage Architects unless otherwise indicated. Images by Arqui9 in collaboration with Mark Foster Gage Architects: p78-79, p94-95, p104-105, p138-139, p230-231, p254-255,p 308-309, p318-319, p395-401, selected images on p456-462, p463, selected images on p466-474, p475. Images by Picksell Studio in collaboration with Mark Foster Gage Architects: p116-117, p121, p123, p124-125, p344-345, selected images on p456-462. Shutterstock.com images with standard licensed acquired by Mark Foster Gage Architects for printing up to 500,000 copies: p0, p6-7 by Fedor Selivanov, p10 by Sainuddeen Alanthi, p14-15 by Leo Morgan, p18-19 by Cpaulfell, p20 by Jennifer Frandsen, p36 by Sainuddeen Alanthi, p60 by Hyserb, p 86 by Tufayel Ali, p110 by pixeltaster, p125 by Jennifer Frandsen, p130 by HaYa-Hns, p140, by John Grummitt, p194 by Muttaz, p232 by Ganasboyz, p262 by Hussam Alduraywish, p278 by John Grummitt, p334 by Hyserb, p346 by The Road Provides, p380 by Ramlan Bin Abdul Jalil, p404 by Osama Ahmed Mansour, p428 by Hyserb, p438 by Aljohara Jewel, p454 by Paul Cowan, p464 by One Design, p476 by Studicon. Common use images from competition organizers and participants: p3, 24, p25, p28, p29, p30, p31, p43, selected images in collages on pages p478-481. Creative commons Zero, public domain dedication: Wiki Commons: p307 photograph of an English muffin.

ORO Editions
Publishers of Architecture, Art and Design
Gordon Goff: Publisher

www.oroeditions.com
info@oroeditions.com

Published by ORO Editions

Editor: Mark Foster Gage
Editorial Assistant: Jean-Emanuel Tremblay
Foreword: Graham Harman
Introduction: Mark Foster Gage
Book Design: MFGA llc with Jean-Emanuel Tremblay, Lauren Hunter and Edwin Maliakkal
Managing Editor: Jake Anderson

10 9 8 7 6 5 4 3 2 1 First Edition

ISBN: 978-1-954081-49-9

Color Separations and Printing: ORO Group Ltd.
Printed in China.

ORO Editions makes a continuous effort to minimize the overall carbon footprint of its publications. As part of this goal, ORO Editions, in association with Global ReLeaf, arranges to plant trees to replace those used in the manufacturing of the paper produced for its books. Global ReLeaf is an international campaign run by American Forests, one of the world's oldest nonprofit conservation organizations. Global ReLeaf is American Forests' education and action program that helps individuals, organizations, agencies and corporations improve the local and global